ONLY IN
LONDON

Duncan J. D. Smith

ONLY IN
LONDON

A Guide to Unique Locations,
Hidden Corners and Unusual Objects

Photographs by
Duncan J. D. Smith

**The
Urban
Explorer**

For those who never tire of exploring London

LONDON, thou art of townes *A per se*.
Soveraign of cities, seemliest in sight,
Of high renoun, riches and royaltie;
Of lordis, barons, and many a goodly knyght;
Of most delectable lusty ladies bright;
Of famous prelatis, in habitis clericall;
Of merchauntis full of substaunce and of myght:
London, thou art the flour of Cities all.

In Honour of the City of London, William Dunbar (1465–1520)

Above: Tiled motoring motif at Michelin House in Chelsea (see no. 74)

Page 2: Toy ducks recall the so-called Winchester Geese buried at Cross Bones Graveyard in Southwark (see no. 87)

Contents

Introduction

"No, Sir, when a man is tired of London, he is tired of life;
for there is in London all that life can afford."
Samuel Johnson (1709–1784), compiler of the first
English dictionary*

London is arguably the world's greatest city. Commercially frenetic, culturally diverse, and historically engaging it contains myriad places to discover – and it's good to know that the famous sights still retain a few surprises. Tourist hotspots aside there are many less well-known locations secreted in London's crooked backstreets, each providing a hidden history of the place. Devotees, like Samuel Johnson before them, declare it is difficult to tire of London!

This book is as much for the carefree stroller as for the determined city explorer. A few minutes' planning with a good street map** will get the reader quickly off the beaten track – and under the city's skin. This is the London of Roman ruins and sci-fi skyscrapers, eccentric museums and novel art spaces, ancient customs and living traditions.

The journeys described in the following pages are the result of the author's odysseys through central London – from St. Pancras in the north down to Westminster, and from Hyde Park in the west across to Tower Bridge. All are potential starting points from where readers can embark on their own voyages of discovery. Although no longer Lord Byron's "mighty mass of brick, and smoke, and shipping" London remains a city with one foot in the past, the other striding confidently ever forwards. Indeed London's flair for reinvention has seen it rise above many grave challenges, from the Great Fire of London in 1666 to the bombing raids of the Second World War. From each era something tangible always remains creating the palimpsest that is London today.

It is the author's intention that the locations described will enable readers to acquaint themselves not only with the surviving treasures of old London but also to savour the delights of the new. Many of them lie within the City – known also as the Square Mile – on the north bank of the Thames. From Roman times to the Middle Ages this relatively small area containing St. Paul's Cathedral constituted almost all of London; no longer walled it is now the financial district and was until recently home to the British press.

In 1857 the many districts of Victorian central London were corralled into half a dozen postal zones, and it is this convention that has been used to divide the material in this book. The City found itself in the eastern central zone (EC), which extends from the river north to

Clerkenwell, flanked by Spitalfields and the start of the East End (E). Immediately west and encompassing the area from Strand to Bloomsbury is the western central zone (WC). This is where London's merchants relocated after the withdrawal of the Romans, and the site of a Victorian slum after they returned to the City. It is now home to the theatres of the West End, universities, law courts, and the British Museum.

Many no less intriguing locations occupy the zones beyond from King's Cross to Mayfair (NW & W), a bustling grid of department stores, hotels and elegant Georgian squares sandwiched between Regent's Park and Hyde Park; others lie in the south west (SW), with its major museums, embassies and royal institutions ranged between posh Knightsbridge and the City of Westminster, the heart of British government. Both areas have long been favoured by the well-to-do being located away from the once overcrowded and smoggy City.

Yet more locations are to be found south of the river in the south east (SE), including Lambeth, the South Bank, and Bermondsey. Once notorious for its bear baiting, brothels and debtors' prisons this area is now home to some fascinating historical remains, as well as some of London's most innovative visitor attractions.

Whilst walking is undeniably the best way to explore London, red double-decker buses, black cabs and hire bikes are convenient, and the ubiquitous London Underground (Tube) is an adventure in itself***. Whether visiting a ghost station on the Piccadilly line, meditating in Soho's Buddhist temple, searching for Florence Nightingale's lamp, or tucking into a plate of Pie'n'Mash, it is hoped that the reader will experience some sense of personal discovery, and thereby take away a more indelible memory. Happy Exploring!

Duncan J. D. Smith, London & Vienna

---

* Dates given after the names of British rulers are regnal years; those after other personalities relate to their birth and death.

** Recommended is the *London A–Z Visitors' Map* published by the Geographers' A–Z Map Co. Ltd., which covers central London, and includes London Underground stations and bus routes (maps of the Underground are freely available at Tube stations). Smartphone users will find postcodes at the start of each chapter.

*** An old-fashioned Routemaster bus runs daily between Tower Hill and Trafalgar Square on Heritage Route 15. Other novel modes of transport include amphibious vehicles (www.londonducktours.co.uk), rickshaws (www.bugbugs.com) and vintage Indian cars (www.karmakabs.com)!

A selection of other locations within easy walking distance is given where applicable at the end of each chapter, and a list of opening times is at the back of the book.

1   The Ruins of Roman Londinium

EC3N 4DJ (The City), a tour of Roman remains including a piece of defensive wall outside Tower Hill Tube station
Circle, District lines to Tower Hill

Humans have long been active on the banks of the Thames. A 7,000-year old Mesolithic structure has been identified in front of the MI6 building on Albert Embankment (SE1), and even older Palaeolithic flints were unearthed in 2014 on the site of the new American Embassy in Wandsworth. But London's story really begins with the Romans.

Roman Londinium – the etymology of the name remains uncertain – was founded in AD 47 on Ludgate Hill and Cornhill on the north bank of the Thames. Now crowned by St. Paul's Cathedral and Leadenhall Market respectively, the two hills were separated by the Walbrook, one of London's 'lost' rivers, with the steep-sided valley of another, the Fleet, providing a natural defence to the west. With easy access to the sea, and the hills conveniently narrowing the Thames's marshy banks to create the ideal place for a bridge, the site was both economically and strategically significant. Despite being razed in AD 60 by Queen Boudicca, Londinium kept on growing and by AD 100 it had become the capital of Roman Britain, with a population of 60,000. It would retain its importance until the Romans' departure from Britain in AD 410.

It is surprising how much of Roman Londinium can still be detected in the modern landscape. Most prominent are the fragments of the defensive wall built around its landward side between 200 and 220 AD. Enclosing a rectangular area between Blackfriars Bridge, the

A statue of Emperor Trajan stands in front of a piece of Roman wall at Tower Hill

Barbican and the Tower of London, the wall was 3.2 km long, 6 metres high, and 2–3 metres thick, and protected by an external ditch (an additional riverside wall was added later).

A well-preserved piece of wall can be examined just outside Tower Hill Tube station, with another behind the Grange City Hotel on Cooper's Row (EC3). It is faced with squared-off Kentish ragstone brought by barge from Maidstone, and infilled with concrete and rubble, with rows of red tiles used as bonding courses. That the wall here is actually 10 metres high demonstrates how during the medieval period it was heightened and used thereafter to define the boundary of the City of London. From the 18th century onwards this wall was gradually demolished or incorporated into later structures, which explains its survival north of Cooper's Row in basements at 1 America Square, Emperor House at 35–36 Vine Street, and Roman Wall House at 1 Crutched Friars (ask at the various receptions if viewing is possible).

Other pieces of wall survive on Noble Street, Monkwell Square and St. Alphege Garden (EC2), where they doubled as the outer walls of a square-shaped fort constructed in AD 120 (the semicircular bastions are medieval). The name of the adjacent Church of St. Giles-without-Cripplegate recalls one of the six gates that connected Londinium with its extramural cemeteries and the wider world beyond. The others were Ludgate, Aldgate, Newgate, Aldersgate, and Bishopsgate, the latter opening onto Ermine Street, where a Roman cemetery and 14th century charnel house have been revealed in Bishop's Square (E1). When eventually the medieval City expanded its jurisdiction beyond the line of the Roman wall several of these old gateways were superceded by toll gates known as bars (e.g. Temple Bar, where the Strand joins Fleet Street, now removed to Paternoster Square (EC4) behind St. Paul's Cathedral).

Archaeologists have long been busy unearthing what remains of the Roman structures enclosed by the wall. These include an amphitheatre in Guildhall Yard off Gresham Street (marked out in black paving stones with visible remains including drains beneath Guildhall Art Gallery), public baths on Milk Street and Huggin Hill (unfortunately no longer visible), a Temple of Mithras on Walbrook (plans are afoot to display its remains in the basement of the new Bloomberg London building), imposing administration buildings under Cannon Street station (where the curious London Stone displayed at 111 Cannon Street is thought to have originated), a huge basilica and forum straddling Gracechurch Street (a footing for a large pier survives in the basement of Nicholson & Griffin at Number 90), a private house and baths beneath 101 Lower Thames Street (visitable during Open House London www.openhouselondon.org.uk), and a timber-built wharf running the

A model in the Museum of London of the Roman wharf

length of the riverbank (Broken Wharf is all that remains with one of its pilings displayed in the churchyard of St. Magnus the Martyr).

To gain an impression of how the Roman basilica, baths and original London Bridge once looked visit the Roman gallery in the Museum of London at 150 London Wall (EC2), where several intricate scale models are on display. The museum also contains a magnificent mosaic floor unearthed by workmen in the 1880s near Queen Victoria Street (EC4), together with hundreds of more humble artefacts from leather shoes to cosmetic skin scrapers known as *strigils*. Recent excavations for Crossrail and other large building projects have enabled archaeologists to unearth many more fascinating objects, including a unique amber amulet in the shape of a gladiator's helmet.

For many years historians were baffled about the fate of post-Roman Londinium. Documents mentioned an Anglo-Saxon settlement but no archaeological evidence could be found for it. All became clear when excavations in Covent Garden in the 1980s revealed the remains of Lundenwic, a Middle Saxon settlement which flourished there between the seventh and ninth centuries. Only in AD 886 did Viking raids force Alfred the Great (871–899) to reoccupy the old Roman walled city of Londinium, which took the name Lundenburgh. The rest, as they say, is history.

Other places of interest nearby: 2, 5

2 Traditions at the Tower

EC3N 4AB (Tower), the Tower of London
Circle, District lines to Tower Hill

The White Tower is the oldest part of the Tower of London

For almost a thousand years the Tower of London has stood sentinel on the north bank of the Thames. It is named after the White Tower, a sturdy Norman keep completed in 1097 by William the Conqueror (1066–1087) to guard and control the city. Still standing the White Tower today is just one of a complex of buildings from different periods protected by two concentric defensive walls and a moat. Over the years the Tower has doubled as a palace, prison and armoury, and variously contained a menagerie, mint, observatory, and public records office. As the sturdiest building in London it is also home to the Crown Jewels, including the royal sceptre, which contains the largest flawless and colourless diamond in the world. Little wonder then that the Tower boasts some of London's most tenacious and colourful traditions.

The best known concerns the Yeoman Warders. They can easily be spotted by their dark blue uniforms trimmed in red and emblazoned with the monarch's cipher and the Tudor Rose. Tasked originally with safeguarding prisoners, as well as the Crown Jewels, they now act as London's most photogenic tour guides. Around 40 of them are employed, drawn exclusively from retired and suitably decorated members of the armed forces, with the first woman admitted in 2007. It is worth noting that their red state uniform trimmed with gold is similar to that of the Yeoman of the Guard, a corps of royal bodyguards known as Beefeaters. Formed by Henry VII (1485–1509), making them Britain's oldest British military corps, their curious name probably re-

According to legend these ravens must never leave the Tower

calls their right to eat as much beef as they wanted from the king's table. When in 1536 Henry VIII (1509–1547) gave up the Tower for St. James's Palace the Tower retained its royal palace status, and with it a dozen Yeoman of the Guard. This detachment was renamed the Yeoman Warders to reflect their new duties.

Each night the Chief Yeoman Warder participates in the Ceremony of the Keys (public admission by written application to Ceremony of the Keys Office, Tower of London EC3N 4AB). At 9.55pm he sets out with the Keys from the Byward Tower to rendezvous with an escort of the Queen's Guard, and together they secure the main gates. At the Bloody Tower, however, the party is challenged by a sentry with the words: "Halt! Who goes there?" After it is explained that it is the ruling monarch's Keys, the command is given to advance. Passing through the Bloody Tower the Chief Warder doffs his Tudor bonnet with a request for God to bless the monarch, to which all reply "Amen". A bugler then plays the *Last Post* from the battlements and the Keys are deposited safely for the night with the Resident Governor of the Tower, who occupies the timber-framed Queen's House on Tower Green. The only time the Keys were delivered late was during an air raid in 1941 – and then only by half an hour! As well as being Keeper of the Jewel House it is the Resident Governor's duty to intruct the Honourable Artillery Company to stage a Royal Salute at the Tower on any given day (62 guns for the anniversary of the monarch's birth, accession and coronation, and 41 for the State Opening of Parliament and the birth of a royal infant).

The Queen's House is entrusted to the Resident Governor by the Constable of the Tower, the Tower's most senior office in existence since the Norman Conquest. The Installation of the Constable occurs every five years on Tower Green and is attended by the Lord Chamberlain, who is the senior officer of the Royal Household. He is handed the Keys by the Constable's subordinate, the Lieutenant of the Tower, who reads out a proclamation from the monarch. The Keys are then handed to the new Constable, who inaugurates his office by inspecting the Yeoman Warders. During the Middle Ages the office of Constable was a profitable one including entitlement to carts tumbling into the Tower's moat and livestock falling off London Bridge. At the Annual Ceremony of the Constable's Dues he still receives a barrel of rum from the Royal Navy recalling the days when every ship coming upstream was obliged to moor at Tower Wharf and give up a portion of its cargo.

On the north side of Tower Green is the Chapel Royal of St. Peter ad Vincula, meaning appropriately St. Peter in Chains. It contains the grave of Anne Boleyn (1501–1536), second wife of Henry VIII, who was privately executed on Tower Green for treason (most prisoners were executed *outside* the Tower in what is today the Merchant Seamen's Memorial Garden on Tower Hill). For many years now on the anniversary of the queen's death a dozen red roses have been placed anonymously on the grave.

Every three years on Ascension Day the Chapel observes the medieval custom of Beating the Bounds, whereby illiterate churchgoers were reminded of the physical extent of their parish by the Chief Yeoman Warder whipping various boundary stones with willow canes. The Church of All Hallows-by-the-Tower on nearby Byward Street does likewise each Ascension Day, and every third year the two stage a mock battle where their boundaries meet, recalling an occasion in 1698 when a boundary dispute erupted into violence.

A Yeoman Warder also acts as the Tower's official Ravenmaster. The birds have been living at the Tower since at least the time of Charles II (1660–1685). He was so taken by the belief that if they departed the monarchy would fall that he removed the Royal Observatory from the Tower to Greenwich rather than remove the ravens, which enjoyed tampering with the observatory's equipment! These days the ravens have their flight feathers clipped to prevent them from leaving and are fed raw meat from Smithfield Market.

Since the 18th century the Druids have gathered on Tower Hill on the 20th or 21st of March to celebrate the Vernal Equinox. Clad in white robes they silently invoke the elements and scatter seeds to encourage a fruitful year ahead.

Other places of interest nearby: 1, 3, 102, 103

3 Monuments to the Great Fire

EC3R 8AH (The City), the Monument at the junction
of Monument Street and Fish Street Hill
Circle, District lines to Monument

Around midnight on 2nd September 1666 the Great Fire of London started in a bakehouse on Pudding Lane (EC3). Over the next four days it swept westwards through the City consuming 13,500 houses, 88 parish churches, and St. Paul's Cathedral. Officially few lives were lost but many of the area's 80,000 inhabitants were made homeless. The diarist Samuel Pepys (1633–1702) described the smouldering ruins as "the saddest sight of desolation that I ever saw".

The huge task of rebuilding began in 1667 but with landowners unwilling to relinquish their plots for redevelopment the City's medieval street plan was retained. The office of architect Sir Christopher Wren (1632–1723) oversaw much of the work, including 51 churches, a new Custom House, and a rebuilt St. Paul's (see nos. 15 & 26). The timber and wattle-and-daub that had fuelled the fire was replaced wherever possible by brick or stone, and insurance companies formed London's first organised fire brigades (durable metal wall plaques like those preserved at 11 Princelet Street (E1) still identify buildings insured with them).

The Monument with its flaming orb stands near where the Great Fire began

Wren also had a hand in designing the Monument, a 61-metre high memorial to the fire at the junction of Monument Street and Fish Street Hill (EC3). Occupying the site of the first church engulfed by the flames it was completed in 1677 in the form of a fluted Doric column. A dizzying 311-step spiral staircase enables energetic visitors to reach an observation platform located beneath a gilded flaming orb.

The height of the Monument supposedly equals the distance from its base to where the fire started. The place where it was stopped – by the dynamiting of houses to create a fire break – is marked by an altogether different memorial. The gilded effigy of a chubby boy at the corner of Giltspur Street and Cock Lane (EC1) is accompanied by an inscription citing the fire's cause as "the Sin of Gluttony". Trading on the novelty that the fire started at Pudding Lane and finished here at what was once called Pye Corner it originally adorned an 18th century tavern (both the French and the Catholics had earlier been blamed).

The only notable new streets built after the fire were Queen Street (EC4) and King Street (EC2) linking the Thames with Guildhall on Gresham Street. On Cloak Lane off Queen Street is an easy-to-miss arcade containing gravestones from the Church of St John the Baptist-upon-Walbrook, one of several medieval stone churches burned and never rebuilt (see no. 19). Guildhall was the only secular stone building to survive having been home to the Lord Mayor and the City of London Corporation since the 12th century. Completed in 1440 its Great Hall and undercroft are now rare examples of medieval civic architecture in the City and can be visited during Open House London (www.openhouselondon.org.uk) (see no. 103).

The City's few timber-framed buildings to escape destruction include a late 16th century private house at 41–42 Cloth Fair (EC1) and the contemporary Hoop and Grapes pub at 47 Aldgate High Street (EC3). Another example known as Prince Henry's Room stands at 17 Fleet Street (EC4). Dating from 1610 it contains London's finest Jacobean plaster ceiling decorated with the Prince of Wales's feathers.

London's second greatest fire broke out in 1861 amongst the riverside warehouses of Tooley Street (SE1). It claimed the life of the Chief of the London Fire Engine Establishment, which had been formed in 1833 when London's various insurance brigades were merged. Calls for London's fire safety to be entrusted to a municipal authority were eventually heeded in 1865 when the Metropolitan Fire Brigade was formed. Both services are documented in the London Fire Brigade Museum at 94a Southwark Bridge Road (SE1).

Other places of interest nearby: 4, 12

4 All Markets Great and Small

EC3V 1LT (The City), a tour of central London markets including
Leadenhall Market on Gracechurch Street
Circle, District lines to Monument; Central, DLR, Northern,
Waterloo & City lines to Bank

The markets of central London have a long history stretching back
centuries. Despite most of the great wholesale markets having moved
away there is still a vibrant market scene here, played out beneath
ornate Victorian canopies as well as open skies.

The oldest market in London is Smithfield (EC1), which occupies
a site where meat has been sold for over 800 years (the cattle market
persisted until 1855, when it was replaced by one trading in butch-
ered meat only, with a capacity of 60,000 carcasses). Its cavernous
covered Central Market was designed by City architect Horace Jones
(1819–1887), who also designed Tower Bridge. Opened in 1868, it still
welcomes wholesale customers each weekday from 4am and is at its
liveliest around breakfast time. It is the only great market not to have
abandoned central London in favour of cheaper, more convenient facilities elsewhere. Jones also designed the adjacent Poultry Market,
rebuilt in the 1960s, with what at the time was Europe's largest con-

Leadenhall Market has been restored to its Victorian glory

crete dome, and the so-called General Market used for the sale of fruit and vegetables. The latter has lain derelict for years and long been threatened with demolition although there is now talk of it becoming the new home of the Museum of London (see no. 18). Time will tell.

Horace Jones also designed Leadenhall Market, which opened in 1881 on Gracechurch Street (EC3). This glorious Victorian arcade takes its name from a lead-roofed house that stood here during the 14th century, when the market was founded by Richard 'Dick' Whittington (see no. 13). Tall entrances in brick and Portland stone give access to cobbled streets enclosed in glass and painted wrought iron. Originally a meat, game and poultry market – some of the original hooks for hanging carcasses can still be seen – it today contains a variety of shops and has twice served as a backdrop for the *Harry Potter* films.

A third market designed by Horace Jones is the Old Billingsgate Fish Market, which opened in 1877 on Lower Thames Street. The site of a wharf in Roman times it became a wholesale fish market in 1699. Although the market relocated in 1982 to the Isle of Dogs, Jones's long French Renaissance façade still retains its fish-shaped weather vanes.

To experience the buzz of modern market life visit Borough Market on Stoney Street (SE1). London's oldest fruit and vegetable market it dates back to the 13th century, when traders selling foodstuffs moved here from the overcrowded London Bridge. Saved from closure in 1755 by local residents it has been providing for the neighbourhood ever since. Between Wednesday and Saturday early birds can see fresh produce arriving from 2am onwards; late risers can enjoy the weekend gourmet market and soak up the atmosphere of the sooty Victorian architecture and the railway rumbling overhead.

Atmospheric, too, is Old Spitalfields Market on Commercial Street (E1), which has been trading since 1638 (its name recalls a medieval hospital founded here in 1197). The present structure was erected in 1887 to service the wholesale fruit and vegetable trade. When it relocated to Leyton in 1991 the building was successfully turned over to general traders (by contrast when the equally ancient Covent Garden relocated in 1974 to Nine Elms its Victorian market halls became a shopping centre and a home to the London Transport Museum). The Old Fruit Exchange across Brushfield Street, where auctions once took place, is set to be demolished leaving only its front elevation intact.

This tour finishes with a clutch of long-established outdoor markets on Brick Lane (E1), Petticoat Lane (E1), and Columbia Road (E2).

Other places of interest nearby: 3, 5, 12

5 Britain's Oldest Synagogue

EC3A 5DQ (The City), Bevis Marks Synagogue off Bevis Marks Circle, Metropolitan lines to Aldgate

Hidden inside a secluded City courtyard is a superlative place of worship. Bevis Marks Synagogue (EC3) is the oldest synagogue in Britain and the only one in Europe to have celebrated Jewish services continuously for more than 300 years.

The first Jews to settle in Britain were invited from Normandy by William the Conqueror (1066–1087). He offered them protection in return for payment but when Edward I (1272–1307) deemed no further revenue forthcoming they were expelled and their property confiscated. Elsewhere in Europe the Jews of Spain and Portugal *(Sephardim)* were being expelled under the Inquisition. Some known as *Marranos* took Spanish names after being forcibly converted to Catholicism, and recommenced trading in England. When war broke out with Spain in 1654, and the property of Spanish merchants in England was seized, one *Marrano* went to court and revealed his true religion. After the court ruled in his favour Jews were officially admitted back into London.

It was these *Sephardim* who opened the Bevis Marks Synagogue in 1701 (its secretive location reflects the fact that Jews were prohibited from building on main roads). With its dignified exterior influenced by the churches of Christoper Wren (1632–1723) the building is little changed. Inside there is much symbolism: the 12 columns supporting the women's gallery represent the tribes of Israel, the seven chandeliers the days of the week, and the ten brass

Bevis Marks Synagogue is well concealed in a City courtyard

candlesticks the Ten Commandments. Contained within the Ark are the sacred *Torah* scrolls, which are read in consecutive instalments each Sabbath over the period of a year. The synagogue's presence has long helped forge links between the Jewish community and the City, with members of its congregation serving not only as Livery Company Masters but also City Sheriffs and Lord Mayors (see no. 16).

In the wake of the *Sephardim* came Jews escaping persecution in Eastern Europe. In 1690 these *Ashkenazim* built a synagogue on nearby Duke's Place. Its destruction during the Blitz, however, means that London's oldest functioning Ashkenazi synagogue is now the one at 4a Sandys Row (E1). Opened in 1854 by poor Dutch immigrants working in the East End it is housed in a former Protestant chapel built a century earlier by silk-working Huguenots (see no. 8).

The Jewish East End reached its zenith around 1900 with a synagogue, school or soup kitchen on most streets. By the 1970s, however, many *Ashkenazim* had relocated to Golders Green as the area's demographics shifted once more. Spitalfields Great Synagogue at 59 Brick Lane (E1), which also began life as a Huguenot chapel, was tellingly converted into a mosque for Bangladeshi Muslims working in the textile trade.

Relocation also affected Bevis Marks. In 1840 a breakaway group established the West London Synagogue of British Jews at 34 Upper Berkeley Street (W1) reflecting a newfound patriotic unity between *Sephardim* and *Ashkenazim*. This had a knock-on effect during the 1980s when the dwindling *Sephardic* congregation at Bevis Marks was bolstered by the arrival of young *Ashkenazim* working in the City's financial institutions. By 1998, when a service was held at the synagogue in honour of the installation of the *Ashkenazi* Lord Levene as the eighth Jewish Lord Mayor of the City of London, it was clear that Bevis Marks had become a centre for all Anglo-Jewry.

The birth register at Bevis Marks includes the name of Benjamin Disraeli (1804–1881). After disagreements with the synagogue's elders his father had him baptised at the Church of St. Andrew Holborn on Holborn Viaduct (EC4) enabling him eventually to become Britain's only Jewish-born Prime Minister.

Other places of interest nearby: 1, 4, 11

6 Hawksmoor's Rockets

E1 6LY (Spitalfields), a tour of three churches by Nicholas Hawksmoor begining with Christ Church Spitalfields on Commercial Street
District, Hammersmith & City lines to Aldgate East; Central, Circle, Hammersmith & City, Metropolitan lines to Liverpool Street

The architect Sir Christopher Wren (1632–1723) made his name rebuilding London after the Great Fire (see nos. 15 & 26). In this enormous task he was assisted by several other architects but for a long time their names remained obscure. Modern scholarship has sought to identify their individual contributions with the most notable being Wren's former apprentice, Nicholas Hawksmoor (1661–1736).

Hawksmoor became Wren's clerk aged just 18 and worked with him on a variety of London projects, including St. Paul's Cathedral. He then cut his teeth further with John Vanbrugh (1664–1726) at Blenheim Palace and Castle Howard. It could be argued that Hawksmoor influenced both architects since by 1700 he had emerged as a major architectural personality in his own right.

Over the next three decades Hawksmoor showed himself to be a master of English Baroque, fusing Classical and Gothic forms in a unique synthesis. He brought his ideas to bear on country houses and universities, and after the death of Wren in 1723 became Surveyor to Westminster Abbey for which he designed the west towers (see no. 85). In London he also contributed six extraordinary designs to the Commission for Building

The spire of Nicholas Hawksmoor's Christ Church Spitalfields

Fifty New Churches to help serve London's rapidly growing conurbation. What follows is a tour of three of them (the others – St. Alfrege's Greenwich, St. Anne's Limehouse, and St. George-in-the-East Wapping – all lie outside the geographical scope of this book).

The tour begins with Christ Church Spitalfields on Commercial Street (E1) (see no. 8). Built in 1714–1729 it was the first and arguably finest of the dozen churches built before the Commission ran out of steam. Viewed from a distance its 69 metre high spire of white Portland stone appears to be a separate entity, like a rocket from a 1950s science fiction film. Audacious steeples are the most recognisable features of Hawksmoor's churches and in its day this one must have been a striking Anglican statement in an area noted for its nonconformity. The richly plastered interior features a 2,000-pipe Georgian organ, which for a century was the largest in England.

Even more extraordinary is the steeple Hawksmoor designed for St. George's Bloomsbury on Bloomsbury Way (WC1). Taking the form of a stepped pyramid it is inspired by Pliny the Elder's description of the Mausoleum at Halicarnassus and is topped off with a statue of George I (1714–1727) dressed as a Roman! The portico beneath is based on that of the Temple of Bacchus at Baalbek in Lebanon. In 1937 Emperor Haile Selassie of Ethiopia attended a requiem here for the dead of the Abyssinian War.

Hawksmoor's only City church is St. Mary's Woolnoth on King William Street (EC4). Its medieval predecessor had been repaired by Wren after the Great Fire but became unsafe and had to be demolished. Hawksmoor's rugged replacement features a tower comprising a Corinthian-style arcade with two square turrets on top. During the 1890s this might also have been demolished to make way for the construction of Bank Tube station. Fortunately a public outcry saved the building and instead it was underpinned and the new station booking hall inserted into its crypt. The church is currently used by London's German-speaking Swiss community.

Hawksmoor's fellow surveyor in the Commission was John James (1673–1746). Together they designed two churches, with Hawksmoor responsible for the steeples. St. Luke's Old Street (EC1) now serves as a music venue for the London Symphony Orchestra, whilst the footings of the demolished St. John's Horsleydown on Tower Bridge Road (SE1) have been reused for the London City Mission.

Other places of interest nearby: 7, 8

7 The Biggest Brewery in the World

E1 6QL (Spitalfields), the Old Truman Brewery at 91 Brick Lane District, Hammersmith & City lines to Aldgate East; Central, Circle, Hammersmith & City, Metropolitan lines to Liverpool Street; London Overground to Shoreditch High Street

For a couple of decades during the mid-19th century the Black Eagle Brewery on Brick Lane (E1) was the biggest in the world. In business for more than three centuries it gave work to thousands and made millionaires of its owners. Since the beer stopped flowing in the 1980s the former brewery has been reinvented as the Old Truman Brewery, one of London's most creative business and leisure quarters.

The Black Eagle Brewery was established in 1670 by the entrepreneur Thomas Bucknall. Its name was derived from an ancient path (now Dray Walk) recalling the rural atmosphere of the place before it was built up (a black eagle adorns the sign that hangs outside the brewery today). Around 1700 Joseph Truman took over the lease and began brewing Porter, a dark, well-hopped beer popular with London's street and river porters. It was the first beer suitable for mass production.

In 1724 the brewery was rebuilt and by the 1740s it was among the biggest brewers of Porter in London. By this time the company had passed to Truman's son, Benjamin, who grew enormously wealthy and bought himself a fine mansion in Hertfordshire, whence he sourced his malt. A knighthood was even bestowed on

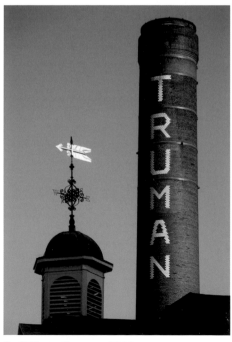

The Old Truman Brewery on Brick Lane

him by George III (1760–1820) for the large loans he made to the Crown to help finance its wars.

By 1799 and with new partners onboard the brewery became the third largest in London, with an annual production of 117,000 barrels. In 1814 mechanical mashing was introduced and like Benjamin Truman before him, the new majority shareholder, Sampson Hanbury, became rich. His nephew, Thomas Fowel Buxton (1786–1845), used much of the wealth he generated from the brewery to improve the lot of the poor weavers who lived in the area (he also assisted in the abolition of slavery as recorded on a Blue Plaque outside the brewery today).

A further influx of new partners saw the brewery expanded and working conditions improved, increasing production to 185,000 barrels by 1818. When drinking tastes changed in the 1830s from Porter to an unaged variety called Mild, production at Brick Lane changed too, and increased once again. Now with its own wharf near St. Katherine's Dock, Truman's beer was being exported as far away as North America and Australia. In 1853 production reached 400,000 barrels making the Black Eagle Brewery the largest in the world.

Within 20 years, however, the mantle of biggest brewer had shifted to Burton-on-Trent, where the water was better for the increasingly popular pale bitter ales. Truman's stuck to what it knew best although by 1930 time had been called on Porter. Around the same time the brick boiler house chimney that still towers over the brewery was built, with Truman's name emblazoned down the side.

The 1960s brought seismic shifts in the brewing industry as traditional practices such as cooperage and the use of dray horses were replaced. An ugly bidding war a decade later saw Truman's sold and merged with Watney's but the writing was on the wall. Customer loyalty fell away, the workforce was cut, and in 1988 the brewery closed forever. Fortunately the historic buildings were saved and today they are home to an assortment of bars, cafés, studios, and galleries. A food hall now occupies the former boiler house and shops have replaced the old stables on Dray Walk.

Equally vibrant is Whitechapel Gallery not far away at 77–82 Whitechapel High Street. This community-driven art space boasts an admirable track record for education and outreach projects.

Other places of interest nearby: 6, 8

8 The Fantasy of Dennis Severs

E1 6BX (Spitalfields), Dennis Severs' House at 18 Folgate Street
Circle, Hammersmith & City, Metropolitan lines to Liverpool
Street; London Overground to Shoreditch High Street

The tangle of narrow streets around Old Spitalfields Market (E1) has the appearance of a film set. The drama in question is set in the late 17th and 18th centuries, when the area was settled by Protestant Huguenot silk weavers fleeing Catholic persecution in France. The mercers controlling this lucrative industry chose Spitalfields to avoid the restrictive legislation of the City's guilds, and built the red-brick terraces and chapels still standing today (see no. 16). Subsequent waves of Irish, Jewish and Bangladeshi immigrants have also left their mark.

Anyone interested in Georgian architecture (1720–1830) should walk these streets. At 56 and 58 Artillery Lane, for example, some of London's oldest wooden shopfronts were added in the 1750s to weavers' houses built in 1715. More well-preserved Georgian terraces line Wilkes Street, Princelet Street and Fournier Street, where the silk for Queen Victoria's Coronation gown was woven. It is sometimes possible to look inside these historic homes, notably on Princelet Street, where Number 13 has been impeccably restored to provide visitor accommodation, and Number 19, which is now a unique museum

An unmade bed in Dennis Severs' House on Folgate Street

illustrating how immigrants have helped shape not only Spitalfields but also all of multicultural Britain.

An unforgettable opportunity is provided by a visit to Dennis Severs' House at 18 Folgate Street. Built in 1724, this red-brick terrace has been transformed by its former owner, Dennis Severs (1948–1999), into something very special indeed. That this Californian-born American was first drawn to London by what he called "English light" speaks volumes about his approach to restoration. When he first arrived on Folgate Street in 1979 the four storey property was in a dilapidated condition. Spitalfields was at the time run-down and popular only with artists in search of cheap living. Severs occupied the property until his death 20 years later and during that time renovated and furnished the building's ten rooms in a style that would have been familiar not only to its original Huguenot occupants but also to those living here until the First World War.

What sets the place apart is Severs' insistence on creating what he called a "still life drama", a series of *tableaux vivants* giving the impression that the occupants have merely stepped outside for a moment. Guttering candles, half-eaten bread, laundry on a drying rack, scented pomanders, and muffled voices in the next room. Severs said that he "worked inside out to create…a collection of atmospheres: moods that harbour the light and the spirit of various ages."

Woven through the house is the story of the fictitious Jervis family (their name anglicised from the original French 'Gervais'). Each room evokes moments from their lives as imagined by Severs. Although it seems a pity he is no longer a physical presence at the property, in dying Severs enabled the place to be opened up to a wider public. He bequeathed the house to the Spitalfields Trust with careful instructions on how best the visitor should experience it: in silence and with an open mind. This advice holds especially true during the candlelit 'Silent Night' tours available by appointment.

> Georgian London continues farther west on Lamb's Conduit Street (WC1) (don't miss London's narrowest alley just 67 centimetres wide at 7 Rugby Street nearby), Bedford Square (WC1), Henrietta Street (WC2), and Queen Anne's Gate (SW1), a superbly-preserved Georgian street with a series of ornately carved wooden door canopies. A little older is Goodwin's Court, an atmospheric gas-lit alley off St. Martin's Lane (WC2), with bow-fronted windows dating from 1690.

Other places of interest nearby: 6, 7

9 London Unseen

EC1Y 1BE (Shoreditch), the Unseen Tour of Shoreditch
commencing at Old Street Tube station
Northern line to Old Street (note: guided tours are
by appointment only)

The 1967 documentary film *The London Nobody Knows* provides a nostalgic glimpse of what remained of old London at that time. Based on a book of the same name by Geoffrey Fletcher it depicts unsung locations and underprivileged people swept aside when the capital was subsequently redeveloped. Fortunately today there are still those intent on revealing London from a different perspective. One example is Unseen Tours (www.unseentours.co.uk), an organisation offering alternative walks celebrating the city's historical and cultural quirks. What makes Unseen Tours different is that all its guides are either homeless or vulnerably housed.

The idea for Unseen Tours evolved from the work of The Sock Mob, a grassroots volunteer network distributing food and socks to London's homeless. Their goal is to present the homeless in a different light, as people with something to offer. It's a logical approach since the homeless know the streets intimately, and out of necessity they tend to be good communicators. Ultimately the lucky ones can secure sustainable work on the very streets where they once slept.

Street Art explained during an Unseen Tour of Shoreditch

It is important to stress that Unseen Tours is not part of any poverty tourism agenda and its itineraries do not focus on impoverished areas. Rather they cover mainstream tourist destinations such as Covent Garden and London Bridge, as well as vibrant alternative locations such as Camden, Shoreditch and Brick Lane. They differ from commercial walking companies in two main ways. Firstly, the guides take the lion's share of the ticket revenues, and secondly because the tours utilise the guides' own stories of homelessness a unique level of social consciousness is achieved. The fact that a homeless person is the tour leader effectively reverses the traditional relationship between homeless and mainstream society.

The five itineraries offered by Unseen Tours are both entertaining and enlightening (and it comes as no surprise that a couple of free places are always reserved for carers and those who can't pay). In Covent Garden, for example, the focus is less on the famous former market and its buskers and more on the area's seedy red light past, and how that ties into the lives of those living on the street today. At London Bridge the emphasis is on the backstreets of Borough, once home to victims of social injustice. The mood lightens somewhat in Camden, a location renowned for its music venues and arts scene, although it remains one of the most polarised boroughs in London in terms of distribution of wealth. The Unseen Tour grapples with this through a combination of historical tales and contemporary anecdotes.

East London is covered by two Unseen Tours. The Shoreditch tour kicks off outside Old Street Tube station and takes in squats, Shakespeare, and the birth of Street Art. Along the way it is explained how this part of London has been gentrified in recent years, and the impact this has had on the lives of the less well-to-do. The Brick Lane tour takes in the backstreets around Old Spitalfields Market. The antithesis of the area's Jack the Ripper tours, the focus here is on multiculturalism (notably the area's Bangladeshi textile workers), trade unions, and women's rights. At the end of the tour the guide will point participants in the direction of a local pub or café. Why not ask them to come along and extend the social experiment pioneered by Unseen Tours?

Several other companies offer tours of East London's street art, including Shoreditch Street Art Tours (www.shoreditchstreetarttours.co.uk), Alternative London (www.alternativeldn.co.uk), and Insider London (www.insider-london.co.uk).

Other places of interest nearby: 10

10 A Hill of Bones

EC1Y 1AU (St. Luke's), Bunhill Fields Cemetery
at 38 City Road
Northern line to Old Street

London in Victorian times witnessed a dramatic increase in population and consequently in the demand for burial space. The City's existing churchyards in use since medieval times became overcrowded and began posing a health hazard. This led to the Burials Act of 1852 by which the old churchyards were closed and new ones opened in the suburbs (see no. 91).

Only one burial ground, Bunhill Fields on City Road (EC1), survived the clearances, and a fascinating place it is. Originally a marshy field in the manor of Finsbury the land was leased in 1315 to the City of London Corporation. When the charnel house of St. Paul's was emptied in 1549, the Corporation brought the remains here. The resulting hill of bones gave rise to the name Bunhill.

Later in 1665 the Corporation earmarked Bunhill as an unconsecrated burial ground for those who could not be buried in conventional cemeteries, notably plague victims. Twenty years later Bunhill became a cemetery predominantly for Nonconformist Protestants and others who worshipped outside the Church of England. By the time of the

A jumble of ancient gravestones at Bunhill Fields Cemetery

Burials Act more than 100,000 of them had been laid to rest in what is today managed as a public garden.

The list of burials at Bunhill reads like a Who's Who of Dissenters. Amongst the mossy memorials are those to the radical preacher and author of *Pilgrim's Progress* John Bunyan (1628–1688), the hymn writer Isaac Watts (1674–1748), the author of *Robinson Crusoe* Daniel Defoe (1660–1731), the visionary and poet William Blake (1757–1827), and the philanthropist Thomas Fowell Buxton (1786–1845), who made his fortune as a brewer in nearby Spitalfields (see no. 7). The majority, however, are unknown, including one Dame Mary Page. The inscription on this stoical lady's headstone reveals that "in 67 months, she was tapped 66 times, had taken away 240 gallons of water, without ever repining at her case or fearing the operation"!

One of the most famous Nonconformists was John Wesley (1703–1791), the founder of Methodism. It is fitting that his former home and chapel containing his tomb lie directly opposite Bunhill Fields at 49 City Road. It is said that Wesley deliberately aligned the chapel with his mother's grave in the cemetery. Wesley's house is well worth visiting since it includes the wooden writing case that he balanced on his saddle, composing sermons as he travelled around the country. It has been calculated that during his lifetime he rode 400,000 kilometres on horseback and delivered some 40,000 sermons! Little wonder that the statue of Wesley standing outside the chapel is inscribed "The world is my parish". The chapel contains a museum of Methodism in its crypt and has the added bonus of some splendid urinals installed by Thomas Crapper in 1891!

Behind Bunhill Fields off Bunhill Row is Chequer Street and the Bunhill Quaker Garden. An estimated 12,000 Quakers are buried here in unmarked graves together with their founder, George Fox (1624–1691).

To learn more about English Protestant Nonconformity visit Dr. Williams' Library at 14 Gordon Square (WC1) bequeathed in 1716 by one of London's leading Nonconformist ministers. To see where Wesley was inspired to found Methodism visit the Museum of London at 150 London Wall (EC2), where a flame-shaped memorial marks the spot. To visit a Nonconformist church visit the Dutch Church at 7 Austin Friars (EC2), founded by Walloon refugees from the Netherlands in 1550. It is the oldest Dutch-language Protestant church in the world.

Other places of interest nearby: 9

11 A Visit to a Turkish Bath

EC2M 3TJ (The City), the former Nevill's Turkish Bath
at 7–8 Bishopsgate Churchyard
Circle, Hammersmith & City, Metropolitan, Northern lines to
Liverpool Street

The street name Bishopsgate is a reminder that one of the seven gates that gave access to the City of London once stood hereabouts (see no. 1). Nothing remains of it today and the area has largely been turned over to modern office buildings. An exception is the 18th century Church of St. Botolph-without-Bishopsgate, and in the churchyard behind it the unexpected remains of a Victorian Turkish bath.

A bath has existed here since 1817 and in the days when most homes lacked bathrooms it would have offered a pleasurable way of keeping clean for those who could afford it. In the late 1880s it was sold as a going concern to Henry and James Forder Nevill, who had previously erected a bath building in Northumberland Avenue (WC2). Realising their new acquisition was old-fashioned by comparison they demolished it, and in 1895 unveiled the exotic Ottoman-style structure seen today.

At first glance Nevill's Turkish Bath appears tiny – but that's because only the flamboyant entrance is visible: the baths themselves lay underground. The entrance takes the form of a kiosk modelled on the Church of the Holy Sepulchre in Jerusalem. Its walls are pierced by Moorish-style ogee windows and clad in blue and brown faience tiles. The deep terracotta cornice

What remains of Nevill's Turkish Bath off Bishopsgate

conceals an attic that once contained the water tanks for the bath, and the whole is crowned with an onion-shaped dome topped off with a golden Turkish crescent.

Male bathers entering the kiosk – mostly City gents from the Stock Exchange and Lloyds – would have descended a winding staircase to reach the ticket desk (3/6d before 7pm and 2/- thereafter). They then proceeded through to a carpeted cooling room divided into cubicles by walnut screens inlaid with blue glass and decorated richly in the style of the Alhambra. Leading off this were three hot rooms with tiled walls, mosaic floors and marble seats, which must have made the bustling City seem far away. All were illuminated by electricity and the hottest room – the Caldarium – was heated to a sultry 270°F. Fresh hot air was supplied through grates near the ceiling, whilst stale air was extracted through ventilators at floor level. After passing through an adjacent shampooing room, customers then had a choice of showers, and finally a bracing dip in a cold plunge pool.

After surviving the Second World War the bath remained open until 1954, when declining numbers and rising fuel costs brought about its closure. Since the 1970s, the remains have been variously used as a restaurant, bar and night club.

To experience a Turkish Bath today visit Ironmonger Row Baths at 1 Norman Street (EC1). Opened in 1931 they provided public washing and laundry facilities at a time when only 4% of the local population had access to a private bath. In 1937 a swimming pool was added and Turkish baths installed in the basement. These popular features ensured that the baths remained viable after the Second World War, when more houses were built with their own bathrooms. Although the original individual slipper baths were subsequently removed and the facilities modernised, the Turkish baths and public laundry are still used today. All that's really changed is the price of admission – and the fact that after a good steam and a massage, customers can no longer enjoy a poached egg on toast for 1/4d!

Other places of interest nearby: 5, 12

12 Where to Hold a Bar of Gold

**EC2R 8AH (The City), the Bank of England Museum
on Bartholomew Lane
Central, DLR, Northern, Waterloo & City lines to Bank**

Emerging from the Tube station at Bank one is brought face-to-face with the buildings that have long represented the power and wealth of the City. They include the Mansion House, the Royal Exchange, and, of course, the Bank of England. Located on Threadneedle Street – the name recalling the nearby Worshipful Company of Merchant Taylors – the bank can be visited during Open House London (www. openhouselondon.org.uk) but one should not expect to see anything very old. It may have been located here since 1734 but the current building dates only from a rebuilding in the 1920s and 30s. Instead visit the Bank of England Museum on nearby Bartholomew Lane, where the British banking system is documented from earliest times.

The Bank of England was founded in 1694 to raise money for William III (1650–1702) in his costly war against France. Whereas banking had previously been in the hands of goldsmiths, who made loans to merchants and the Crown, the broader-based Bank of England could provide the government with share capital in return for interest. In doing so it became one of the world's first privately-owned national banks. Still essentially a private business it acts today as central bank

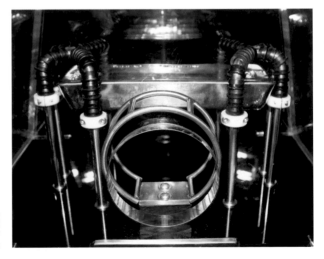

Visitors can touch this heavily-protected gold bar in the Bank of England Museum

for the United Kingdom, setting interest rates to control inflation, issuing banknotes, and working to help maintain a healthy economy.

The Bank of England Museum conveys all this in a surprisingly entertaining and interactive way. The first section is centred on a reconstruction of the original banking hall used from 1793 until the bank was rebuilt. Designed by the renowned architect Sir John Soane (1753–1837) it features mahogany counter tops and oak ledger rests brought to life by mannequins of bank clerks.

The next section covers the early years of the bank's history. Exhibits include the original terms of operation drafted by the Scottish merchant William Paterson (1658–1719), a book containing the names of those who subscribed to the initial loan of £1,200,000, and the bank's Charter granted by William III. Mention is also made of the so-called Restriction Period, when the war with France saw the bank's falling gold reserves force a curb on payments of its notes in gold. It was during this period that the bank was nicknamed 'The Old Lady of Threadneedle Street' after a political cartoonist depicted it as an elderly dame being wooed by then Prime Minister, William Pitt the Younger.

Next comes the Rotunda which is supported by *caryatids* rescued from the original building. It provides a suitably grand backdrop for the museum's display of precious metals, including a heavily-protected bar of 99.79% gold that visitors can touch (the doormen outside the bank wear gold-trimmed top hats as a reminder that the bank still controls Britain's gold reserves). Also exhibited here are the pikes and muskets once used to protect the bank. The gallery beyond charts the development of paper money from banknotes written out by clerks in longhand (and signed individually by cashiers) to today's mass-produced counterfeit-proof notes.

The museum's final section covers money in the modern economy, where it's worth remembering that today's pound sign (£) is ancient having developed from the letter 'L' of the word *libra*, an ancient Roman unit of weight.

Those interested in precious metals should also visit the London Silver Vaults at 53–64 Chancery Lane (WC2), a unique retail silver outlet housed in the former Chancery Lane Safe Deposit opened in 1876.

Other places of interest nearby: 4, 11, 14

13 Heroes and Villains

EC4R 2RL (The City), the stained-glass window of Dick
Whittington in the Church of St. Michael Paternoster Royal
on College Hill
Circle, District lines to Mansion House or Cannon Street

The long story of London features many local heroes and one of the
first was medieval merchant and politician Richard Whittington (1358–
1423), who provided the real-life inspiration for the folk tale *Dick Whittington and his Cat*. According to the tale Dick Whittington was a poor
country boy who walks to London to seek his fortune, where he finds
work in the kitchen of a merchant called Fitzwarren. To control the
mice in his bedroom Dick keeps a pet cat, which eventually finds its
way to the vermin-infested court of a foreign king. Dick leaves London
but at Highgate Hill he hears the bells of Bow Church encouraging him
to return. Once back in London he receives a fortune in gold paid by
the grateful king, he marries the merchant's daughter, and eventually
becomes Lord Mayor.

As with all good folk
tales there are elements of
truth here. The real Richard Whittington did indeed
hail from the country – but
his father was a wealthy
landowner. When his older
brother inherited the family
estate Whittington moved
to the City and joined the
Worshipful Company of
Mercers. He grew rich supplying the Royal Court with
luxury imported fabrics
and in 1397 was made Lord
Mayor of the City of Lon-
don, a position he eventually filled four times.

It is also true that Whittington married a woman
called Fitzwarren. She pre-
deceased him and in the

Dick Whittington and his cat in the Church of St. Michael
Paternoster Royal

absence of heirs he left his considerable fortune to the City. Amongst other things the money was used to found Guildhall Library, to rebuild Newgate Prison, and to create a charity that still helps London's disadvantaged. Whittington also financed the rebuilding of the Church of St. Michael Paternoster Royal on College Hill (EC4) near to where he once lived. He is buried there and although his tomb is now lost a search for it in 1949 revealed a mummified cat! Unfortunately it only dates from a rebuilding of the church by Sir Christopher Wren (1632–1723). Both Whittington and his cat appear today in a stained-glass window in the church.

London also has its share of villains, including the dashing French highwayman Claude Duval (1643–1670), who was hung at Tyburn for robbing stagecoaches. Legend has it that he liked to dance with his female victims and that several society beauties attended his funeral at the Church of St. Paul Covent Garden on Bedford Street (WC2). It was at the same church during a puppet show in 1662 that another villain, the anarchic Mr. Punch, was first documented by diarist Samuel Pepys (1633–1703), an event marked on the second Sunday in May by an extraordinary church service for puppetmasters.

London's most infamous villain was Victorian serial killer Jack the Ripper, who operated in the poverty-stricken slums around Whitechapel. Attacks against the area's prostitutes were rife and of the eleven murdered here between 1888 and 1891 five bore the hallmarks of a single killer, namely deep cuts to the throat and abdominal mutilations. The fact that the perpetrator was neither caught nor identified has maintained interest in the case to this day.

Three of the murder scenes lie within the parameters of this book: 29 Hanbury Street (EC1), where the Ripper's second victim Annie Chapman was murdered; Mitre Square (EC3), where the body of fourth victim Catherine Eddowes was found; and the alley known formerly as Dorset Street behind the Old London Fruit Exchange on Brushfield Street (E1), where the final victim Mary Jane Kelly met her end. She is said to have picked up clients outside the Ten Bells Pub around the corner at 84 Commercial Street.

Of the many Ripper-themed walking tours available one of the best is that devised by retired police officer and published Ripperologist Donald Rumbelow, who remembers patrolling Mitre Square when it was still gaslit (www.jacktheripperwalk.com).

Other places of interest nearby: 14, 15

14 London's Alternative Royal Family

EC2V 6AU (The City), the Costermongers' Harvest Festival
in the Church of St. Mary-le-Bow on Cheapside
Central line to St. Paul's; Central, District lines to Mansion
House; Central, DLR, Northern, Waterloo & City lines
to Bank

London revels in its customs and traditions and many involve royalty. Uniformed soldiers, ushers, chamberlains and other officials accompany (and sometimes deputise for) the monarch in a variety of annual ceremonies. Some such as Remembrance Day and Trooping the Colour are well-known and attended by the public, whereas others including the State Opening of Parliament and Royal Epiphany take place largely behind closed doors (see nos. 2, 77 & 86). One of the most curious is the Quit Rents Ceremony, which occurs in October in the Royal Courts of Justice on the Strand (WC2), whereby the City of London Corpora--

Pearly royalty gathering in Guildhall Yard

Members of the London Pearly Kings and Queens Society

tion's solicitor makes a payment to the Monarch's Remembrancer (a legal officer of the Crown) in the form of two faggots, six horseshoes and 61 nails. This act relieves the Corporation of its obligation to pay rent on a blacksmith's forge in the parish of St. Clement Danes given in 1235 by Henry III (1216–1272). Apart from the Coronation it might well be the oldest surviving ceremony in England.

London's royal pageantry, however, is not restricted solely to the monarch. The capital boasts an alternative royal family in the form of its Pearly Kings and Queens, with their own distinctive flair for tradition. The Pearlies began life as Victorian costermongers, street vendors who distributed market produce around London by handcart (the name is derived from the word 'costard' being an extinct medieval variety of apple). By 1860 there were 30,000 costers in London and considerable rivalry had developed between them. They wore flamboyant clothes to maintain customer loyalty and developed their own dialect to avoid the attentions of the police. To help keep the peace respected senior costers were elected 'kings', who identified themselves by sewing mother-of-pearl buttons on their garments. The fashion caught on and by 1911 all 28 metropolitan boroughs of London boasted their own Pearly royal family.

As retail patterns changed so the profession of costermongering declined. Instead London's Pearlies embraced a charity role, attending events in all their finery to help raise money for good causes. Their magnificent outfits are a sight to behold with many handed down through the generations. Some are adorned with as many as 35,000 buttons and weigh up to 30 kilos!

The most important event in the Pearly calendar is the Costermongers' Harvest Festival. The London Pearly Kings and Queens Society attend theirs on the last Sunday in September in the Church of St. Mary-le-Bow on Cheapside (EC2), after congregating in Guildhall Yard. They celebrate another on the second Sunday in October in the Church of St. Paul Covent Garden on Bedford Street (WC2). Meanwhile the Original Pearly Kings and Queens Association attend theirs on the first Sunday in October in the Church of St. Martin-in-the-Fields on Trafalgar Square (WC2). In the crypt here stands the life-sized statue of Henry Croft (1861–1930), a road sweeper who in 1880 was so impressed by the Pearly tradition that he covered himself in buttons from head to toe. Dressed in this so-called "smother suit" he raised a small fortune for local hospitals in the days before the National Health Service. By the time he died he was a London celebrity and his funeral was attended by 400 fellow Pearlies.

The Church of St. Clement Danes on the Strand (WC2) hosts another London custom. In 1919 its carillon was altered to ring out the traditional nursery rhyme *Oranges and Lemons* (daily every three hours between 9am and 9pm) in which "the bells of St. Clements" are mentioned. Since then a service has been held in the third week of March during which citrus fruits are presented to schoolchildren. The church of St. Clement's Eastcheap on Clements Lane (EC3) also lays claim to the rhyme since it stands nearer to the wharf where the fruits were once unloaded. Whatever the truth the origin of the nursery rhyme, which refers to the bells of several churches within or close to the City of London, remains obscure. Suggestions have included child sacrifice, public executions and even the marital difficulties of Henry VIII!

Other places of interest nearby: 12, 13, 15, 16, 17

15   Secrets of St. Paul's

EC4M 8AD (The City), St. Paul's Cathedral in St. Paul's Churchyard
Central line to St. Paul's (note: be prepared for a high admission charge and a ban on photography; tours of the *Triforium* are by appointment only)

A consideration of St. Paul's Cathedral should really begin on Bankside (SE1). This is where the architect Sir Christopher Wren (1632–1723) lived while supervising the cathedral's construction, and from where he had an unimpeded view of the work in progress. A plaque identifying Number 49 as Wren's house was removed here from his actual home a few doors away when it was demolished.

For fourteen centuries a cathedral dedicated to Saint Paul has stood on the summit of Ludgate Hill. Rising majestically over the City, Wren's cathedral is the fifth structure on the site to bear the name of London's patron saint. The suggestion that a Roman temple to the goddess Diana stood here has never been proven.

The first cathedral was a wooden one erected in AD 604, when the Frankish abbot Mellitus, sent by Pope Gregory I (540–604) to convert the Kingdom of Kent to Christianity, was made first Bishop of London. After being destroyed by fire it was rebuilt in 675 in stone only to be destroyed in the 9th century by the Vikings and rebuilt again in 962. In 1087 this too burned and its replacement, known as Old St. Paul's, was erected. Completed in 1314 with what at the time was the highest spire ever built it remained in use until its destruction in 1666 during the Great Fire (see no. 3).

Of Old St. Paul's nothing remains except for the outline of an octagonal chapter house south of the present nave. The street names surrounding the present cathedral, however, probably originated in processions through the walled precincts of Old St. Paul's. The Lord's Prayer would have been sung on Paternoster Row and completed at Amen Court, followed by the Hail Mary in Ave Maria Lane and the Credo in Creed Lane.

After the fire Wren was commissioned to design an entirely new cathedral. Influenced by Renaissance and Baroque trends it is not surprising that his early designs were rejected by the puritanical Church Commissioners. His fifth design, however, was accepted with a "noble cupola…of wonderful grace" between the nave and choir.

Despite being a well-known building, St. Paul's still retains some secrets. Look closely at the pediment over the entrance into the South Transept. It is said that when the site was cleared Wren asked a workman to fetch a stone to mark the centre of the new building. The man brought a broken gravestone inscribed with the word *Resurgam*, meaning "I shall

St. Paul's Cathedral seen from Bankside

rise again", which Wren had inscribed here beneath a phoenix rising from the flames. The adjacent blank second storey walls are used to conceal Gothic flying buttresses supporting the cathedral's clerestory, whilst eight hidden columns support the dome.

Inside the Great West Door on the right-hand side is the superbly cantilevered Geometrical Staircase. It spirals up through the southwestern tower to the *Triforium*, a secret arcade running down both sides of the nave. Here can be found the Cathedral Library and the Trophy Room containing Wren's Great Model, his third design for the cathedral.

The painted dome encircled by the famous Whispering Gallery – reached by 257 steps – is actually the innermost of three domes. Above it rises an unseen brick cone supporting the stone lantern topped out in 1708, and around that is a lead-sheathed timber dome forming the roof (the lantern's Golden Gallery is 85 metres above the cathedral floor and can be reached by 528 steps). In the choir beyond the dome are much-admired stalls carved by Grinling Gibbons (1648–1721) but don't overlook the wrought iron screens by the mysterious Jean Tijou. Here can also be found the ghostly effigy of poet and cleric John Donne (1572–1631) and William Holman Hunt's bewitching painting *The Light of the World*.

It is entirely fitting that Wren is buried in the cathedral's crypt, where his tomb is inscribed thus: *Lector, si monumentum requiris, circumspice* (Reader, if you seek his memorial, look around you).

Other places of interest nearby: 13, 14, 16, 17, 23

16 The Worshipful Company of Goldsmiths

EC2V 6BN (The City), Goldsmiths' Hall at
13 Foster Lane
Central line to St. Paul's (note: tours are by appointment
only between October and March)

London is home to more than a hundred livery companies. These historic trade associations based predominantly in the City developed out of informal medieval guilds established to protect, support and regulate particular professions. Most company's trading rights are enshrined by Royal Charter, which also allows them to wear their own unique ceremonial robes (or livery) and in many cases to use the honorific prefix 'Worshipful Company'.

There are livery companies not only for traditional professions – Bakers, Brewers, Saddlers, and Shipwrights – but also newer ones, including Information Technologists, Management Consultants, and Security Professionals. Since 1515, when the 48 companies in existence at the time were listed according to economic and political power, the top dozen have been known as the 'Great Twelve'. They are the Mercers, Grocers, Drapers, Fishmongers, Goldsmiths, Merchant Taylors, Skinners, Haberdashers, Salters, Ironmongers, Vintners, and Clothworkers. Those established *after* 1515 are ranked in order of creation making the Worshipful Company of Arts Scholars, which received livery status in 2014, the 110th to be formed.

Many companies still continue their original professional function. The Hackney Carriage Drivers, for example, only admit those who have passed the 'Knowledge of London' test. Others such as the Tallow Chandlers, whose trade is now obsolete, have evolved into charitable and educational foundations. Past or present they all retain an important social and networking function, and are governed by a Master and several Wardens.

Royal Charters also granted livery companies the right to build meeting halls and 39 still possess one. Although none are original each is unique, from the tiny Georgian Watermens' Hall at 16–18 St. Mary-at-Hill (EC3) to the Victorian splendour of Drapers' Hall on Throgmorton Avenue (EC2). The oldest extant hall built in 1672 belongs to the Apothecaries on Blackfriars Lane (EC4) and has unicorns carved over its door. That this company's banner hangs in the nearby Church of St. Andrew-by-the Wardrobe is a reminder that livery companies were once tied closely to Rome.

Goldsmiths' Hall at 13 Foster Lane (EC2) was one of the first to be built in 1339. Rebuilt in the 1630s and again in 1835 in Neo-Classical style it is the second largest after Plaisterers' Hall at 1 London Wall (EC2). Although most halls

The gilded splendour of Goldsmiths' Hall

are now rented out for business and other events relatively few people ever get to see inside them. Goldsmiths' Hall is one of the easier ones to access by virtue of its free monthly tours between October and March (www.thegoldsmiths.co.uk). Highlights include the Main Staircase, the Drawing Room, with a carpet into which is woven the Company's coat of arms, and the magnificent Livery Hall itself, with its Corinthian columns, ornate ceiling, and crystal chandeliers.

Outside Goldsmiths' Hall on Gresham Street (EC2) is a tiny park, where the Church of St. John Zachary stood until its destruction during the Great Fire. The Goldsmiths installed the park gate adorned with the leopard's head used by their Assay Office to hallmark precious metals since the 1300s. This makes it the oldest company in Britain to trade continually from the same site. Each spring the Goldsmiths test the quality of coins made by the Royal Mint in an ancient ceremony known as the Trial of the Pyx (a *pyx* being the wooden box containing the sample coins).

Also on Gresham Street is Guildhall, where the Lord Mayor of the City of London Corporation resides. Livery companies are eligible to vote in the annual election of the Lord Mayor (not to be confused with the Mayor of London) and of the two City Sheriffs from which he or she is drawn. After being elected the new Lord Mayor rides from Guildhall to the Royal Courts of Justice on the Strand (WC2) to take the oath before the Lord Chief Justice. Known as the Lord Mayor's Show the procession occurs on the second Saturday in November. One of the Lord Mayor's duties is to preside over the City's Court of Aldermen (one from each of the City's 25 wards), which meets at Guildhall to oversee the formation of new livery companies.

Swan Upping recalled outside the Church of St. James Garlickhythe

Numerous archaic traditions are associated with the livery companies. When the Vintners, for example, process to the Church of St. James Garlickhythe on Garlick Hill (EC4) after electing a new Master on the second Thursday in July they are preceded by a wine porter in traditional smock and top hat. He sweeps the pavement with a birch broom in a tradition dating back to the days when horses dirtied the streets. Outside the church is a sculpture entitled *Barge Master and Swan* commissioned by the Vintners in 2007. It is a reminder that during the third week in July the Vintners join with the Dyers in the custom of Swan Upping, when cygnets on the Thames as far as Henley are tagged as a means of monitoring the swan population. The custom dates back to 1473 when Edward IV (1461–1470) borrowed money from the two Companies in return for ownership of several royal swans, which each year were identified by a distinctive nick made in their beaks.

Another watery custom is the Doggett's Coat and Badge sponsored since 1715 by the Fishmongers' Company. The prize for this annual Thames boat race between London Bridge and Chelsea Bridge is a red coat and a silver badge named in honour of Thomas Doggett, who launched the race in 1716. As such it is the oldest continually staged annual sporting event in the world.

Fishmongers' Hall on the riverside at London Bridge (EC4) contains the dagger used by Sir William Walworth (d. 1385) in 1381 to end the Peasants' Revolt by stabbing the rebel Wat Tyler in the presence of Richard II (1377–1399). Walworth was not only a fishmonger but also twice Lord Mayor of the City of London.

Other places of interest nearby: 14, 15, 17, 18, 19

17 Postman's Park

EC1A 7BX (The City), Postman's Park on King Edward Street
Central line to St. Paul's (note: the park is only open during
daylight hours)

Standing outside the former General Post Office Headquarters on King
Edward Street (EC1) is a bronze statue on a granite plinth. Unveiled
in 1882 it commemorates Rowland Hill (1795–1879), who in 1840 pioneered the Penny Post, the world's first prepaid postal system. As the
first country in the world to print stamps Britain retains the unique
privilege of not having to depict the country of origin on its postal
stationery.

The statue and the building are not, however, the only reminders
here of the British postal system. Across the road is the 18th century
Church of St. Botolph-without-Aldersgate. In 1880 its graveyard was
cleared in line with the Burials Act of 1852 and replaced by a public
park. This was soon nicknamed Postman's Park because of its popularity with postal workers on their lunch breaks (see no. 91).

Around the same time George Frederick Watts (1817–1904), a popular painter and outspoken socialist, came up with the idea of com-

The author examines the Watts Memorial to Heroic Self Sacrifice

memorating the bravery of ordinary Londoners who had died trying to save the lives of others. Accordingly he gave funds for glazed ceramic tablets to be made and for a wooden loggia to be constructed in the park to house them. On each tablet, several of which were manufactured by Royal Doulton in Lambeth, the story of an everyday Victorian hero would be recorded.

Opened in 1900 the Watts Memorial to Heroic Self Sacrifice had an intended capacity of 120 tablets, although initially only four were installed. By the time Watts died another nine had been added, after which Watts' wife took over the running of the memorial. Over the next few years another 35 tablets were installed, as well as a memorial to Watts himself. Thereafter, however, with interest waning and money tight, the project was wound down and by the time of Mrs Watts' death in 1938 the total number of tablets totalled only 53.

Despite their melodramatic tone the stories on the tablets are moving. Take Ernest Benning, for example, who drowned saving another "one dark night off Pimlico Pier", or Frederick Alfred Croft "who saved a lunatic woman from suicide at Woolwich Arsenal Station but was himself run over by the train". Then there is the Battersea sugar refinery worker "fatally scalded in returning to search for his mate", and the mother who perished "saving her family and house by carrying blazing paraffin to the yard".

There is an interesting corollary to the story of the Watt's Memorial. In 2004 scenes for the film *Closer* were shot in Postman's Park and interest in the memorial rekindled. As a result in June 2009 a new tablet was added to the memorial for the first time in 78 years. It commemorates Leigh Pitt, a young print technician from Surrey, who died in 2007 trying to rescue a boy from a canal in Thamesmead. At the behest of Pitt's fiancée and colleagues the Diocese of London arranged for his selfless act to be recorded on the Watts' Memorial.

George Frederick Watts was also a sculptor but rarely worked in the genre because of an allergy to plaster. An exception is his equestrian bronze *Physical Energy* in Kensington Gardens (W2). To explore further the history of the British postal system visit the Royal Mail Archive in Freeling House on Phoenix Place (WC1), part of the huge Mount Pleasant sorting office.

Other places of interest nearby: 14, 15, 16, 18, 19

18 A History of London in Eight Objects

EC2Y 5HN (Barbican), the Museum of London at
150 London Wall
Circle, Hammersmith & City, Metropolitan lines to Barbican;
Circle, Hammersmith & City, Metropolitan, Northern lines to
Moorgate; Central line to St. Paul's

For an institution documenting the history of a city and its people, the Museum of London is perfectly located. Sandwiched between St. Paul's Cathedral and the post-war Barbican Estate it overlooks the ruined walls of Roman Londinium, where the story of London really begins (see no. 1). The museum opened in 1976 and is designed so that the visitor follows a single route through eight galleries, taking in some 7,000 objects displayed chronologically. What follows is a brief description of the contents of each gallery together with one iconic object:

1) *London before London (450,000 BC–AD 47)* explores the prehistory of the Thames Valley until the arrival of the Romans. The area was a wilderness inhabited by few people and many Aurochs, a huge wild ox immortalised in prehistoric cave paintings and the ancestor of today's domestic cattle. The skull displayed comes from Ilford northeast of London and is dated between 245,000 and 186,000 BC.

2) *Roman London (AD 47–410)* brings together evidence for Roman Londinium until the Roman departure in AD 410. Building work continues to throw up fascinating remains including an extraordinarily well-preserved pair of 1st century leather briefs from the bottom of a well in Queen Street (EC4)!

3) *Medieval London (AD 410–1558)* details the post-Roman period until the mid-16th century during which London experienced inva-

A Vespa motor scooter in the Museum of London represents the Swinging Sixties

sion, famine, and religious and political upheaval yet still grew into one of Europe's most important cities. It was the age of the crusader knights and the pewter model of one dated c. 1300 is amongst the earliest mass-produced metal toys in England.

4) *War, Plague and Fire (1550s–1660s)* covers London from the time of Elizabeth I (1558–1603) until the Great Fire of London in 1666, and details the Great Plague that claimed 100,000 lives. On display is the plaster death mask of Parliamentarian Oliver Cromwell, whose Protectorship (1653–1658) came in the wake of the English Civil War (1641–1651) and the execution of Charles I (1625–1649).

5) *The Expanding City (1670s–1850s)* shows how London was rebuilt after the Fire and transformed into the capital of a vast trading empire. To enable the expanding population to escape the throng, Georgian pleasure gardens were built and the one at Vauxhall is recreated here, with a display of costumes from the period.

6) *The People's City (1850s–1940s)* depicts Victorian London as the world's wealthiest city but one divided between rich and poor. Charles Booth's colour-coded poverty maps sit alongside a 1920s *Art Deco* lift from Selfridges' department store, a glamorous symbol of the well-to-do West End. Two World Wars went some way to bridging the gap.

7) *The World City (1950s–today)* brings London's story up to date and focusses on the city as a fashion capital. On display is a Vespa scooter recalling the Swinging Sixties and its epicentre, Carnaby Street.

8) *The City Gallery* contains the magnificent gilded Lord Mayor's State Coach of 1757, which takes to the streets each November for the Lord Mayor's Show.

Tours of the museum finish in the Sackler Hall, where there is a café surrounded by an elliptical LED curtain on which a whirl of interesting London statistics are presented.

The Barbican Estate is a residential complex of towers and terrace blocks built in the 1960s and 70s in an area of the City devastated during the Second World War. An important example of concrete Brutalist architecture it contains the Barbican Centre on Silk Street, one of Europe's largest performing arts venue. Guided tours are available.

Other places of interest nearby: 16, 17, 19, 20

19   Medieval Church Survivors

EC1A 9DS (The City), a walking tour of the City's medieval churches beginning with the Church of St. Bartholomew the Great on West Smithfield
Circle, Hammersmith & City, Metropolitan lines to Barbican (note: with the exception of St. Bartholomew's the Great most City churches are only open on weekdays)

It is remarkable to think that by the end of the Middle Ages there were over a hundred parish churches in the City of London, an area barely more than 1.5 kilometres square. In 1666 the Great Fire destroyed 88 of them, after which 51 were rebuilt by the office of Sir Christopher Wren (1632–1723) (see no. 3). Depopulation, war and the demands of developers have reduced those remaining to around 40. What follows is a tour of the City's eight extant medieval churches, which today form a convenient arc inside the City's boundary (for a tour of post-medieval City churches see no. 26).

The tour begins with St. Bartholomew's the Great on West Smithfield (EC1). Surely one of London's most atmospheric churches, the building seen today is all that remains of an Augustinian Priory founded in 1123 with St. Bartholomew's Hospital by the monk Rahere (St. Bartholomew's the Less serves the hospital itself and retains a medieval tower). The church is approached by means of a quaint gatehouse, a remnant of the priory's west front. A garden path then

Sturdy Norman columns in the Church of St. Bartholomew the Great

crosses what was once the nave, demolished at the time of the Dissolution. The present church occupies the original chancel, its sturdy columns representing the only substantial Norman architecture left in the City. Filmgoers will recognise it from the films *Shakespeare in Love* and *Four Weddings and a Funeral*. Don't miss the Chapel of the Holy Icon, its walls blackened from when it was used as a blacksmith's forge after the Dissolution!

At the end of nearby Giltspur Street is St. Sepulchre's-without-Newgate (the suffix signifies it stood just outside a gate in the now demolished city wall). Rebuilt in 1440 and again after the Great Fire it still retains its Gothic tower, as well as an 18th century watch-house erected to deter grave-robbers. A handbell displayed in the nave was rung outside the cells of the condemned in Newgate Prison, which once stood opposite the church on Old Bailey (see no. 53).

Walk north-east now passing the ruined 17th century Christ Church Greyfriars to reach St. Giles'-without-Cripplegate on Fore Street (EC2). Gutted during the Blitz the Gothic walls of this church have been fully restored. This is where Oliver Cromwell (1599–1658) married and where the likes of explorer Martin Frobisher (1535–1594) and poet John Milton (1608–1674) are buried.

Continue to St. Ethelburga's Bishopsgate at 78 Bishopsgate. Rebuilt in 1400 this is the smallest church in the City. Fortunate in being located just north of where the Great Fire stopped it also survived the Blitz only to be ruined in 1993 by an IRA bomb. Rebuilt once again it is now used as a Centre for Reconciliation and Peace, and incorporates a Bedouin tent in its churchyard, where people of all faiths can find sanctuary. By contrast the largest church in the City is the 12th century St. Helen's Bishopsgate on nearby Great St. Helen's (EC3), its unique double nave once split between the parish and a nunnery. In the north wall is a rare hagioscope or squint (now blocked) through which sick nuns were once able to glimpse their altar.

Around the corner on St. Mary Axe is the 16th century St. Andrew's Undershaft (the name recalls the fact that a maypole stood here in the early 1500s) (see front cover). It contains an alabaster memorial to John Stow (1525–1605), a former parishioner and author of the famous *Survey of London*, in whose hand the Lord Mayor places a new quill pen every three years (www.lamas.org.uk).

Continue southwards to the 15th century Gothic St. Olave's Hart Street. Diarist Samuel Pepys (1633–1703) worshipped here and the skulls over the churchyard gate prompted Dickens to dub it "Saint Ghastly Grim"!

This tour finishes across the road with All Hallows-by-the-Tower on Byward Street. The City's oldest church it includes a 7th century Saxon arch, a Norman column, and a fascinating museum in the crypt containing a Roman pavement and the crow's nest from Ernest Shackleton's Antarctic vessel *Quest*.

The Norman keep of the Tower of London, the so-called White Tower, was originally enclosed within the City wall and contains the perfectly-preserved Chapel of St. John built around 1080.

Other places of interest nearby: 16, 17, 18, 20, 21

20 From Plague Pit to Pension House

EC1M 6AN (Farringdon), the London Charterhouse on Charterhouse Square
Circle, Hammersmith & City, Metropolitan lines to Barbican
(note: guided tours are by appointment only)

Crossing Charterhouse Square it is sobering to think one is walking over a medieval plague pit! Between 1348 and 1430 some 50,000 victims of the Black Death were buried here on waste land beyond the City wall. By contrast much of the area today is taken up by the London Charterhouse, surely England's most historic home for pensioners.

The story of the London Charterhouse is a long and fascinating one. The plague pit on which it stands was established in an act of philanthropy by Walter Manny (1310–1372), a soldier of fortune who proved his worth fighting for Edward III (1327–1377). In 1371 he founded a Carthusian priory on the site for two dozen monks (the name Charterhouse is an English corruption of Carthusian, which itself derives from Chartreuse, where the order originated). Manny stipulated in his will that he be buried in the priory church so the monks could pray for his soul.

Thereafter the priory became an important centre for ecclesiastical learning, attracting such visitors as the young Thomas More (1478–1535), who became advisor and chancellor to Henry VIII (1509–1547). When Henry abandoned Rome in 1535 to make himself supreme head of the English church, More began to question his loyalty. The monks at Charterhouse felt the same way for which their prior was hung at Tyburn Tree gallows (see no. 53). More was executed, too, and in 1537 the priory passed to the Crown. Little wonder, in the light of his brutal dissolution of religious establishments across the land, that Henry's last words were "Monks! Monks! Monks!"

In 1545 the abandoned priory was granted to the peer Sir Edward (later Lord) North (1496–1564), who constructed a fine Tudor mansion on the site. In 1558 Elizabeth I (1558–1603) stayed at the house for five days before proceeding to Westminster Abbey for her coronation. The mansion was then sold to Thomas Howard, 4th Duke of Norfolk (1536–1572). Another important guest was James VI of Scotland (1567–1625), who upon succeeding to the English throne as James I (1603–1625) came to Charterhouse from Edinburgh and held his first council in what is now the Great Chamber.

A new chapter in the history of Charterhouse opened in 1611, when Norfolk's son, Thomas Howard, 1st Earl of Suffolk (1561–1626), sold the mansion to Thomas Sutton (1532–1611). Between 1568 and 1594 Sutton had held the post of Master of the Ordnance in the Northern Parts, and his involvement with the coal trade, property dealing, and money lending had made him the wealthiest commoner in England. He used his fortune to endow a charitable foundation at Charterhouse, with a school for boys and an almshouse for the care of elderly men, known as brothers. Pupils at what

Winter sun highlights a detail of the London Charterhouse in Farringdon

became known as Sutton's Hospital included John Wesley (1703–1791), founder of the Methodist Church, and the novelist William Makepeace Thackeray (1811–1863). The writer Daniel Defoe (1660–1731) called it "the greatest and noblest gift that ever was given for charity, by any one man, public or private, in this nation."

In 1872 the school relocated to Godalming in Surrey and the site was turned over to various medical colleges. The almshouse, however, with its 15th century gateway remained in use, and to this day still serves its original function. The only difference is that the 40 brothers fortunate enough to reside here – all single retired gentlemen over the age of sixty – are more likely to be former teachers, writers and clergymen rather than the "decrepit or old captaynes...merchants fallen on hard times...or those ruined by shipwreck" of earlier times!

Other places of interest nearby: 18, 19, 21

21 The Legendary Knights of Saint John

EC1M 4DA (Clerkenwell), the Museum of the Order of St. John
in St. John's Gate on St. John Lane
Circle, Hammersmith & City, Metropolitan lines to Farringdon

Stories of crusading knights have long fired the public imagination, moreso in the wake of bestselling books such as *The Da Vinci Code*. But who were these fighting men of the cloth and what became of them? A good place to find out is the Museum of the Order of St. John on St. John Lane (EC1) in Clerkenwell.

A model of a knight in the Museum of the Order of St. John in Clerkenwell

Following the conversion to Christianity in 312 AD of Roman Emperor Constantine, pilgrims began making the long and hazardous journey to the Holy Land. Hostels (known as 'hospitals') were built in Jerusalem to provide the weary pilgrims with accommodation and medical assistance. Later during the First Crusade (1069–1099) two Roman Catholic Orders of Chivalry evolved out of these institutions. One of them, the Knights Hospitallers of St. John, established their own hospital in Jerusalem in 1080. The other, the Knights Templar, was founded to safeguard Jerusalem after its capture by the Crusaders in 1099.

In England the Knights Templar established their London headquarters south of Fleet Street in an area still known as Temple (the Royal Courts of Justice on the Strand occupy the site of the knights' tilting ground). They remained there until their suppression by the Pope in 1312 for becoming too powerful. The less threatening Knights of St. John established their headquarters in a priory in Clerkenwell. Consecrated in 1185 it is where the Grand Prior lived in considerable style and from where prospective hospitallers sallied forth on their journeys east.

After the Knights Hospitallers were dissolved by Henry VIII (1509–1547) their priory was demolished leaving only the priory church and gatehouse intact. The gatehouse served subsequently as offices for the Master of the Revels, where Shakespeare's plays were licensed, then as a coffee house run by the father of artist William Hogarth (1697–1764), and as a printing house for *The Gentleman's Magazine* on which Samuel Johnson (1709–1784) worked. It also served as the Old Jerusalem Tavern, which was frequented by Charles Dickens (1812–1870) (the tavern has subsequently relocated to a former Georgian watchmaker's shop around the corner at 55 Britton Street).

Eventually during the 1870s the revived Order of St. John reacquired the gatehouse for use as its London headquarters and for that of its main humanitarian subsidiary, St. John Ambulance. It also now houses the museum, which uses everything from antique suits of armour to modern nurses' uniforms to tell the 900 year long story of the Order. Visitors will learn how the Order moved to Cyprus in 1291 after Palestine was recaptured by the Muslims, and then to Rhodes where it remained until being ousted by the Ottomans. In 1565 Sultan Suleiman the Magnificent pursued the order to Malta, which the knights defended successfully, building the new capital, Valetta, in the process (weapons and other equipment from this time are included in the collection). Although Malta was lost to Napoleon in 1798 the Order retained its headquarters in Rome, where it remains to this day.

A tour of the museum also includes the adjacent 19th century Church of St. John Clerkenwell beneath which the priory's atmospheric 12th century crypt remains undisturbed, one of London's rare Norman survivals. The circular footprint of the former priory church has been marked out at pavement level in St John's Square.

The Knights of St. John no doubt prized the sweet waters of the well after which Clerkenwell is named. The setting for medieval miracle plays performed by parish clerks, it still exists inside a modern building at 14–16 Farringdon Lane (EC1). To visit contact the Clerkenwell & Islington Guiding Association (www.ciga.org.uk).

Other places of interest nearby: 19, 20, 22

22 A Corner of Cambridgeshire

EC1N 6SJ (Farringdon), the Church of St. Etheldreda
at 14 Ely Place and Ye Olde Mitre at 1 Ely Court
Central line to Chancery Lane; Circle, Hammersmith
& City, Metropolitan lines to Farringdon (note: the gates
to both Ely Place and Ely Court are closed at 10pm)

At first glance Ely Place seems little more than a cul–de-sac of smart Georgian terraced houses – but look again. The clue to its unexpectedly colourful history is the little gatehouse standing at one end. It carries a street sign lacking the usual EC1 district number and it houses a beadle who locks the gates each evening at 10pm. By passing through them one leaves London and enters a corner of Cambridgeshire instead.

Ely Place is one of the last privately owned streets in London and finds its origins in 1290, when an exclave of Cambridgeshire was established here for the powerful Bishops of Ely. In common with the Bishops of Canterbury and Winchester they held high state offices requiring the maintenance of a London residence. Long subject to its own ancient rights and privileges the area is still managed by its own body of commissioners.

In medieval times the self-supporting community, which included a palace and extensive gardens and orchards, was separated from the City and its laws by a high wall. All that remains of the place today, however, is the Church of St. Etheldreda at Number 14. Once the Bishops' private chapel, it is unusual in being a pre-Reformation church that is still used as a Catholic place of worship. It is also one of London's few surviving buildings from the reign of Edward I (1239–1307). The desiccated hand of St. Etheldreda is preserved in a jewelled casket alongside the altar and her unfortunate death from a neck tumour gives added poignancy to the 'Blessing of the Throats' ceremony held in the church on February 3rd each year. Despite being badly damaged during the Second World War the church has been restored. Its undercroft is perfectly preserved and now used for candlelit wedding celebrations and banquets.

The chapel gardens were once renowned for their strawberries, so much so that Shakespeare has the Duke of Gloucester compliment the Bishop of Ely accordingly in his *Richard III* and they are still recalled in an annual strawberry fair in June. Shakespeare also uses the palace (known as Ely House) as the setting for John of Gaunt's famous "This royal throne of kings, this sceptre'd isle" speech. The nobleman lived here after the Savoy Palace was destroyed during the Peasants' Revolt of 1381.

Many famous people visited the Bishops in their palace, including Henry VIII (1509–1547) and his first wife Catherine of Aragon, who attended a five-day feast here in 1531. The historian John Stow (1525–1605) records that the menu included 13 dozen swans, 37 dozen pigeons, 91 pigs, and 340 larks! Another noteworthy visitor was Elizabeth I (1558–1603), who in 1578 granted the freehold of the estate to her favourite, Sir Christopher Hatton (1540–1591). He had already secured a lease on the property and spent money renovating it, which the incumbent Bishop of Ely was unable to reimburse.

The gatekeeper's lodge at the entrance to Ely Place

Hatton renamed the property after himself and in 1587 became Lord Chancellor. He is remembered around the corner in Hatton Garden, where a passage alongside Number 8 gives access to Ely Place via Ely Court. Here can be found Ye Olde Mitre, a quirky tavern built for the Bishops' servants in 1546 and rebuilt in 1772, when the estate was sold to the Crown (in the same year the Georgian cul-de-sac was built and a new home for the Bishops found at 37 Dover Street (W1) in Mayfair). Just inside the tavern door is the trunk of a cherry tree around which a love-struck young Elizabeth is said to have danced. Although the pub license is no longer sought in Cambridgeshire the opening hours remain strictly in line with those of the gates.

Other places of interest nearby: 24, 39

23 An Historic Pub Crawl

EC4V 4EG (The City), a walking tour of City pubs beginning with the Black Friar at 174 Queen Victoria Street
Circle, District lines to Blackfriars

In describing 12th century London the Norman cleric William Fitzstephen (d. 1191) wrote that it suffered from two plagues, namely fire and drink. Neither the Great Fire of London in 1666 nor the emergence of the Victorian temperance movement would therefore have surprised him. These days of course London's historic taverns are tourist attractions and enjoying a drink in them is considered a quintessentially English experience. From centuries-old watering holes to Victorian Gin Palaces they all have a story to tell.

This tour takes in a handful of City pubs and begins with the Black Friar at 174 Queen Victoria Street (EC4). Rebuilt in 1905 it occupies a wedge-shaped plot of land defined by London's pre-Great Fire medieval street plan and the railway to its rear. Its name commemorates a 13th century Dominican friary that once stood nearby – a wall fragment remains in Ireland Yard – and its external decoration includes a mosaic of a pair of friars fishing in the lost River Fleet, which empties under nearby Blackfriars Bridge (see no. 56). The interior is even more extraordinary with whimsical bas-reliefs of friars at work amidst some wonderful Arts and Crafts decoration.

At the other end of Queen Victoria Street is Ye Olde Watling at 29 Watling Street (EC4). The plaque outside states it was built in 1688 by Sir Christopher Wren (1632–1723) for workers building St. Paul's Cathedral, and constructed from reused ships' timbers, although it has been restored several times. Watling Street is one of the oldest roads in the City and in Roman times stretched from Dover to Wroxeter.

Continue eastwards along Cannon Street to find Martin Lane (EC4) on the right-hand side. Just a stone's throw from where the Great Fire started, the Olde Wine Shades at Number 6 retains a lead drain hopper inscribed with the date '1663'. As such it is the City's only pre-Great Fire tavern still in business and boasts a walled-up smugglers' tunnel in its cellar running down to the Thames.

Time for a brisk stroll now passing the Counting House at 50 Cornhill (EC3), one of several ornate Victorian bank buildings converted recently into pubs. Dating from 1893 it features some glorious woodwork and a domed ceiling. Turn left onto Bishopsgate (EC2) to reach the final port of call. Dirty Dick's Old Port Wine & Spirit House at

Dusk at the Black Friar on Queen Victoria Street

Number 202 was known originally as the Old Jerusalem and its name change has a curious origin. During the 18th century a well-to-do iron-monger called Richard Bentley lived nearby. Distraught at losing his fiancée he gave up on life and lived in self-imposed squalor until his death in 1809. By then he had become a celebrity eccentric and the

An intact set of snob screens in the Lamb on Lambs Conduit Street

pub capitalised on this by renaming itself after him and displaying a collection of his musty belongings still visible in the cellar today, including a mummified cat!

Pub building in Britain reached its peak in the late 19th century with the construction of lavishly appointed establishments known as Gin Palaces (although gin drinking had declined in popularity by this time the name provided continuity from the old dram shop gin counters to the new-look pub bars). Their decoration typically included polished mahogany, etched glass, polychrome tiles and embossed ceilings, with 'snugs' to separate different classes of drinker. Surviving examples include the Argyll Arms at 18 Argyll Street (W1), the Red Lion at 2 Duke of York Street (SW1), and the Princess Louise at 208 High Holborn (WC1), which still retains its original stoneware gents' urinals. The Lamb at 94 Lambs Conduit Street (WC1) features a set of 'snob screens' – pivoting frosted glass shutters at head height designed to provide drinkers with privacy – and a rare working *Polyphon* music box. The Viaduct Tavern at 126 Newgate Street (EC1) opened in 1869 contains four oil paintings representing Agriculture, Commerce, Fine Arts, and Science, which also feature on the nearby Holborn Viaduct, the world's first flyover opened the same year.

London's oldest wine bar is Gordon's at 47 Villiers Street (WC2), which opened in 1890 in the cellar of a demolished Georgian house once occupied by Samuel Pepys (1633–1702).

Other places of interest nearby: 15, 24

24 C is for Cat

EC4A 3DE (The City), Dr. Johnson's House at 17 Gough Square
Central line to Chancery Lane

An estimated 750,000 cats live in London although few of them will ever be memorialised. An exception is Hodge, whose bronze effigy stands outside 17 Gough Square (EC4), the former home of his owner, Dr. Samuel Johnson (1709–1784). Hodge is depicted sitting atop a copy of Johnson's famous *Dictionary of the English Language* together with a pair of empty oyster shells.

The son of a Staffordshire bookseller, Johnson rose from poverty to become one of the great literary figures of the 18th century. After walking to London he made a modest living writing magazine articles. Then in 1746 he was commissioned to compile the first comprehensive English dictionary and moved to Gough Square to work on it. Publication of the dictionary in 1755 assured his everlasting fame.

Now an independent museum, Dr. Johnson's House is one of the last Georgian remnants in the City. The charming red brick building retains many of its original architectural features, including sash windows and a fanlit front door of 1775. Displayed inside are editions of the famous dictionary together with numerous personal effects, including Johnson's walking stick.

Johnson shared his home not only with his cat but also his Jamaican valet, Francis Barber, who was sent by friends to console Johnson after the death of his wife. The pair remained together for the rest of Johnson's life, with Barber assisting whenever the dictionary required updating. A strong opponent of slavery Johnson left Barber a generous annuity and a gold watch in his will, and the advice that he move to Lichfield in Staffordshire, Johnson's place of birth. This Barber did and it is said his descendants still live there today.

Johnson chose Gough Square because of its proximity to Fleet Street (EC4), which for almost 300 years was home to the British press. Despite the departure of the press in the 1980s the street remains synonymous with the newspaper industry. A tiled mural on Magpie Alley off Bouverie Street gives a potted history beginning with the first printing works set up in 1500 and the media boom sparked by the expiry of England's censorship laws in 1695. Various former newspaper offices bolster the tale, including 12 Ludgate Circus (EC4), where London's first daily newspaper, *The London Courant*, was published in 1702. Others include the *Art Deco* black-glass-and-chrome *Daily Express*

Hodge the cat sits atop his master's English dictionary on Gough Square

building at 120 Fleet Street, with the more staid Neo-Classical *Daily Telegraph* building at Number 135. The *News of the World* opted for 30 Bouverie Street beneath which a ruined medieval crypt was discovered in 1867. Part of the former Whitefriars Monastery it was hoisted out in one piece when the site was redeveloped in the late 1980s and lowered back in a more convenient position!

Fleet Street boasts numerous other connections with Johnson. A sociable man he probably enjoyed a drink at Ye Olde Cheshire Cheese at Number 145, which still boasts open fires and sawdust on the floors. Its warren of cosy rooms was also frequented by Dickens, Tennyson, Conan Doyle, and Mark Twain. Johnson attended Mass at the Church of St. Bride Fleet Street, the so-called Journalists' Church, as did poet John Milton and diarist Samuel Pepys (see no. 26).

Other places of interest nearby: 23, 25, 26, 27, 28

25 The World's Oldest Debating Society

EC4A 2LT (Temple), the City of London Cogers in the Old Bank of England at 194 Fleet Street
Circle, District lines to Temple (note: non-members may attend meetings for a nominal fee)

Readers looking to improve their public speaking skills, or just looking for some stimulating conversation, look no further! Each second Monday of the month between 7 and 9.15pm a debating society known as the City Of London Cogers meets in the Old Bank Of England public house at 194 Fleet Street (EC4). Founded in 1755 it is the oldest debating society in the world.

The Society of Cogers (pronounced 'Koh-jers') finds its origins in the taverns and coffee houses of Fleet Street during the reign of George II (1727–1760). At that time such venues doubled as centres of trade and commerce and were frequented by merchants, publishers, journalists and lawyers. Not only would they conduct business but also take time out to discuss the day's news. The society's curious

A 19th century engraving of a London Cogers' meeting in full swing

name derives from French philosopher Rene Descartes' maxim, *Cogito Ergo Sum* (I think therefore I am).

The first meeting of the society took place above a tavern in Bride Lane. It was convened by the friends of John Wilkes (1725–1795), a Radical journalist who agitated for greater freedom of the press. The society soon included politicians, judges and authors, and avoided suppression by adopting a policy of strict political neutrality. This meant that over the years it provided a platform for people of all political persuasions – from monarchists to republicans.

The society still meets in various licensed premises in the City and in 1997, after being reconstituted as the City of London Cogers, it selected the Old Bank of England for its meetings (in a previous incarnation this gloriously-appointed public house provided banking facilities to the Royal Courts of Justice next door).

The form taken by a Cogers' meeting is curious to behold. At 7pm the moderator ("The Grand") reveals the 'Apple of Discord', a symbol from Greek mythology representing dissension between individuals. The first person asked to speak is referred to as "The Opener" and it is their responsibility to recap on the most important news stories that have occurred since the group last met. Tradition insists that they also pass comment on the recent activities of the Royal Family. Called 'Loyal Reference' this custom dates back to the time of the American and French Revolutions, when Home Office spies infiltrated debating societies to evesdrop on any seditious language.

After "The Opener" has suggested possible themes for discussion "The Grand" invites assembled members (and any visitors) to speak, usually for around five minutes at a time. All speeches must be addressed to "My Grand" and delivered from a position known as 'The Box'. Like the Speaker of the House of Commons, "The Grand" does not participate in discussions but instead moderates challenges (or 'heckles') from the floor (to prevent any despotism a new "Grand" is appointed at each meeting). Finally at 9.15pm "The Grand" elects an 'Evaluator', who comments on the speeches and awards the 'Apple of Discord' to the speaker considered most eloquent.

Another bank serving the Royal Courts of Justice is Lloyds at 222 Strand. Unlike the Old Bank of England it still fulfils its function having previously served as the Palsgrove Hotel. This explains the unexpectedly ornate Doultonware decoration adorning its vestibule and banking hall.

Other places of interest nearby: 24, 26, 27, 28, 29

26 More City Church Survivors

EC4A 2HR (The City), a walking tour of some of the City's post-Great Fire churches beginning with St. Dunstan's-in-the-West at 186a Fleet Street
Circle, District lines to Temple (note: most City churches are only open on weekdays)

In 1666 the Great Fire of London destroyed 88 of the City's hundred or so parish churches (see no. 3). Afterwards Sir Christopher Wren (1632–1723) was commissioned to rebuild 51 of them. Depopulation, war and the demands of developers have reduced to around 40 those still standing. What follows is a tour of some of Wren's reconstructions, together with a few by other architects for good measure.

The tour begins with St. Dunstan's-in-the-West at 186a Fleet Street (EC4). After narrowly escaping the Great Fire it was rebuilt in 1832 by John Shaw (1776–1832). Note the public clock installed in 1671 (the first in London to feature a minute hand), the octagonal interior and matching tower making good use of the constricted build-

The unusual octagonal tower of St. Dunstan's-in-the-West on Fleet Street

ing plot, and the porch of the adjoining former parochial school, with its figures of Elizabeth I and the legendary King Lud from the now-demolished Ludgate.

Continue eastwards to reach St. Bride's Fleet Street, the Journalists' Church. The seventh church to occupy this site it was rebuilt by Wren and features his tallest spire, its tiered design said to have inspired countless wedding cakes! Inside is a rare medieval brass lectern and an ancient crypt.

Now drop down New Bridge Street onto Queen Victoria Street to reach Wren's St. Benet's Paul's Wharf. Today the City's Welsh Church it also serves the College of Arms opposite. Continue along Queen Victoria Street and onto Watling Street to reach St. Mary's Aldermary, Wren's only Gothic-style reconstruction, with some superb fan vaulting and a very pleasant café.

A couple of streets north on Cheapside (EC2) is another Wren church, dedicated to St. Mary-le-Bow. To be born within earshot of its bells defines a true Cockney, which explains why the church is a venue for the annual Costermongers' Harvest Festival (see nos. 14 & 58). In the churchyard is a statue of former parishioner Captain John Smith, who founded Virginia and was allegedly saved by Pocahontas.

Return to Queen Victoria Street to find St. Stephen's Walbrook (EC4). Its interior remains much as Wren left it demonstrating clearly his interest in restrained Baroque forms. The Samaritan's movement was founded here in 1953 and their original telephone is on display. Doubling back onto King William Street reveals St. Mary's Woolnoth designed by Wren's pupil, Nicholas Hawksmoor (see no. 6). At the bottom of the same street is St. Mary's Abchurch, another Wren original with a fine domed ceiling.

Wren's work continues down on Lower Thames Street (EC3) with St. Magnus the Martyr's. Its proximity to the river explains the stones in the churchyard from earlier incarnations of London Bridge. From here climb St. Mary at Hill – pausing to explore the leafy ruins of Wren's St. Dunstan's-in-the-East on the right-hand side – to reach St. Margaret Pattens' on Eastcheap. This Wren church contains unique canopied pews inscribed with the architect's initials and an unusual iron hourglass mounted on the pulpit. Now walk east along Fenchurch Street to St. Katherine's Cree on Leadenhall Street. Unlike the rest of this tour it dates from *before* the Great Fire and is the City's only Jacobean church. Note the ceiling bosses decorated with the arms of the City's livery companies (see no. 16).

This tour finishes at St. Botolph's-without-Aldgate on Aldgate High Street (the suffix signifies that it stood outside one of the gates through the City's wall). Built in 1741 by George Dance the Elder it contains the oldest church organ in England.

In addition to the nine Wren City churches described above there are 15 others extant. Add to these one interior (Temple Church), five more ruins, two relocations (including Mary Aldermanbury to America) and 19 demolitions and destructions, and all of Wren's 51 City churches are accounted for.

Other places of interest nearby: 24, 25, 27, 28, 29, 30

27 Everyone Enjoys a Cuppa!

**WC2R 1AP (The City), Twining's Tea Shop at 216 Strand
Circle, District lines to Temple**

The British taste for tea is legendary, the beverage having played an integral part in the building of empire and the winning of wars. As "the cup that cheers but does not inebriate" and despite fierce completion from coffee it still plays an important role in everyday British life. Cutting across all social and cultural barriers it seems that everyone enjoys a good cuppa!

To uncover the story of tea visit Twining's Tea Shop at 216 Strand (WC2). In 1706 the company of merchant Thomas Twining (1675–1741) became one of the first importers of tea into Britain, and this has been their flagship store since 1717. The carved Chinese figures over the doorway are a reminder that tea drinking originated in China over 4,500 years ago, making it the world's second oldest manmade beverage after beer.

Initially the price of tea imported from China was astronomical: £160 for 100g! This explains why Twining's first business on the site was actually selling coffee. Only later, with the establishment of the British East India Company – their old warehouses still stand on

A Chinese man sits over the entrance to Twining's Tea Shop on the Strand

Devonshire Square (EC2) – did they shift to tea. So it was that tea went from being a luxury enjoyed only by the rich to a cheap drink for the masses.

At the back of Twining's tea shop is a sampling counter and a small museum. Amongst the old teapots, tea caddies, and trade advertisements are numerous fascinating objects, including a copy of the Royal Warrant granted to the company by Queen Victoria in 1837, which explains the royal crest outside. There is also a wooden box inscribed with the letters T.I.P., an acronym for 'To insure promptness'. Coins were placed in the box by patrons to encourage speedy service although whether it actually gave rise to the verb "to tip" remains a moot point.

The Chinese philosopher T'ien Yiheng said "Tea is drunk to forget the din of the world." It is therefore little wonder that bustling London is where the tradition of Afternoon Tea originated. It is attributed to Anna, 7th Duchess of Bedford (1783–1857), who as lady-in-waiting to Queen Victoria felt sustenance was needed to avoid any empty feeling between lunch and dinner, which at the time was not served until 8pm. The habit spread and soon all of fashionable London was taking tea served with sandwiches and cakes – and observing the etiquette that went with it.

In 1865 the Langham at 1C Portland Place (W1) became the first grand hotel to serve Afternoon Tea and the tradition is still going strong there, as it is at the Dorchester on Park Lane, which opened in 1931. Brown's Hotel at 33 Albermarle Street serves Afternoon Tea in its cosy wood-panelled tearoom, whilst not far away on Piccadilly the Park Lane Hotel does likewise in its Palm Court, a sumptuously-appointed 1920s *Art Deco* lounge. At the other end of the scale is the cheerful and chintzy tearoom over the Coach & Horses pub at 29 Greek Street, and the no-nonsense formica tables of the century-old family delicatessen Paul Rothe & Sons at 35 Marylebone Lane. Whatever the venue most punters take their tea the English way – with milk – and their scones with a dollop of strawberry jam and clotted cream. Delicious!

Over a hundred teas and almost as many coffees can be bought at the Algerian Coffee Store at 52 Old Compton Street. Established in 1887 this wonderful old shop retains many of its original fittings.

Other places of interest nearby: 24, 25, 26, 28, 29, 30, 36

28 The Most Extraordinary Office in England

WC2R 3BD (Temple), Two Temple Place on Victoria Embankment
Circle, District lines to Temple (note: the house is only open during exhibitions between January and April or by appointment)

Two Temple Place (WC2) is one of London's hidden architectural gems. Only open to the public since 2011 this late Victorian mansion was built for the businessman and politician, William Waldorf Astor (1848–1919). As one of the world's wealthiest men he ensured that no expense was spared in its construction and that it reflected his life and personal interests. The result is a building as eccentric as it is opulent.

Born into a prominent American family, William Waldorf Astor was an only child. After being privately tutored in Europe he returned home to New York to practice law then turned his hand to politics. His wealthy background and his failure to enter Congress, however, made him a target for the press. As a result he spent the early 1880s in Rome, where he developed a lifelong interest in art.

Back in New York, Astor inherited his father's vast fortune and in 1890 built the Waldorf Hotel. Around the same time a family feud prompted him to relocate his family to England, where in 1892 he purchased the *Pall Mall Gazette* and the Cliveden estate in Buckinghamshire. It was to manage these new business ventures that he commissioned Two Temple Place.

Completed in 1895 to a design by the Gothic Revival architect John Loughborough Pearson (1817–1897), the exterior of Two Temple Place is rendered entirely in Portland

Carved figures adorn the staircase at Two Temple Place

stone. High above the machicolated parapets is a copper weather vane representing the caravel in which Columbus sailed to America. It symbolises the path taken in 1784 by Astor's German ancestor, John Jacob Astor – and Astor's own journey the other way. The bronze lamp standards flanking the main entrance demonstrate Astor's modernity by including cherubs using a telephone and an electric light!

Crossing the threshold an imposing vestibule gives onto the richly-decorated Staircase Hall. Panelled in oak it features a Pavonazetto marble fireplace and a floor inlaid with chalcedony, jasper, porphyry and onyx. That Astor was a fan of historical fiction is clear from the mahogany staircase, the newel posts of which support characters from his favourite novel *The Three Musketeers*. On the first floor is a gallery with ten columns of ebony topped off with more sculptures. Inspired this time by American literature they feature characters from *The Last of the Mohicans* and *Rip Van Winkle*. Above these runs a frieze depicting 82 characters from the plays of Shakespeare, the whole being lit by a glorious stained-glass cupola.

Leading off the first floor gallery is the Great Hall, which extends the full length of the building's riverside frontage. This is where Astor worked and it is surely the most extraordinary office in England. Entered through a door decorated with heroines from Arthurian legend it features stained-glass windows at either end representing Swiss landscapes at sunrise and sunset. Overhead is a hammerbeam roof made of Spanish mahogany. The cedar-lined walls are surmounted by a frieze in which a further 54 characters from history have been carved in relief and then gilded, with a dozen freestanding figures above. How curious it is to see Bismarck and Martin Luther mingling with Robin Hood and Maid Marion!

Known originally as the Astor Estate Office, Two Temple Place is now owned by the Bulldog Trust, a philanthropic organisation providing support and advice to various charities. It also offers educational facilities in tandem with its unique annual exhibitions of publically-owned art from collections outside London. Staged between January and April these provide an ideal opportunity to visit this unique building.

Other places of interest nearby: 24, 25, 26, 27, 29, 30, 36

29 Ghost Stations on the Piccadilly Line

WC2R 1LS (Strand), a tour of ghost stations on the Piccadilly line finishing with Aldwych at the corner of the Strand and Surrey Street
Circle, District lines to Temple (note: guided tours of Aldwych station are provided occasionally by the London Transport Museum)

The London Transport Museum on Covent Garden Piazza (WC2) illustrates well the complexity of the capital's transport infrastructure. Whilst the horse-drawn trams and motorised buses are interesting, it's the material relating to the London Underground that really fascinates. Pride of place goes to a wooden railway carriage used on the Metropolitan line between Paddington and Farringdon, the world's first underground passenger railway, which opened in 1863. Since then the Tube has expanded dramatically and helped transform London from a congested Victorian city into the massive conurbation it is today.

Aldwych Tube station was originally named Strand

An intriguing facet of the Tube is its ghost stations of which there are more than 40. Whilst some closed due to lack of customers others were abandoned when rival companies merged or else were reworked to increase capacity. A handful of them are located conveniently on the Piccadilly line, which opened in 1906, and it makes for quite an adventure finding them.

First stop is Brompton Road (SW3), which closed in 1934 be-

Aldwych Tube station has been closed since 1994

cause of its proximity to the busier stations at South Kensington and Knightsbridge. As early as 1909 some services were already passing through without stopping. During the Second World War the station served as the Royal Artillery's anti-aircraft control centre for London. Although the platforms are no longer visible from passing trains, part of the façade above ground still survives on Cottage Place, with its distinctive arches and maroon tiling designed by architect Leslie Green (1875–1908).

Next stop is the former ticket hall at Hyde Park Corner (SW7), which closed in 1932 when it was replaced by a new underground ticket hall with the same name and its escalators replaced by lifts. The redundant Leslie Green façade is now part of a hotel.

Like Brompton Road, Down Street (W1) was another station that proved unpopular, this time because of its proximity to Hyde Park Corner and Dover Street (today Green Park). It too closed in 1932 and again a Leslie Green façade survives above ground. Below ground a change in tunnel surface from cast iron segments to brickwork on the right-hand side denotes where the platforms have been walled off. Behind them was an air raid shelter used in 1940 by Winston Churchill before his Cabinet War Rooms were ready (see no. 84).

The next station, Dover Street, was rendered obsolete when escalators and a new underground ticket hall were installed in 1933, at which time the station was renamed Green Park.

The most atmospheric ghost station on the Piccadilly line is undoubtedly Aldwych (WC2) at the corner of the Strand and Surrey Street. Originally intended to be the southern terminus for one of the companies that merged to form the Piccadilly line, Aldwych instead became the terminus of a short branch line. Opening as Strand station in 1907 (the station façade still bears this name) it provided a shuttle service up to Holborn but by 1918 had been renamed and its service curtailed. During the Second World War it provided shelter for 1500 people together with the British Museum's Elgin Marbles. The station closed completely in 1994 after the cost of replacing its lifts was deemed uneconomic. Since then the mothballed station with its old-fashioned ticket office, wood-panelled lifts, original tiling and peeling posters has proved a popular film location (it is also where electronic band The Prodigy filmed their memorable *Firestarter* video). Occasional guided tours are provided by the London Transport Museum (www.ltmuseum.co.uk) although plans to sell off London's ghost stations might one day make it more accessible.

London once had three other underground railways. Of the London Pneumatic Despatch Railway, which carried light freight out of Euston Station between 1863 and 1874, only a solitary vehicle survives in the collection of the Museum of London at 150 London Wall (EC2). Of London's tram network, which criss-crossed the city until the early 1950s, the abandoned Kingsway tunnel of 1906 remains, with entrance at the bottom end of Southampton Row (WC2) and beneath Waterloo Bridge. Nothing is currently visible of the driverless narrow gauge Mail Rail, which from 1927 to 2003 transported millions of letters daily for the Post Office between Paddington and Whitechapel. Plans are afoot to open parts of the mothballed system to visitors in 2020 as part of a revamped British Postal Museum & Archive at the Mount Pleasant sorting office (WC1).

Other places of interest nearby: 25, 26, 27, 28, 30, 31, 36, 37

30 Somerset House Revisited

WC2R 1LA (Strand), Somerset House on the Strand
Circle, District lines to Temple

Amongst the greenery of Victoria Embankment Gardens (WC2) there lurks a curious Baroque archway erected in 1626 for the Duke of Buckingham. His mansion, York House, stood on the Strand and the archway served as a water gate giving him direct access to the Thames. The construction of Victoria Embankment in the 1860s explains why it is now seemingly marooned.

York House was one of a string of great homes built along the Strand by those seeking influence at Westminster. All have been demolished except for Somerset House, which still retains some secrets from its colourful past. The story begins in 1547 with the death of Henry VIII (1509–1547). Since his son was too young to accede, his ambitious uncle, Edward Seymour (1500–1552), proclaimed himself Duke of Somerset and the boy's protector. Having already obtained a riverside plot from Henry he set about building an imposing residence. A courtyard house in the Tudor tradition, this early manifestation of Somerset House was the first Renaissance palace in England. Seymour had little time to enjoy it though as his enemies tried him for treason and had him executed on Tower Hill.

The palace then became the property of the Crown. During the 17th century the wife of James I (1603–1625), Anne of Denmark, commissioned Inigo Jones (1573–1652) to upgrade the building as a venue for masques and balls (it was the first building in England with parquet flooring). In 1630 Jones built a chapel where the wife of Charles I (1625–1649), Henrietta Maria of France, could practise her Catholicism. A small cemetery was attached and a handful of its gravestones can still be seen in the subterranean passage surrounding the present quadrangle.

During the English Civil War the palace served as a military headquarters and in 1658 the body of Oliver Cromwell was laid in state here. Royalty returned with the Restoration and in 1685 the widow of Charles II (1660–1685), Catherine of Braganza, used the palace to stage the country's first Italian opera. With the Glorious Revolution, however, Somerset House fell out of favour and in 1775 it was demolished.

With the site's royal associations severed a new public building soon rose in place of the palace. Designed in Palladian style by Sir William Chambers (1723–1796) it was probably the first purpose-built office block ever constructed, and contained everything from the Navy Board to the Hackney Coach Office, with a trio of water gates enabling boats to sail right inside the building.

During the 19th century further wings were added as government departments came and went, including the Register of Births, Marriages and Deaths and an Inland Revenue laboratory established to prevent the adulteration of tobacco products. King's College and the Courtauld Gallery are still there; the rest are remembered in long-redundant names inscribed over the doors.

Refurbishment in the late 1990s has made Somerset House a popular visitor destination, with exhibitions, film screenings, a riverside café, and a winter ice rink in the quadrangle. There is even the gilded state barge of the Lord Mayor of the City of London parked in the building's basement.

A mysterious subterranean passage surrounds the quadrangle at Somerset House

Not far from Somerset House on Savoy Street is the Queen's Chapel of the Savoy. Once part of a paupers' hospital founded by Henry VII (1485–1509) it still belongs to the monarch as part of the Savoy Estate, the Duchy of Lancaster's principal London land holding. The chapel is a Royal Peculiar in that it falls under the jurisdiction of the monarch rather than a bishop, whilst remaining within the Church of England. Richard D'Oyly Carte's Savoy Theatre stands nearby.

Other places of interest nearby: 26, 27, 28, 29, 31, 36

31 Egypt on the Thames

WC2N 6BL (Strand), Cleopatra's Needle on Victoria
Embankment near Waterloo Bridge
Bakerloo, Central, District, Northern lines to Embankment

Where is the oldest outdoor statue in London? Some would say Trinity
Church Square (SE1) in Newington, where there is a 14th century effigy of Alfred the Great (871–899) allegedly removed from Westminster
Hall. Others suggest the Church of St. Dunstan-in-the-West on Fleet
Street (EC4), which is adorned with a statue of Elizabeth I (1558–1603)
carved in 1586 and removed from the now-demolished Ludgate. The
correct answer, however, involves something much older. Displayed
above the entrance to Sotheby's at 34–35 New Bond Street (W1) is a
black basalt sculpture of the ancient Egyptian lion-goddess Sekhmet.
Dating to around 1320 BC it's been there since the 1880s, when it was
sold at auction for £40 but never collected (it provides an interesting counterpoint to sculptor Henry Moore's abstract *Time-Life Screen*
(1953) farther along the road at Number 153).

The European craze for things Egyptian goes back to Napoleon's
expedition to the Nile in 1798. As news of his discoveries filtered back
so a demand was created for ancient artefacts, as well as for new art
and architecture with an Egyptian flair. After British troops defeated
the French in Egypt in 1801 this demand spread to England, and in-
tensified after the Rosetta Stone was installed in the British Museum
on Great Russell Street (WC1). Used to decipher the ancient Egyptian
hieroglyphs, the stone remains one of the museum's most visited objects together with the ever popular mummy rooms.

Amongst the other ancient Egyptian artefacts that arrived in London was the alabaster sarcophagus of the Pharaoh Seti I, which now
graces Sir John Soane's Museum in Holborn (see no. 38). The most celebrated artefact, however, is undoubtedly the 21-metre high, rose-red
granite obelisk known as Cleopatra's Needle on Victoria Embankment
(WC2), near Waterloo Bridge. The story of how the obelisk reached
London is as interesting as the obelisk itself.

Nothing actually to do with Queen Cleopatra the obelisk was
one of a pair erected around 1450 BC by Pharaoh Tuthmosis III in the
ancient city of Heliopolis outside modern Cairo. Relocated to Alexandria by the Romans in 12 BC and toppled thereafter it was not until
1819 that one of the pair was presented to Britain by the Turkish viceroy of Egypt, Muhammad Ali, in gratitude for expelling the French (the

other found its way to New York).

The obelisk was towed to London in a cylindrical iron barge named the *Cleopatra*. All went to plan until a storm blew up in the Bay of Biscay during which six sailors drowned and the barge was set adrift. Only when it was retrieved several days later could the journey be safely completed. The obelisk was eventually erected in London on 12th September 1878.

The Egyptian theme permeates the area surrounding Cleopatra's Needle. As well as two bronze sphinxes flanking the obelisk, the public benches overlooking this section of the Thames are supported by winged sphinxes and occasionally kneeling camels. The latter recall the short-lived Imperial Camel Corps, which fought in Palestine and the Sinai during the First World War. The Imperial Camel Corps monument in the nearby Victoria Embankment Gardens commemorates the 346 British, Australian and New Zealand men who perished as a result.

One of a pair of bronze sphinxes guarding Cleopatra's Needle

As an alternative to the British Museum why not visit the relatively little-known Petrie Museum of Egyptian Archaeology on Malet Place (WC1)? Exhibits include ancient wills written on papyrus, painted funerary masks from Roman mummies, and beads that are the oldest manmade iron ojects ever found.

To see an ancient Egyptian toy mouse made from Nile clay visit the wonderfully nostalgic Pollock's Toy Museum at 1 Scala Street (W1). Founded in 1956 this small but quirky museum is particularly strong on toy theatres, modern versions of which can be purchased in the museum shop.

Other places of interest nearby: 29, 30, 80, 93

32 A Closer Look at Trafalgar Square

WC2N 5DU (Strand), Nelson's Column on Trafalgar Square
Bakerloo, Northern lines to Charing Cross

It has been said that if you wait long enough in Trafalgar Square you will eventually encounter someone you know. Certainly it is one of London's most popular open spaces, attracting visitors with its public art, celebrations and demonstrations. Whilst waiting why not take a closer look at this famous meeting place?

The area occupied today by Trafalgar Square once formed part of the stables for the Palace of Whitehall, as well as a labyrinth of cook-shops nicknamed Porridge Island (see no. 81). In 1812 when the architect John Nash (1752–1835) set about creating a ceremonial route for the Prince Regent – later William IV (1830–1837) – he proposed "an open square in the Kings Mews opposite Charing Cross". When this was opened to the public in 1844 it was named in honour of Britain's great naval victory at the Battle of Trafalgar.

Trafalgar Square subsequently underwent numerous changes, notably in 1838 when the National Gallery was erected along its north side (see no. 33). But when the building's lack of grandeur drew criticism the architect Sir Charles Barry (1795–1860) had the sloping square in front excavated down to the level of the Strand, so that the gallery would appear more imposing. Don't miss the late 19th century set of brass Imperial Measures installed at the bottom of the gallery steps giving archaic units of length such as perches, poles, and chains.

Barry also approved two plinths in front of the gallery. A bronze equestrian statue of George IV (1820–1830) was placed on the eastern one but the other was left empty when the money for a statue of William IV ran out (since 1998 it has been used to display commissioned and often controversial temporary works of art). Two more plinths were added later on the south side of the square. Barry also sanctioned two fountains, the purpose of which was to reduce the space available for riotous assemblies (this also explains the presence of a tiny police station installed in 1926 inside a granite lamp post in one corner of the square). During the 1930s the fountains were shipped to Canada and the current fountains designed by Edwin Lutyens (1869–1944) put in their place.

At the heart of the square is Nelson's Column erected in 1843 by public subscription. Soaring 51.6 metres high the granite monument was designed by William Railton (1800–1877), the sandstone statue of Nelson at its summit facing towards his fleet in Portsmouth. The bronze reliefs around the pedestal were cast a decade later from captured French cannon (look out for the sole African crew member of Nelson's flagship *Victory*). The damage to the stonework at the base of the column dates not from the Second World War as might have been expected but rather 1918, when soldiers celebrating the Armistice accidentally set fire to a workmen's hut! The bronze lions guarding the column are by Edwin Landseer (1802–1873) and were added in 1867 (excavations in the square in 1960 revealed the bones of very real lions from the last interglacial period).

The bronze reliefs on Nelson's Column are made from captured French cannon

Before leaving the square notice the old-fashioned gas lamps lining the roadside. Now converted to electricity they were installed by William Sugg & Co., a pioneering firm of Westminster gas engineers responsible for illuminating Tower Bridge.

On the traffic island below Trafalgar Square is an equestrian statue of Charles I (1625–1649). It occupies the former site of a cross marking the last leg of the funeral cortège of Queen Eleanor of Castille, wife of Edward I (1272–1307), on its way to Westminster. A plaque states that all distances to and from London are measured from here. A Victorian replica of the cross stands today in front of Charing Cross station.

Other places of interest nearby: 33, 34, 35, 80

33 Walking on Greta Garbo

WC2N 5DN (Strand), the National Gallery on Trafalgar Square
Bakerloo, Northern lines to Charing Cross

The nearest London ever came to having a grandiose street plan came late in the reign of George III (1760–1820), when madness necessitated his eldest son George to rule as Prince Regent. Keen to carve out an alternative court he commissioned architect John Nash (1752–1835) to create a ceremonial route – Regent Street – between his personal palace, Carlton House in St. James's, and Regent's Park. When he acceded to the throne as George IV (1820–1830), however, he deemed Carlton House inadequate and had it demolished. Instead Nash began transforming one of the old king's properties, Buckingham House, into something more suitable. The result, Buckingham Palace, has been the London residence and principal workplace of all Britain's monarchs since Queen Victoria (1837–1901).

But that is not quite the end of the story of Carlton House. In the late 1820s Nash proposed the construction of a National Gallery on the north side of Trafalgar Square (WC2). Economic recession, however, prevented his grandiose plan from being realised and instead the tender was thrown open. The winning design by William Wilkins (1778–1839) was unveiled in 1838 but immediately drew criticism. The existence of a workhouse and barracks behind the site meant the gallery could only be one room deep, which meant the entrance porticoes had to be constructed at either end. For reasons of economy columns from the demolished Carlton House were reused in the construction of these porticoes – but their relative shortness diminished the gallery's intended visual impact. The resulting elevation with its central dome and flanking turrets was described by one underwhelmed critic as resembling "the clock and vases on a mantelpiece, only less useful"!

Considerable energy was subsequently expended on making the gallery appear more imposing, notably in the 1840s when architect Charles Barry (1795–1860) lowered the level of Trafalgar Square (see no. 32). The demolition of the workhouse in the 1870s permitted construction of a new, richly decorated wing called the Barry Rooms. By the 1920s, however, public taste was moving away from the overly decorous interiors favoured by the Victorians, which were whitewashed or boarded over to create a more neutral backdrop.

It was during this period that an extraordinary new decorative feature began taking shape in the gallery's main stairwell. Between 1928

The National Gallery depicted in a Victorian engraving

and 1952 the Russian mosaicist Boris Anrep (1883–1969), who had arrived in London after meeting the Bloomsbury Group, commenced work on a uniquely playful set of mosaics. Financed primarily by the industrialist Samuel Courtauld they poke fun at the overly serious approach to interior design taken by the gallery's Victorian builders. Thus *The Labours of Life* (1928) in the west vestibule illustrates man's creative nature and includes everything from washing a pig (representing farming) to studying a dinosaur in the Natural History Museum (science). *The Pleasures of Life* (1929) in the east vestibule depicts man's love of recreation and shows a girl on a motorcycle (speed) and a figure performing the Charleston (dance). On the landing *The Awakening of the Muses* (1933) includes Anrep's contemporaries doubling as figures from Greek mythology. Apollo (played by Sir Osbert Sitwell) and Bacchus (Clive Bell) are shown awaking the muses, with Virginia Woolf as Clio, Diana Mitford as Diana, and a golden-haired Greta Garbo as Melpomene. The final mosaic, *Modern Virtues* (1952), in the north vestibule, depicts intellectual life in the 1930s and 40s, and features T. S. Eliot contemplating the Loch Ness Monster!

Adjoining the National Gallery is the National Portrait Gallery on St. Martin's Place. Opened in 1856 it is the largest and oldest collection of its type in the world.

Other places of interest nearby: 32, 34, 35, 64

34 An Art Deco Picture Palace

**WC2H 7LQ (Soho), the Odeon Leicester Square at
22–24 Leicester Square
Northern, Piccadilly lines to Leicester Square**

In the heart of London's West End lies Leicester Square (WC2), an area of popular entertainments since the mid-19th century. The Alhambra music hall, Bartholomew's Turkish Baths, and Wyld's Great Globe all once stood here. Now boasting a handful of cinemas it is today the epicentre of London's cinemaland.

The jewel in the crown is undoubtedly the Odeon. Erected on the site of the Alhambra to an exciting *Art Deco* design by architect Harry Weedon (1887–1970) it opened in 1937 with a screening of *The Prisoner of Zenda*. The flagship of the Odeon chain the building still impresses with its polished black granite façade and tall tower displaying the name. Blue neon outlines the building at night creating the same sense of excitement as it did in the thirties.

The auditorium was also a bold foray into *Art Deco*: a sinuous ribbed ceiling concealing the lighting, two bas relief nymphs leaping out from the walls towards the screen, and seats upholstered in faux leopard skin. Although most of it was lost to insensitive modernisation during the 1960s much has subsequently been restored.

Superlatives abound in describing the Odeon's facilities. Despite its audience capacity being reduced from 2,000 to 1,683 to create extra leg room it remains the largest single-screen cinema in Britain. In 1953 the first ever wide-screen was installed here, and in the same year CinemaScope made its British debut with the Biblical epic *The Robe*. Later in 1999 the Odeon became Europe's first cinema to have a digital projector installed. Little wonder it has long been the venue for the annual Royal Film Performance, necessitating the installation of a Royal Retiring Room for visiting monarchs.

It's a sad fact, however, that most screenings these days are automated, without the need for trained projectionists. But fortunately there is one original feature that will always require the human touch. Concealed beneath the orchestra pit is a fully-functioning Compton cinema organ. Featuring everything from strings to trumpets it must have been a wonderful sight as it rose up towards the screen, the organist silhouetted against colourful illuminated side panels. Nicknamed the Duchess it still puts in an appearance at special events (www.theduchess.org.uk).

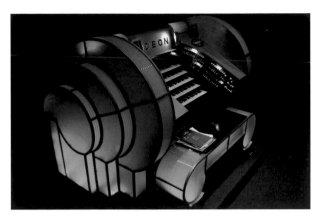

A Compton cinema organ hides beneath the stage of the Odeon Leicester Square

The second largest cinema in Leicester Square is the Empire built in 1928. It occupies the site of Barker's Rotunda, a Victorian music hall, where in 1896 the Lumière Brothers projected the first moving pictures in Britain. Another cinema on historic ground is the nearby Prince Charles Cinema at 7 Leicester Place. In the 17th century Leicester House stood here, which for a while contained the *Holophusikon*, a museum of curiosities acquired by Captain Cook. The cinema is today renowned for its sing-along screenings of popular musicals.

Historic, too, is the Hippodrome on nearby Cranbourn Street, erected in 1900 to a design by renowned theatre architect Frank Matcham (1854–1920). Originally a hippodrome for circus and variety performances it became a theatre in 1909 and is where Tchaikovsky's *Swan Lake* received its English première (it is today an award-winning casino).

To discover more about the history of cinema visit the London Film Museum at 45 Wellington Street (WC2) and the Cinema Museum at 2 Dugard Way (SE11). The latter is housed in the former Lambeth Workhouse, where Charlie Chaplin (1889–1977) lived as a child.

London's finest *Art Deco* interior is Brasserie Zédel at 20 Sherwood Street (W1). Its opulent Bar Américain was once part of the Regent Palace Hotel and features striped walls and Jazz Age columns. The London School of Hygiene & Tropical Medicine on Keppel Street (WC1) is also *Art Deco* and has gilded insects worked into its balconies. It can be visited during Open House London (www.openhouselondon.org.uk).

Other places of interest nearby: 32, 33, 35, 64

35 London's French Connection

WC2H 7BX (Soho), a tour of French London concluding
with the Church of Notre Dame de France at
5 Leicester Place
Northern, Piccadilly lines to Leicester Square

Immigrant communities have long left a mark on London's landscape from Bengali street signs and curry houses in Spitalfields' Banglatown to the red lanterns and restaurants of Soho's Chinatown, although neither community predates the 1970s. French London is low-key by comparison – but much older. The first significant influx was that of Huguenot silk weavers, who arrived in 1675 and built their fortunes in the East End textile industry (see no. 8).

Modern French London is centred on the Institut Français in well-heeled South Kensington (SW7). A clutch of Parisian-style cafés and bookshops enhance the Gallic scene but there is little in the way of colourful history. For that the Francophile should venture northeast into Soho, where three locales make up for the shortfall.

The first is the Church of Notre Dame de France at 5 Leicester Place (WC2), which opened in 1868 to service London's lower class French in the days when Soho was a French enclave. Although the original building was destroyed during an air raid in 1940 it was rebuilt in 1955 to the same circular plan, inspired by a rotunda containing a panorama of the Battle of Waterloo that occupied the site in the 1790s. Circular churches are a rarity in Britain but this one is made unique by its murals of the Crucixion created in 1960 by the French artist and writer Jean Cocteau (1889–1963).

The French connection continues a couple of streets north with Kettner's at 29 Romilly Street (W1). This authentic brasserie was established in 1867 by Auguste Kettner, onetime chef to Emperor Napoleon III (1808–1873), at a time when French cuisine was considered exotic. Famous habitués have included Oscar Wilde and Edward VII (1901–1910), who courted his mistress the actress Lillie Langtry here.

Even more storied is the French House around the corner at 49 Dean Street (W1). Originally called the Wine House this pub was opened in 1910 by a German but following his deportation during the First World War it was acquired by a Belgian, Victor Berlemont. Although he renamed the pub the York Minster, regulars soon began calling it "the French house". The French connection was cemented during the Second World War with the fall of France, when General Charles de Gaulle escaped to London and formed the Free French Forces. His famous speech rallying the French people – "À tous les Français" – is said to have been written in the pub.

Later under Gaston Berlemont a bohemian clientele was encouraged, including writers, artists and actors, as well as prostitutes and tramps. A sozzled Dylan Thomas famously left the manuscript of his *Under Milk Wood* beneath a chair here.

Bizarrely the pub's name was officially changed to the French House after a fire swept through the real York Minster in 1984. Contributions for that building's restoration began arriving at the pub in error, whilst several consignments of claret ended up in Yorkshire! Despite Berlemont's retirement in 1989 his rules regarding no music or television make the place a haven for conversationalists.

A detail of Jean Cocteau's murals in the Church of Notre Dame de France

Continuing the French theme is the Wallace Collection on Manchester Square (W1). This former private art collection includes French 18th century paintings, furniture, and porcelain, as well as the famous Dutch painting *The Laughing Cavalier*. For more things Dutch visit De Hems at 11 Macclesfield Street (W1), London's only Dutch café-bar. It is named after a Dutch seaman, who leased the place as an oyster bar in the 1890s, and is where members of the Dutch Resistance met during the Second World War.

Other places of interest nearby: 32, 33, 35, 61, 64, 79

36 Theatreland

WC2B 5JF (Covent Garden), a tour of the Theatre Royal Drury Lane
Piccadilly line to Covent Garden; Central, Piccadilly lines to Holborn; Circle, District lines to Temple

The term 'West End' was coined in the early 19th century to describe the fashionable area of London west of Charing Cross. Close to Westminster and away from the cramped City and the slums of Holborn and Covent Garden, it was developed from the 17th century onwards as a place of residence for the well-to-do. Since the late 19th century, when the slums were cleared, the term has been used to describe the broader shopping and entertainment areas west of the City.

A distinct area within the West End is London's Theatreland bound by Regent Street, Oxford Street, Kingsway and the Strand. Successor to earlier theatre districts in Shoreditch and Bankside, it today boasts 47 separate venues from the massive Edwardian 2,356-seat London Coliseum on St. Martin's Lane (WC2) to the intimate modern 70-seat Jermyn Street Theatre (SW1) in a former restaurant staff changing room (see no. 98). The record for the world's longest theatrical run goes to St. Martin's Theatre on West Street (WC2), which since 1952 has helped stage over 25,000 performances of Agatha's Christie's *The Mousetrap*.

The first venue to open in Theatreland was Lincoln's Inn Theatre on Portugal Street (WC2) in 1660. Its appearance signalled not only the Restoration of the Monarchy under Charles II (1660–1685) but also the end of the ban on plays first imposed on moral grounds by the Puritans and continued under Cromwell for political reasons. Long since demolished it was the country's first modern theatre to feature a proscenium arch and moveable scenery.

Theatreland's oldest extant venue today is the Theatre Royal Drury Lane, with its main entrance on Catherine Street (WC2). Opened in 1663, with the present building dating from 1811, it is the oldest theatrical site in Britain. An entertaining way to discover its long history is to join a *Through the Stage Door* tour available at the theatre twice-daily from Monday to Saturday. Led by professional actors dressed in period garb they are theatrical performances in miniature. Highlights include the magnificent Georgian Grand Saloon, the Royal Box, and the hidden walkways beneath the stage. There are all sorts of fascinating stories, too, including how the words "crew" and "rigging" come from

Looking out across the auditorium of the Theatre Royal Drury Lane

the days when sailors were employed to hoist the heavy scenery. Colourful characters encountered along the way include the orange seller-turned-actress Nell Gwyn (1650–1687), who later became Charles II's mistress, and the Regency-era clown, Joseph Grimaldi (1778–1837). His ghost is one of five said to still haunt the theatre!

There is one thing, however, that even an official tour won't reveal to visitors. On the twelfth night after Christmas a special cake is baked for the players using money bequeathed in 1792 by fellow actor Richard Baddeley. Theatrical superstition has ensured the survival of this longstanding tradition ever since.

Several other Theatreland venues also offer tours, including the London Coliseum on St. Martin's Lane (WC2), the Royal Opera House on Bow Street (WC2), the London Palladium on Argyll Street (W1), and the Theatre Royal Haymarket on Suffolk Street (SW1).

Other addresses in Theatreland with a connection to the stage include the actors' Church of St. Paul Covent Garden on Bedford Street (WC2), where Dame Ellen Terry (1847–1928) is buried, the Sarastro Restaurant at 126 Drury Lane (WC2), with its opera box tables, and the Salisbury at 90 St. Martin's Lane (WC2), a Victorian Gin Palace popular with theatregoers. Shops include the ship's chandler Arthur Beale at 194 Shaftesbury Avenue (WC2), which supplies theatres with rigging.

Other places of interest nearby: 28, 29, 30, 37, 38

37 Mysterious World of the Freemasons

WC2B 5AZ (Covent Garden), Freemasons' Hall at 60 Great Queen Street
Piccadilly line to Covent Garden; Central, Piccadilly lines to Holborn

One of the most remarkable buildings in London was until recently one of its best kept secrets. Freemasons' Hall at 60 Great Queen Street (WC2) is the imposing headquarters of the United Grand Lodge of England, the governing body of freemasonry in England, Wales and the Channel Islands. The third Masonic building to occupy the site – the first opened in 1775 – it was built in the *Art Deco* style between 1927 and 1933, as a memorial to the 3,225 Freemasons who perished in the Great War.

The exterior of Freemasons' Hall is certainly impressive but it's the interior that is most remarkable. At its heart is the Grand Temple, the meeting room for the Grand Lodge, which can be visited as part of a guided tour. Entered through a pair of bronze doors, each weighing more than a ton, the room is almost 40 metres long with seating for 1,700. The ceiling is decorated with motifs and symbols pertinent to Masonic ritual, with corner figures representing the four cardinal virtues – Prudence, Temperance, Fortitude, and Justice. Also featured are the arms of Prince Arthur, the youngest son of Queen Victoria, who as Grand Master from 1901 until 1939 proposed the dedication of the current building as a war memorial.

In addition to the Grand Temple, Freemasons' Hall contains a further 23 smaller temples and meeting rooms, all of which are distinctively decorated. One of them combines *Art Deco* with Egyptian designs, whilst another doubles as a portrait gallery of former Grand Masters. Unfortunately, they rarely feature on the guided tour because they are permanently in demand by over a thousand other provincial and private Masonic Lodges. Also off-limits is an entire floor from where the four major national masonic charities are administered (the Freemasons' Grand Charity, the Royal Masonic Trust for Girls and Boys, the Royal Masonic Benevolent Institution, and the Masonic Samaritan Fund). These act as a reminder that whilst the Freemasons may have originally come into being as a secretive guild designed to protect the rights of medieval stonemasons they are known today for their charity work and espousal of good working practices.

As the oldest Grand Lodge in the world, it seems fitting that Freemasons' Hall should also be home to the Library and Museum of Freemasonry. The library is more for the serious student and contains works on every facet of Freemasonry, including its mystical and esoteric traditions so beloved by writers of fiction. The museum is more accessible to the general public, with its extensive collection of objects sporting Masonic insignia, including embroidered membership aprons and a miniaturised depiction of a Lodge meeting inside a glass bottle. Elsewhere amongst the jewels, regalia, engravings and clocks are items that once belonged to famous and even royal Freemasons, including Mozart, Sir Henry Irving, Winston Churchill, and Edward VII. The collection also reveals much about the different ranks and offices of Freemasonry, so often misunderstood by the unitiated, as well as the meaning behind the organisation's penchant for symbolism. Finally, there are items relating to non-Masonic fraternal societies, including the Oddfellows, the Ancient Order of Foresters, and the Sons of the Phoenix.

Inside the Grand Temple at Freemasons' Hall

Several streets north of Freemasons' Hall is a very different museum. The diminutive Cartoon Museum at 35 Little Russell Street (WC1) preserves and promotes British cartoon art, comic art, and caricature from the 18th century to the present. There is everything here from Dennis the Menace to biting political satire.

Other places of interest nearby: 29, 30, 36, 38, 44

38 Sir John Soane's Pasticcio

**WC2A 3BP (Holborn), Sir John Soane's Museum
at 13 Lincoln's Inn Fields
Central, Piccadilly lines to Holborn**

Despite being the son of a humble bricklayer the architect Sir John Soane (1753–1837) rose to the pinnacle of his profession. He applied his penchant for Classical clean lines and considered proportions to the Bank of England and the Dulwich Picture Gallery, and yet it is his own house at 13 Lincoln's Inn Fields (WC2) that most excites devotees today.

Soane purchased the house in 1806 and set about creating a distinctive place in which to live and work. He added a projecting Portland Stone loggia, installed public rooms at the front of the house, and created a drawing office and museum to the rear. After his wife's death in 1815 Soane lived here alone, embellishing his impressive collection of architectural fragments, antiquities and other works of art.

The legal heir to Soane's remarkable home was his son, George, but unfortunately the two had for years been locked in a fierce family feud. Soane disapproved of his son's debts, jobless state, and even his marriage, and set about disinheriting him. The result was an extraordinary Private Act of Parliament requiring that the house and its contents be preserved for the nation in the state left by Soane at the time of his death. His wishes have been carried out to the letter.

Visiting Sir John Soane's Museum is a memorable experience. Crossing the threshold one immediately gets a sense of the man's architectural and collecting sensibilities, indeed there is the feeling that he might make an entrance any moment. That visitor numbers are restricted, labelling kept discreet, and the fact there is no café only enhances this intimacy.

The Dining Room-and-Library comes first, its rich red decoration inspired by a fragment of wall plaster pocketed by Soane during a visit to Pompeii. The Study beyond contains Soane's writing desk, as well as a collection of Roman architectural fragments. To one side it overlooks a lightwell called the Monument Court at the centre of which is the so-called *Pasticcio*. This column made from disparate pieces of decorative masonry embodies more than anything else Soane's eclectic interests in architecture ancient and modern. It comprises an Ionic column pedestal, an Islamic capital from the Alhambra, a chunk of Norman stone from Rochester Cathedral, a Corinthian capital of the type used by Soane at the Bank of England, and a cast iron pinnacle.

A corridor beyond is lined with more pieces of architecture and leads to the Picture Room, where large folding wall panels ingeniously enable three times as many works to be hung as normal (staff will demonstrate these). The corridor additionally gives access to the basement, which contains the Monk's Parlour and Yard, with medieval stonework from the Old Palace of Westminster. Also located here is the atmospheric Crypt containing the alabaster sarcophagus of Egyptian Pharaoh Seti I.

Back on the ground floor is the Colonnade and Dome area toplit by concave skylights in the same revolutionary way that Soane illuminated his public buildings. Whilst

A riot of sculpture in the Dome area of Sir John Soane's Museum

candlelit tours of the museum are available each first Tuesday in the month, only a daytime visit will demonstrate this important architectural innovation. Equally innovative is the domed ceiling of the Breakfast Room daringly inset with convex mirrors.

The tour concludes with Soane's private rooms on the first floor and a dining room with a *trompe l'oeil* ceiling giving the impression of being under a garden pergola.

Soane also designed Holy Trinity Church on Marylebone Road (W9), a so-called 'Waterloo church' built to mark the end of the Napoleonic wars. Its crypt served as a storeroom for Penguin Books when they were based on Great Portland Street.

Other places of interest nearby: 36, 37, 39, 43

39 Waters, Walks and Gardens Green

WC1R 5ET (Holborn), a walking tour of London's Inns of Court
beginning with Gray's Inn on Gray's Inn Road
Central line to Chancery Lane (note: this walk should be
conducted on weekdays during office hours when the Inns
of Court are open)

In his poem *The Prelude* William Wordsworth (1770–1850) wrote that
the lawyers of London "look out on waters, walks and gardens green".
He was describing the so-called Inns of Court, where the country's barristers have been trained and regulated since the 14th century. Visiting
the Inns today reveals that the passage of time has barely touched
these tranquil precincts of learning.

England's legal system finds its origins in the mid-12th century
with the establishment of Common Law based on the principle of precedent. At that time law was only taught by the clergy in the City of
London. This changed in 1234 when Henry III (1216–1272) closed the
City's law schools and the clergy were banned from teaching by papal
bull. Instead London's lawyers relocated to new dwellings (or 'inns')
in the hamlet of Holborn, which was the closest they could get to the
Law Courts of Westminster (see no. 86).

This tour begins at Gray's Inn on Gray's Inn Road (WC1) named
after the De Gray family, who leased their property to several lawyers
and their families in the early 14th century. By the reign of Elizabeth I
(1558–1603) it was the largest Inn of Court, with an established system
of education common to all Inns that culminated in students being
called 'to the Bar' (the 'bar' in question was a physical barrier in an
Inn separating senior members from their students, whence the term
'barrister' is derived). The entire process could take up to 14 years,
with some students commencing their studies at an Inn of Chancery (a
dedicated legal training institution) such as the timber-framed Staple
Inn on High Holborn.

Gray's Inn still retains its 16th century layout, namely a gatehouse
opening onto a peaceful courtyard surrounded by 'Sets' of barristers'
chambers, a library, chapel, and a hall for dining and moots. A walled
garden known as Gray's Inn Walks was added by Francis Bacon (1561–
1626) during his tenure as Treasurer. Consisting of a broad gravelled
path lined with London plane trees it remains a popular promenade

Barristers' chambers overlooking Gray's Inn Walks

despite the encroachment of solicitors' offices, including the one where the young Charles Dickens (1812–1870) worked as a junior clerk (see no. 59).

South of High Holborn is Lincoln's Inn on Chancery Lane (WC2), which also evolved out of an association with nobility, in this case Henry de Lacy, 3rd Earl of Lincoln (1251–1311), who was instrumental in encouraging lawyers to move to Holborn. Its medieval gatehouse and hall, 17th century chapel, and open undercroft by Inigo Jones

A quiet corner of Inner Temple

(1573–1652) all remain intact, as does its Victorian Great Hall and library. Ede & Ravenscroft at 93 Chancery Lane still supply barristers with horsehair wigs!

Between Fleet Street and Victoria Embankment are London's two other Inns of Court: the Inner Temple and Middle Temple. Both were established on land occupied formerly by the Knights Templar, who were suppressed in 1312 for becoming too powerful (see no. 21). After the Reformation the land became the property of the Crown until 1608, when James I (1603–1625) granted it to the Inns in perpetuity. The cobbled streets, fountain courtyard and gas lights of Middle Temple imbue a magical atmosphere, as does its lovely hall where Shakespeare's *Twelfth Night* was premiered in 1602. The highlight of Inner Temple, where this tour finishes, is the Temple Church on Inner Temple Lane (EC4). Constructed by the Templars in 1185 it imitates the rotunda of the Church of the Holy Sepulchre in Jerusalem and contains several marble effigies of recumbent knights in armour.

The Inns of Court have had their own regiment in the British Army since 1584, when 95 lawyers pledged to defend London against the threat of Spanish invasion. They subsequently defended the City during the Gordon Riots, fought in the Boer War, and most recently (as 68 Signal Squadron) served in Iraq and Afghanistan. The regiment's history is given in the Inns of Court and City Yeomanry Museum at 10 Stone Buildings (WC2), where amongst the weapons and uniforms is the Army's oldest complete set of drums.

Other places of interest nearby: 22, 38

40 Lenin and Marx in London

WC1X 9HD (Clerkenwell), some sights associated with Lenin
and Marx including Bevin Court on Holford Street
Northern line to Angel (note: the interior of Bevin Court is
open to residents only)

The Russian Communist revolutionary Vladimir Ilyich Lenin (1870–1924) visited London six times before becoming the Soviet Union's first leader. Masquerading as one Jacob Richter he was a regular in the reading room of the British Museum, where Karl Marx (1818–1883) had written *Das Kapital* half a century earlier. The political theory resulting from his studies – known as Marxism-Leninism – gave rise eventually to Stalinism, Trotskyism, and Maoism.

There are numerous sites in London associated with Marx and Lenin. Needless to say, several of the premises they once occupied are marked with blue plaques. During the 1850s, for example, Marx lived in a squalid apartment at 28 Dean Street (W1), where three of his children died. Lenin, on the other hand, occupied various safe houses inhabited by fellow revolutionaries, including 36 Tavistock Place (WC1), where he stayed in 1908.

During an earlier visit in 1905 Lenin resided at 16 Percy Circus (WC1), whilst attending the third congress of the Russian Social Democratic Labour Party (RSDLP) (the party's eventual split would see the Bolsheviks become the Communist Party of the Soviet Union). Just around the corner from here on Holford Street is Bevin Court. This large housing complex commissioned in the early 1940s stands on the site of Holford Square, where Lenin lived in 1902–03. The complex was designed by the Russian Constructivist architect, Berthold Lubetkin (1901–1990), and was originally to be called Lenin Court. However, by the time the building was completed in 1954 the Cold War was in full swing, and so instead it was named Bevin Court, after Britain's staunchly anti-Communist Foreign Secretary, Ernest Bevin (1881–1951).

Visiting Bevin Court today it is easy not to see any connection whatsoever with Lenin but back in 1942 a significant Lenin memorial also by Lubetkin stood outside. After repeated acts of vandalism, however, Lenin's bust was removed to Islington Museum at 245 St. John Street (EC1) and the rest of the memorial was incorporated quietly (and invisibly) into Bevin Court's impressive central stairwell. Lubetkin's original idea of relocating the memorial immediately outside the main

Bevin Court in Clerkenwell was originally to be named after Lenin

entrance was never realised although a viewing hatch designed to allow the doorman to keep an eye on it still exists, as does a mural in the foyer by Lubetkin's sometime collaborator Peter Yates (1920–1982). It is made up of stylised elements taken from the heraldic arms of Finsbury, the London borough in which Bevin Court stands.

The lives of Lenin and Marx converge again at 37a Clerkenwell Green (EC1). In April 1902 Lenin relocated the publishing office of the RSDLP newspaper *Iskra* here. In the early 1930s the building became the Marx Memorial Library, which today contains not only Lenin's tiny former office but also an extensive archive of Marxist literature. On the wall is a mural entitled *The Worker of the Future Upsetting the Economic Chaos of the Present* depicting a barechested labourer with Lenin and Marx looking on. As the labourer releases his chains so Big Ben tumbles on top of the capitalists below.

To walk in the footsteps of Marx visit www.marxwalks.com. Readers wishing to see where Lenin enjoyed a drink should visit two former pubs: the Crown and Woolpack at 394 St. John Street (EC1) and the Pindar of Wakefield at 328 Gray's Inn Road (WC1), now a music venue where Bob Dylan played his first British concert. The claim that Lenin met Stalin for the first time at the Crown Tavern at 43 Clerkenwell Green (EC1) is unfortunately apocryphal.

41 Foundlings and the Messiah

**WC1N 1AZ (Bloomsbury), the Foundling Museum
at 40 Brunswick Square
Piccadilly line to Russell Square**

Coram's Fields in Bloomsbury is a unique children's playground. It occupies the former site of the Foundling Hospital, England's first home for abandoned children. Created in 1936 using private donations the park has been administered by an independent charitable trust ever since.

A trinket left with an abandoned child at the Coram's Fields' Foundling Hospital

The poignant story of London's foundlings is given in the Foundling Museum, which overlooks Coram's Fields at 40 Brunswick Square (WC1). It is sobering to learn that in the early 18th century nearly a thousand babies a year were abandoned on the streets of London. In 1739 this statistic prompted retired shipbuilder and philanthropist Captain Thomas Coram (1668–1751) to establish the Foundling Hospital, where infants up to two months old could be left by poverty-stricken parents. Identified by little more than a scribbled scrap of paper or a cheap trinket, a typical entry in the admissions book reads "Paper on the breast, clout on the head".

Walking through Coram's Fields today it is difficult to imagine the brick hospital with its two wings and a chapel built around a large open courtyard (the wings were designed to segregate the sexes). All that remains of it today is a stone alcove on Guildford Street, where the unwanted infants were deposited, and a Georgian colonnade, where older children once toiled to earn their keep.

In 1756 the hospital's admission age was raised to 12 years and collection centres established countrywide. A flood of illegitimate children began arriving at the hospital from the country's workhouses to be cared for until they could be apprenticed out (boys at 14 years into various occupations and girls at 16 into servitude).

One of the hospital's original governors was the artist and social critic William Hogarth (1697–1764). He designed the children's uniforms and also set up an art gallery featuring works by contemporary painters. It was the country's first public exhibition space and led to the creation in 1768 of the Royal Academy of Arts. Another hospital governor was composer George Frideric Handel (1685–1759), who in 1750 donated the chapel organ and thereafter annually directed his *Messiah* to raise funds (see no. 55). The benefits of music at the hospital were significant, with many foundlings later joining military bands.

When in the 1920s the hospital relocated to the country the Coram Fields' site was sold and the hospital demolished. Later, however, the hospital bought back some land alongside the park and built their headquarters on it. With the tide now turning against the institutionalisation of children the Foundling Hospital began promoting adoption and foster care instead. Known today simply as Coram it remains one of London's largest children's charities. The Foundling Museum was created here, too, where Hogarth's gallery and much Handel memorabilia can again be enjoyed against a reconstructed 18th century backdrop. Not surprisingly many of the museum's events are aimed at a young audience.

On Handel Street behind the Foundling Museum is the little-known St. George's Gardens, an early 18th century burial ground now also used as a park. It still contains the chest tomb of Oliver Cromwell's granddaughter, Anna Gibson, and holds the dubious distinction of being the first London cemetery to attract body-snatchers.

Another relic from the early days of caring for London's underprivileged children are the effigies of boys and girls outside former charity schools. Dating from the mid-16th century onwards they wear the uniforms of the day, which were often blue since that was the cheapest clothing dye available at the time (their yellow socks were dyed with saffron as that was thought to deter rats from biting their ankles!). This explains why such establishments were known as Bluecoat Schools. Such Effigies can still be seen on Caxton Street (SW1), Duke's Place (SW3), and Hatton Garden (EC1).

Other places of interest nearby: 42

42 The Horse Hospital and Other Galleries

WC1N 1JD (Bloomsbury), some unusual art galleries including the Horse Hospital at the junction of Herbrand Street and Colonnade
Piccadilly line to Russell Square (note: the Horse Hospital is only open during exhibitions and special events)

Art spaces in London come in all shapes and sizes from imposing traditional venues, such as the National Gallery on Trafalgar Square, to temporary 'Pop-ups' in the East End. Some of them occupy unusual premises, too. The Ditch, for example, is in the basement of the former Shoreditch Town Hall on Old Street (EC1), the Photographers' Gallery occupies an adapted Edwardian warehouse at 16–18 Ramillies Street (W1), T. J. Boulting is beneath a converted Arts and Crafts stove factory at 59 Riding Hosue Street (W1), and White Cube at 152–154 Bermondsey Street (SE1) occupies a reworked storage space from the 1970s. Another is the Horse Hospital in Bloomsbury, where all things *Avant-Garde* rub shoulders in a former stable for cab drivers' sick horses.

The Horse Hospital is concealed in a cobbled mews behind the luxury Hotel Russell, at the corner of Herbrand Street and Colonnade (WC1). Built in 1797 from handmade bricks (known as London stocks) it still retains the ramps by which horses once entered the building, as well as the iron rings used to tether them. Also still in place are the cast iron pillars that helped support the weight of horses stabled on the

The Horse Hospital is an arts venue with a difference

first floor. It is easy to forget that as late as 1900 there were still 300,000 horses working in London.

Against this historic backdrop the Horse Hospital was founded in 1993 by punk pioneer Richard Burton, who gained fame designing Vivienne Westwood's legendary World's End boutique on Kings Road. Now one of London's most progressive arts venues it provides an interactive space that promotes synergy between the related media of film, fashion, music and art. Propelled by artistic rather than financial motives the eclectic events staged here embrace a spirit of experimentation not seen since the Arts Lab movement of the late 1960s. The Contemporary Wardrobe Collection in the basement houses thousands of historic garments dating back to 1945, which Burton rents out to the film, television and fashion industry.

Another unusual not-for-profit arts venue is Village Underground in Shoreditch. Opened in 2007 it consists of an exhibition-cum-concert space in a Victorian warehouse, as well as carbon friendly studios installed in several recycled Jubilee line rail carriages. These are perched high above Great Eastern Street (EC2) on a disused portion of the Broad Street Rail Viaduct.

A very different experience is provided at 123 Kennington Road (SE11), where Danielle Arnaud has been curating exhibitions in her home since 1995. There has been a tradition of London gallerists displaying art at home ever since Maureen Paley (b. 1953) opened the doors of her East End Victorian terraced house in 1984. Although Arnaud hosts her exhibitions in a smart Georgian townhouse her aim is the same, namely to encourage artists to develop their talents without market constraints. The chance to wander at leisure through elegantly furnished rooms whilst appreciating modern art is not something usually associated with this part of London.

Other unusually-sited London galleries include the Victoria Miro Gallery at 16 Wharf Road (N1) inside a former furniture factory. Offering one of the largest commercial spaces for contemporary art in London it boasts a strikingly modern, whitewashed roof extension, with floor-to-ceiling windows looking out over a restored stretch of the Regent's Canal. By contrast one of London's smallest art spaces is the Subway Gallery in a pedestrian underpass beneath Edgware Road and Harrow Road (W2). Occupying a former 1960s retail kiosk, its glass walls create an intriguing interface between the subversive art inside and the passers-by outside. The smallest art space of all must surely be White Cubicle located in the ladies' toilet of the George & Dragon Pub at 2 Hackney Road (E2)!

Other places of interest nearby: 41, 43

43 Strolling Bloomsbury's Squares

WC1A 2RJ (Bloomsbury), a tour of Bloomsbury's squares
beginning with Bloomsbury Square
Central, Piccadilly lines to Holborn

A nightingale may have sung in Berkeley Square but it would have been equally at home in Bloomsbury. Defined by Euston Road, Gray's Inn Road, High Holborn, and Tottenham Court Road, Bloomsbury is named after a Norman noble, who was given the land by William the Conqueror (1066–1087). The area's peaceful squares, located so close to the bustle of UCL and the British Museum, exemplify how London can change character within a very short distance.

The names of Bloomsbury's squares, and the elegant terraces they contain, recall the aristocrats who created them. "This whole area is well-crafted," noted the architectural historian Nikolaus Pevsner (1902–1983) in 1930, "a pleasure to the eye with

Elegant architecture in Bloomsbury Square

its trees and squares, the product of centuries of a very self-aware bourgeoisie." Unlike Berkeley Square, however, which is now shorn of many of the residential buildings that once defined it, the squares of Bloomsbury remain largely intact.

This tour begins with the oldest, the eponymous Bloomsbury Square, which was first laid out as Southampton Square in the 1660s by Thomas Wriothesley, 4th Earl of Southampton (Henry VIII had presented the land to Wriothesley's ancestor during the Dissolution of the

Monasteries, Bloomsbury having previously been in the hands of the Carthusian monks of Charterhouse). The Earl erected a city residence for himself on the north side of the square and lined the other three with fine terraced houses for the aristocracy.

Renamed Bloomsbury Square in the 1730s it later passed by marriage to the Russell family, whose main title was the Dukedom of Bedford. By 1800 Bloomsbury Square was no longer considered fashionable and so the 5th Duke moved away and replaced the original buildings with handsome new terraces for middle class professionals (still extant they now serve mainly as offices). He also laid out a new road on the site of his old back garden leading to Russell Square, where a statue of the duke stands today (as well as a tree planted in memory of those killed by the terrorist bombings of July 2005). Bloomsbury Square today reflects the Regency-era layout imposed on it by landscape gardener Humphry Repton (1752–1818).

The building activities of the Russells are further evidenced a couple of blocks west in Bedford Square. Created between 1775 and 1783 it is one of London's finest set pieces of Georgian architecture. Built for the upper middle classes it attracted many distinguished residents, which explains the many Blue Plaques hanging there today. The square still retains an air of exclusivity notably its private residents' garden, one of several in Bloomsbury that can be visited during the annual Open Garden Squares Weekend (www.opensquares.org). Another is Mecklenburgh Square, east of Coram's Fields.

In north-west Bloomsbury two further squares lie side-by-side. Tavistock Square takes its name from the courtesy title given to the eldest sons of the Dukes of Bedford, namely Marquess of Tavistock. It contains a bust of the writer Virginia Woolf (1882–1941), who was a founding member of the Bloomsbury Group of writers and artists. They met at the home of Woolf's sister, the artist and interior designer Vanessa Bell (1879–1961), at Number 46 in the adjacent Gordon Square. Others members included the economist John Maynard Keynes (1883–1946), who occupied the house after Vanessa left, and the writer and biographer Lytton Strachey (1880–1932), who lived at Number 51. Woolf herself lived at 29 Fitzroy Square (W1), the only London square designed by renowned Georgian architect, Robert Adam (1728–1792).

Since 2006 the annual Bloomsbury Festival has helped reinvent the cultural lineage of the area by partnering with local libraries and galleries.

Other places of interest nearby: 38, 42, 44

44 The Treasures of Room 41

WC1B 3DG (Bloomsbury), the British Museum on Great Russell Street
Central, Piccadilly lines to Holborn; Central, Northern lines to Tottenham Court Road

When the British Museum opened by royal decree in 1759 barely 80 people a day came to see it. These days that figure can exceed 30,000 making the museum the second most visited in the world after the Louvre in Paris. Both the building and the collections have grown, too, with almost 90 rooms used to display just one percent of the museum's total holdings of six million objects.

So how should one go about visiting such a huge museum? Initially a half day whistlestop tour is required just to get a sense of its vast scope. Everything is here from world class exhibits, including the Rosetta Stone and the Elgin

A reconstruction of the Sutton Hoo helmet in the British Museum [Photo © www.gernot-keller.com]

Marbles, to less well known treasures such as the enigmatic crystal skull in Room 24 and the leathery remains of Lindow Man in Room 50.

The visitor is then advised to retreat to the café in the museum's Great Court to reflect on all they've seen. If time and energy permits they can then return refreshed and perhaps examine a single room more closely. The author opted for Room 41 on the first floor, which contains early medieval objects from the period known as the Dark Ages (AD 300 to 1100). Until recently this room was ignored by many visitors as they rushed headlong towards the Egyptian mummy rooms. Refurbished displays and better labelling, however, have now made Room 41 a must-see.

The objects displayed bring to life the fierce, fantastical world recorded in *Beowulf*, England's oldest vernacular epic. Indeed it could be the great warrior hero himself who grabs the visitor's attention in the shape of the Sutton Hoo helmet in the centre of the room. It was unearthed in 1939 in the hold of a wooden ship, which had been hauled onto dry land to serve as the tomb of a 7th century king. The helmet has a forceful air about it, a dragon-like bird forming the nose guard, its outstretched wings covering the eyebrows and a toothed head filling the furrow in between. Over the top of the head slides an equally ferocious serpent, the two creatures joined at the mouth. It is conjectured that such creatures afforded supernatural protection to the helmet's wearer.

The Sutton Hoo helmet is a spectacular piece of craftsmanship, as are the other grave goods associated with it. These include a superb *cloisonné* purse lid, a great gold belt buckle, and a pair of shoulder clasps so masterfully crafted that goldsmiths would struggle to replicate them today. These objects reflect a surprisingly sophisticated society influenced by late Roman, Scandinavian, Frankish and Byzantine arts and crafts.

Joining the treasures from Sutton Hoo are others from farther afield: Roman glass vessels (the so-called Lycurgus Cup is one of the very finest), Germanic ivory and crystals, Byzantine textiles, Anglo-Saxon brooches, and Viking metalwork. This was a time of great migrations and taken together these objects reveal a cultural interconnectedness that now renders the term 'Dark Ages' a misnomer.

At the centre of the British Museum's Great Court is the magnificent Round Reading Room used by the British Library when it was a department of the museum. Famous readers have included Karl Marx, Oscar Wilde, Mahatma Gandhi, Virginia Woolf and George Orwell. Since the library's relocation to St. Pancras in 1997 the room has served as an exhibition space and is currently being refurbished.

Contemporary with the Round Reading Room is the less well-known dodecagonal reading room of the King's College Maughan Library on Chancery Lane (WC2).

Other places of interest nearby: 37, 43, 61

45 Pickled Toads and Dodo Bones

WC1E 6DE (Bloomsbury), the Grant Museum of Zoology and
Comparative Anatomy in the Rockefeller Building
at 21 University Street
Circle, Hammersmith & City, Metropolitan lines to Euston
Square; Northern line to Goodge Street; Northern, Victoria
lines to Warren Street

London's Natural History Museum is considered one of the world's greatest repositories of objects pertaining to the natural world – but it's not the capital's only such collection (see no. 73). Although tiny by comparison, the Grant Museum of Zoology and Comparative Anatomy at University College London offers its own unique take on natural curiosities.

The museum was established in 1828 by the Scotsman Robert Edmond Grant (1793–1874), one of the foremost biologists of his time. A year earlier he had been made the first Professor of Comparative Anatomy at the newly-founded London University – now University College London (UCL) – where he quickly identified the need for a teaching

Just a few of the 60,000 specimens in the Grant Museum of Zoology

collection of zoological specimens. On his death Grant bequeathed his own personal collection of specimens to the museum since when further donations have been received from other university collections, hospitals, and even London Zoo.

In 2011 the museum was moved from the Darwin Building on the UCL campus – Grant influenced the young Charles Darwin, who once occupied a house on the site – to new premises in the Rockefeller Building at 21 University Street (WC1). Today the entrance to the museum is adorned with the skeletons of a walrus, a baboon and a giant iguanadon beyond which can be found over 60,000 zoological specimens, many of which are preserved in glass vials and jars. As such this museum is probably not for the squeamish.

To the untrained eye the exhibits might at first appear disorganised but on closer inspection it will be seen that they are carefully categorised into evolutionary groups. The entire animal kingdom is represented here from jars of humble worms and pickled toads to monkey skeletons and huge elephant skulls. The curled up skeleton of a 250-kilo anaconda is particularly memorable!

Amongst the exhibits are some real oddities. Take for example the enormous skull of a Giant Deer *(Megaloceros giganteus)*, which was unexpectedly found hanging in an Irish hotel. Once a denizen of Europe and Asia, the Giant Deer's last refuge 10,000 years ago was Ireland giving rise to the misleading name of Irish Elk. Then there is a skeleton of the extinct Quagga, a partially-striped sub-species of Plains Zebra hunted to extinction during the 1870s. It had long been in the museum but only identified in 1981. The box of Dodo bones, an extinct flightless bird so famous it has entered modern English parlance (hence "dead as a Dodo"), was stored away for a century before being rediscovered in 2011. And don't overlook the fossilised remains of *Rhamphorhynchus*. This Jurassic-era pterosaur was assumed to be a plaster cast until it turned out to be the real thing. Definitely a cast but no less interesting for that is an example of *Archaeopteryx* believed by some to represent the missing link between saurian reptiles and birds.

Wrongly perceived as a purely Victorian collection, the Grant Museum of Zoology today stages modern and innovative temporary displays designed to be of interest to a non-professional audience. These attract not only university students but also schoolchildren, artists and other curious visitors. As a further nod to modernity they are encouraged to share their opinions on iPads positioned alongside the exhibits.

Other places of interest nearby: 46, 59

46 The Mummified Philosopher

WC1E 6BT (Bloomsbury), the Jeremy Bentham Auto-Icon
in the South Cloisters of the Wilkins Building at University
College London on Gower Street
Circle, Hammersmith & City, Metropolitan lines to Euston
Square; Northern line to Goodge Street; Northern, Victoria
lines to Warren Street

Whilst still a child the philosopher and jurist Jeremy Bentham (1748–1832) was discovered at his father's desk reading a history of England. Later aged just 12 he was sent to Queen's College Oxford in the hope he would emulate his father by practising law – but it was not to be. Instead the brilliant Bentham settled eventually in Westminster, where he spent the rest of his life criticising the existing legal system and suggesting ways for its improvement.

Bentham is remembered for his doctrine of Utilitarianism and its axiom that actions are right if they benefit the majority. But that was only the starting point for his radical critique of society. Along the way Bentham mused on

The Jeremy Bentham Auto-Icon at UCL

subjects as diverse as prison reform, religion, poor relief, and even animal welfare. A visionary far ahead of his time he advocated universal suffrage, the abolition of slavery, and the decriminalisation of homosexuality.

With all this in mind it is not surprising that Bentham's will was also extraordinary. In it he stipulated that his body be dissected in public for the benefit of science and that his skeleton be preserved and displayed in a lifelike state. Accordingly his bones were padded out with straw and then dressed in Bentham's own clothes. His head was mummified but not successfully and soon replaced by one made of wax topped off with Bentham's own hair. The finished work, after being placed inside a glazed mahogany cabinet on wheels, was dubbed an Auto-Icon or 'man in his own image'. Since 1850 it has been displayed in the South Cloisters of the Wilkins Building at University College London (UCL) on Gower Street (WC1). Quite why Bentham wished to be preserved this way remains a mystery.

Numerous legends have grown up around the Auto-Icon. It is said, for example, that it presides over meetings of the College Council and that it is recorded in the minutes as being "present but not voting". Whilst untrue it did attend the 100th and 150th anniversaries of the founding of the college. It is also claimed that Bentham's head was once stolen by students from rival Kings College and used as a football! Although the head was indeed stolen in 1975 it was returned unharmed following the payment of a ransom. The head is far too delicate and is now kept in the university's safe.

Unfounded, too, is the belief that Bentham was a founder of UCL. When it opened in 1826 he was almost 80 years old and played no part in the campaign to create it although quite likely his ideals inspired it. The myth stems from a fantastical mural in UCL's Flaxman Gallery showing the architect William Wilkins submitting plans to Bentham for his approval. Another myth states that in 1955 the Auto-Icon was removed to a storeroom from where each night the disgruntled philosopher sallied forth to wreak havoc. The irony is that Bentham had a fear of ghosts and in later life only slept accompanied by a servant. That he would reappear as one seems therefore unlikely!

Alongside Bentham stand the so-called Koptos Lions. Dating to around 3,000 BC they are the oldest ancient Egyptian sculptures displayed anywhere in England.

Jeremy Bentham is not London's only modern mummy. In the belfry of the Church of St. James Garlickhythe on Garlick Hill (EC4) there is a dessicated 300 year old corpse (viewing by appointment only). Nicknamed Jimmy Garlick – French wine and garlic was once unloaded at a nearby wharf (or 'hythe') in medieval times – it was discovered beneath the chancel floor in the mid-19th century.

Other places of interest nearby: 45, 47, 59

47 Harry Houdini's Handcuffs

**NW1 2HD (Euston), the Magic Circle Museum at
12 Stephenson Way
Circle, Hammersmith & City, Metropolitan lines to Euston
Square (note: the museum is open by appointment only)**

It seems entirely fitting that a museum of magic should be well hidden and infrequently open, and London's Magic Circle Museum is both. Less than a minute's walk from the bustle of Euston Station it is tucked away at 12 Stephenson Way (NW1), the door marked only by cryptic symbols. Although the casual visitor will not gain access, those booking ahead through the museum's website (www.themagiccircle. co.uk) will be extended a warm welcome. After all, the Magic Circle is essentially a private society for magicians, and they guard their secrets well.

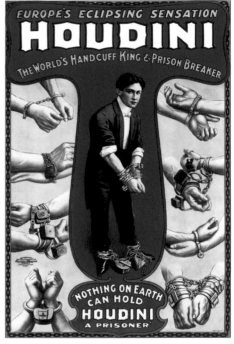

No handcuffs on earth can hold Houdini!

The society was founded in 1905, when a group of professional and amateur magicians congregated at a London restaurant. Dedicated to promoting and advancing the art of stage magic its first official meeting was held in Soho. Later meetings took place at St. George's Hall in Langham Place (W1). The renowned magician David Devant (1868–1941) performed there regularly and became the society's first president.

Another celebrated magician, John Nevil Maskelyne (1839–1917), edited the society's newsletter, *The Magic Circular*. Still published today its cover is adorned with the signs of the Zodiac together with the Latin inscription *Indocilis Private Loqui* meaning 'not apt to disclose secrets' (members contravening this basic house rule are liable to expulsion). The newletter is distributed to a worldwide membership including many women, who have been allowed to join the society since 1991. The greatest growth in membership, however, has been in the society's Young Magicians' Club, triggered by the enormous popularity of the *Harry Potter* franchise.

The Magic Circle opened its premises in 1998 and they can be visited on a two hour Monday morning tour called The Magic Circle Experience. Commencing at 11.30am a society member divulges the fascinating history of stage magic in the hallowed Club Room, where magicians from around the world meet to discuss their art. Visitors can then make a wish whilst turning three times on the Magic Circle emblem in the magnificent stairwell, where a series of murals depict the history of magic from earliest times. Bringing things up to the present day visitors are then treated to a display of modern magic in the intimate Magic Circle Theatre.

The tour concludes in the Magic Circle Museum, which contains a treasure trove of artefacts recalling the great magicians of the past. Witness original equipment used by the French conjuror Robert-Houdin! Be amazed at the handcuffs used by his namesake the escapologist Harry Houdini! Gasp at how the illusionist Chung Ling Soo was shot dead when a performance in 1918 went wrong! See the rifle used by Maurice Fogel in his 1940s 'bullet catch' routine! Hear how a magician was commissioned by the British Army to render the Suez Canal invisible to enemy bombers in 1941! There is even the cup and ball set used by HRH Prince Charles of Wales during his Magic Circle entrance exam in 1975!

Visitors wishing to try their own hand at magic should afterwards visit Davenports Magic Shop at 7 Charing Cross Underground Arcade (WC2). Founded in 1898 it is the oldest family-owned magic shop in the world.

As well as being a magician, John Nevil Maskelyne is credited with inventing the lockable toilet. Requiring the insertion of a penny coin to operate, it gave rise to the euphemism "to spend a penny". Many equally beguiling inventions are displayed not far from the Magic Circle in the Wellcome Collection at 183 Euston Road (NW1), including the first X-ray taken by its inventor Wilhem Röntgen (1845–1923).

Other places of interest nearby: 45, 46

48 The Most Wonderful Railway Station

NW1 2AR (St. Pancras), St. Pancras International railway station and St. Pancras Renaissance Hotel on Euston Road
Circle, Hammersmith & City, Metropolitan, Northern, Piccadilly, Victoria lines to King's Cross St. Pancras

Not without reason has St. Pancras been called "the most wonderful railway station in the world". A marvel of Victorian engineering it consists of a colossal train shed fronted by a glorious Neo-Gothic hotel. After defying calls for its demolition the station was successfully reinvented in 2007 as St. Pancras International, with the refurbished hotel opening four years later.

The Midland Railway unveiled St. Pancras in 1868, as the southern terminus of a new mainline connecting London with the industrial heartlands of the East Midlands and Yorkshire. The consultant engineer on the project was William Henry Barlow (1812–1902), who was responsible not only for the permanent way from Bedford down to London but also the terminus station on Euston Road.

To enable the line to cross Regent's Canal, and accommodate the sloping site of the station itself, Barlow set his platforms five metres

John Betjeman looks up at the roof of the railway station he helped save

above pavement level on a forest of cast iron columns and girders. The resulting undercroft was used for the storage of beer from the breweries of Burton-upon-Trent. Barlow protected the platforms themselves with a cast-iron and glass canopy. Measuring 75 metres side-to-side it was at the time the world's largest single-span roof. The ribs supporting it were sprung directly from platform level and still carry the name of the Derbyshire company that made them.

The Midland Grand Hotel opened five years later in 1873. A competition for its design was won by the Gothic Revival architect, George Gilbert Scott (1811–1878), who also designed the Albert Memorial in Hyde Park. He provided for 250 bedrooms behind an extravagant Italianate façade of polychromatic brick. The building was not only luxuriously appointed, with a grand staircase, wall-to-wall Axminster carpets and a fireplace in every room but also featured many technical innovations, including the country's first revolving door.

Despite such a promising start, St. Pancras declined steadily throughout the 20th century. The Railways Act of 1921 forced the creation of the London, Midland and Scottish Railway, which adopted Euston as its principal London terminus. Services into St. Pancras were reduced accordingly and the hotel, which had proved difficult to modernise, closed in 1935 and was converted into offices. A campaign in the 1960s spearheaded by the poet John Betjeman (1906–1984) staved off the threat of demolition.

Redemption came in the 1990s with the decision to adapt St. Pancras as the terminus for the new cross-Channel Eurostar service. After much effort and expenditure the new-look station was reopened by the Queen. To accommodate a terminal for trains to continental Europe and another for domestic services to the north and south-east of England the old train shed was extended, and a shopping mall opened in the former undercroft. Likewise the hotel was enlarged and its public rooms painstakingly restored to their former glory. A new lobby occupies what was once the covered taxi rank and the former ticket office is now a bar. Fascinating guided tours of the re-branded St. Pancras Renaissance Hotel are available by appointment.

St. Pancras is flanked by two other historic railway stations. King's Cross opened in 1852 as the southern terminus of the East Coast Main Line. A blue plaque commemorates Nigel Gresley (1876–1941), designer of the world's fastest steam locomotive *Mallard*, and there is a much-photographed sign for Platform 9¾ inspired by the film *Harry Potter*. Euston opened in 1837 as the terminus of the West Coast Main Line and plans are afoot to rebuild the grand Doric arch that once graced its forecourt.

49 The Mystery of Baker Street

NW1 6XE (Marylebone), the Sherlock Holmes Museum at
221B Baker Street
Bakerloo, Circle, Hammersmith & City, Jubilee, Metropolitan
lines to Baker Street

Surely one of London's most famous addresses is 221B Baker Street. It was in lodgings here between 1881 and 1904 that writer Arthur Conan Doyle (1859–1930) installed his fictional super sleuth, Sherlock Holmes, along with dependable sidekick, Dr. John Watson. But as with all good detective stories not all is quite as it seems.

Baker Street certainly existed when Conan Doyle wrote his books but the house numbers only reached as far as 85 (beyond lay York Place and then Upper Baker Street). The area was a well-to-do residential district, and Holmes' apart-

A statue of the unmistakeable Sherlock Holmes outside Baker Street Tube station

ment – had it existed – would probably have been part of a Georgian terrace. It is described in *A Study in Scarlet* (1897) as comprising "a couple of comfortable bed-rooms and a single large airy sitting-room, cheerfully furnished, and illuminated by two broad windows".

Only after Conan Doyle's death in 1930 was the name Baker Street extended from its original terminus at the junction with Crawford Street, northwards to Park Road. The existing houses in this new section were renumbered, with the block of odd numbers from 215 to 229 being assigned to an *Art Deco* building constructed in 1932 for the Abbey National Building Society. With 221 now a real address, post addressed to Sherlock Holmes began arriving, so much in fact that for many years a full-time secretary was employed to deal with it!

Fast forward 60 years and the plot thickens. In 1990 a wall plaque identifying 221B Baker Street was installed outside the newly-opened Sherlock Holmes Museum – at Number 239! Immediately a dispute arose over who should rightfully receive letters addressed to the detective. Certainly the museum had a good case, since it occupied a Georgian building that had actually served as a boarding house between 1860 and 1934. The Abbey National, on the other hand, occupied the correct address although 221 was only part of a much larger building. The issue was only resolved in 2002, when the Abbey National vacated its premises and the Royal Mail recognised the museum's right to the post.

The regular queues outside the museum today are testimony to the enduring popularity of Sherlock Holmes despite the fear expressed by Conan Doyle's daughter that its existence might reinforce the notion that the detective was real. She was probably right since even the blue wall plaque outside mimics those erected elsewhere in London in honour of people who really existed. Either way an undoubted highlight of any visit is the atmospheric reconstruction of the famously cluttered sitting room-cum-study overlooking Baker Street, replete with Holmes' trademark pipe, Stradivarius and magnifying glass. It is not difficult to imagine him standing at the window musing on his next case against the backdrop of Victorian suburban London.

Those who can't get enough of Holmes should also visit the Sherlock Holmes Pub at 10–11 Northumberland Street (WC2). It contains another replica of the Baker Street apartment created this time by the Abbey National and Marylebone Borough Library for the 1951 Festival of Britain. It was acquired by Whitbread's Brewery in 1957.

The first life-size statue of Sherlock Holmes was erected in 1988 near the Reichenbach Falls in Switzerland, where Conan Doyle's attempt to kill off his hero resulted in a public outcry so fervent that he was forced to revive the character. A decade later the Abbey National commissioned another statue outside London's Baker Street Tube station. A wax effigy of actor Robert Downey Jr. as Holmes is displayed currently at nearby Madame Tussauds.

50 Worship beneath a Golden Dome

NW8 7RG (St. John's Wood), the London Central Mosque at 146 Park Road
Bakerloo line to Marylebone; Bakerloo, Circle, Hammersmith & City, Jubilee, Metropolitan lines to Baker Street; Jubilee line to St. John's Wood (note: shoes must be removed before entering the prayer hall)

Glinting in the sun on the edge of Regent's Park is a golden dome. It is the prayer hall of the London Central Mosque at 146 Park Road (NW8) to which worshippers are drawn by a 43-metre high minaret. Together with the Islamic Cultural Centre attached to it, the mosque is one of the most important and active centres of Sunni Islam in the Western world.

The idea for a mosque in central London was first mooted in the early 20th century, when the British Empire contained more Muslims than Christians. Amongst these early initiatives was

The golden dome of the London Central Mosque in St. John's Wood

one spearheaded by Rowland Allanson-Winn, 5th Baron Headley (1855–1935), who was a prominent English convert to Islam. With money donated by the Nizam of Hyderabad, the foundation stone of a mosque was laid in 1937. Little else happened, however, until 1940 when the

Secretary of State for the Colonies sent a memo to the Prime Minister pointing out that "London contains more Moslems than any other European capital but…it was anomalous and inappropriate that there should be no central place of worship". Consequently Churchill's War Cabinet allocated funds for the acquisition of a site near Regent's Park, which was officially inaugurated in 1944 by George VI (1936–1952).

Several designs for the mosque were submitted but the necessary planning permission was withheld. Only in 1969 was an international competition staged, which attracted over a hundred designs from both Muslim and non-Muslim architects. The winning entry by the English town planner Frederick Gibberd (1908–1984) provided for a main prayer hall for men overlooked by a balcony for women, a minaret and a library, with a lecture hall and imam's office attached. Kick-started with a donation of two million pounds from Saudi Arabia and the United Arab Emirates, work on the mosque was largely completed by 1978.

The mosque's prayer hall today is simply furnished with a *mihrab* or prayer niche facing towards Mecca, a chandelier, and a vast carpet. Together with the foyer and courtyard it can accommodate 5,000 worshippers. Thousands of Muslims visit each week with up to 25,000 attending prayers during the festival of Eid. They also come to receive education and legal advice in the Islamic Cultural Centre, which hosts various conferences and courses, and includes a library, bookshop and halal café.

Non-Muslims are very welcome to visit as part of the mosque's outreach programme designed not only to facilitate conversion to Islam but also to engender mutual respect between Britain's various faith communities. Around 16,000 non-Muslims visit the mosque annually, including tourists, schoolchildren, and politicians. Tours are conducted by a native British Muslim and include a visit to the Exhibition Islam, a permanent display aimed at providing visitors with a better understanding of Islam and its main tenets as revealed in the Qur'an.

One of London's least known green spaces is the roof garden of the Ismaili Centre in Cromwell Gardens (SW7). Inaugurated in 1985 in the presence of the Aga Khan the centre was the first in the West to be designated specifically for use by the Shia Ismaili community. The Persian-style *Charbagh*, or four-part Paradise garden, is delineated by a series of rills running outwards from a central fountain. A minimalist combination of stone, water and plants creates an oasis of calm above the busy streets below. For occasional opening times visit www.opensquares.org.

Other places of interest nearby: 51

51 Bowling Balls and Cricket Bats

NW8 8QN (St. John's Wood), the Marylebone
Cricket Club Museum at Lord's Cricket Ground
on St. John's Wood Road
Jubilee line to St. John's Wood

The circular garden at the centre of Finsbury Circus (EC2) was laid out in 1606, which makes it the oldest public park in London. Earlier during the Middle Ages the area was part of a boggy fen created when a culvert in the City wall – through which the River Walbrook passed – became blocked. Its use as a dumping ground means archaeologists have unearthed some interesting artefacts here, including a wooden bat used in a Tudor version of cricket.

These days bowling is enjoyed on this ancient spot. The City of London Bowling Club has held matches here since its founding in 1924. That all changed in 2010, however, when Crossrail served a compulsory purchase order on the club as a necessary part of their construction of a new rail link through central London. The club hopes to return in 2018 after the work is finished but until then those with an interest in London's sporting legacy must look elsewhere.

The Ashes takes pride of place at the Marylebone Cricket Club Museum

One hallowed location is Lord's Cricket Ground on St. John's Wood Road (NW8). The home of Marylebone Cricket Club (MCC) it is named after its founder and professional cricketer Thomas Lord (1755–1832), who opened his first ground in 1787 on what is now Dorset Square (NW1). After a dispute over the rent he relocated to Lisson Grove in

1809, where the subsequent cutting of the Regent's Park Canal forced a further relocation in 1814 to the ground's present site.

Lord's today is also home to the Marylebone Cricket Club Museum. Opened in 1953, it is the world's oldest sporting museum and tells the story of cricket from its first appearance in southern England in the 16th century up to the present day. As well as artefacts relating to legendary batsmen such as W. G. Grace (1848–1915) there are several oddities relating to the game, including the sparrow killed in 1936 by bowler Jahangir Khan and the copy of the *Wisden Cricketers' Almanack* read by journalist E. W. Swanton in a Japanese prisoner-of-war camp. Pride of place goes to the Ashes, a tiny terracotta urn said to contain a burnt bail, which was presented to England Captain Ivo Bligh during the 1882–83 tour of Australia. It is now the notional prize in Test cricket between the two countries.

To buy your own cricket equipment visit Lillywhites at 24–36 Regent Street (SW1). The world's oldest sports shop it was founded in 1863 by James Lillywhite (1842–1929), who as the first-ever captain of the English cricket team lead two Tests against Australia in 1876–77. A bronze plaque at the shop entrance depicts him playing cricket in a top hat!

London's sporting legacy has also left its mark elsewhere. In 1863, for example, in the New Connaught Rooms on Great Queen Street (WC2) the Football Association met to establish its rules. Attendees unhappy with the proposed ban on carrying the ball withdrew to form the Rugby Football Union, hammering out its own set of rules at the Mall Restaurant at 1 Cockspur Street (SW1). Ping Pong fanatics will love Bounce at 121 Holborn (EC1), a purpose-built table tennis venue where the game was patented in 1901. And devotees of winter sports should visit the Broadgate Ice Rink on Exchange Square (EC2), which hosts a Canadian skateless version of ice hockey called Broomball. The modern architecture, however, means the setting is a far cry from the days when Londoners skated freely on the frozen Thames and attended frost fairs. Fortunately these bygone spectacles have been documented for posterity in a series of engraved panels in the pedestrian tunnel at the southern end of Southwark Bridge (SE1).

Other places of interest nearby: 50

52 The Man Who Saved Millions

W2 1NY (Paddington), the Alexander Fleming Laboratory
Museum in St. Mary's Hospital on Praed Street
Bakerloo, Circle, District lines to Paddington

"When I woke up just after dawn on September 28, 1928, I certainly didn't plan to revolutionise all medicine... But I suppose that was exactly what I did." With these words the Scottish scientist Sir Alexander Fleming (1881–1955) described his discovery of the antibiotic substance penicillin, a breakthrough that saved millions of lives and earned him a Nobel Prize.

Antibiotics did not exist when Fleming was a boy and consequently a quarter of hospital patients succumbed to gangrene after surgery. This grim statistic may have stayed that way had Fleming not made an important decision after graduating from St. Mary's Hospital Medical School on Praed Street (WC2). He gave up the idea of becoming a physician and became a bacteriologist at the hospital instead.

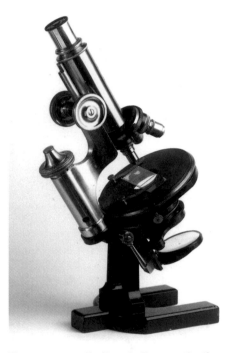

The microscope used by Alexander Fleming to identify penicillin

Fleming made his momentous discovery by accident in his cramped second-floor laboratory, whilst investigating the properties of the bacteria *staphylococcus*. Returning from a holiday he noticed that a fungus had entered the laboratory through an open window and appeared to be impeding the growth of one of his cultures. Fleming initially called the mystery active ingredient "mould juice" until he identified it scientifically as *Penicillium notatum* renaming it penicillin for convenience. Realising his discovery could save lives he was confounded about how to manufacture it commercially. The answer was eventually found in

America during the Second World War in response to the enormous demand for drugs to treat infected wounds. Penicillin was first used on a mass scale on D-Day 1944, since when it has been used to save more than 200 million lives.

The laboratory where Fleming worked between 1919 and 1933 is now preserved as the Alexander Fleming Laboratory Museum and can be identified from outside by a plaque mounted beneath the famous window. His worktop is cluttered with test tubes, microscopes, and leatherbound medical books. Even the mouldy Petri dish is there in which the effects of penicillin were first observed, although the original is held by the British Library.

Fleming at work in his laboratory

Fleming was a modest man and he accepted his newfound celebrity gracefully. For the last decade of his life he toured the world giving lectures on his discoveries. By the time he died he was an international celebrity and his ashes were interred in St. Paul's Cathedral, beneath a stone tablet framed with Scottish thistles.

Many other pioneers who changed the world have lived and worked in London. They include John Logie Baird (1888–1946), who first demonstrated television at 22 Frith Street, and Samuel Morse (1791–1872), who invented his famous code at 141 Cleveland Street (both W1). Some, like Fleming, warrant their own museum. The Benjamin Franklin House at 36 Craven Street (WC2), for example, is where the American statesman and inventor of the lightning conductor lodged from 1757 until the start of the American War of Independence. The laboratory of Michael Faraday (1791–1867), the discoverer of electromagnetic induction, is preserved as the Faraday Museum in the Royal Institution at 21 Albemarle Street (W1). It also includes the miner's safety lamp invented by Humphry Davy (1778–1829), the first ever vacuum flask invented by James Dewar (1842–1923), and the glass tube used by John Tyndall (1820–1893) to explain why the sky is blue.

53 Execution in Mayfair

W2 2EN (Mayfair), the site of the Tyburn Tree gallows at the
junction of Bayswater Road and Edgware Road
Central line to Marble Arch

The last public hanging in England occurred outside Newgate Prison on 26th May 1868. Before a crowd of 2,000 onlookers the Fenian Michael Barrett was executed for detonating a bomb in Clerkenwell in support of Irish nationalism. Thereafter until the prison's demolition in 1902 hangings were conducted *inside* away from the public gaze.

Newgate Prison was built in 1188 by order of Henry II (1154–1189). It was located just inside the City wall at the corner of Newgate Street and Old Bailey (EC4), the latter lending its name to the Central Criminal Court, which occupies the site today (a court has existed on the site since 1585). All that remains of the prison today is a stretch of brickwork concealed in Amen Court, off Warwick Lane. The novelist Henry Fielding (1707–1754) described the prison as a "prototype for hell" with outbreaks of disease that killed inmates

This sign outside Tyburn Convent depicts the three-legged
Tyburn Tree gallows

and officials alike. To this day at the start of each session judges carry a floral posy like those once used to mask the stench.

Although Newgate was sturdily constructed it was not always secure. The burglar Jack Sheppard (1702–1724) managed to escape its confines twice and became a celebrity in the process. When he was eventually executed for his crimes he was taken to the Tyburn Tree gallows in Mayfair, where public executions had been carried out since the late 12th century (see no. 56). On the day preceding his death Sheppard would have witnessed a grim tradition. At midnight the clerk of the nearby Church of St. Sepulchre-without-Newgate visited the prison to ring a handbell outside the cells of the condemned, whilst reciting the following verse: "All you that in the condemned hold do lie, prepare you, for tomorrow you shall die." The bell can still be seen in a glass display case in the church nave (see no. 19).

Hanging days were usually Mondays, and Sheppard's was no exception. Sometime after 9am with the great bell of St. Sepulchre ringing his shackles were struck off and he climbed onto a horsedrawn cart. Accompanied by a mounted City Marshall and liveried Javelin Men the cart then moved slowly westwards along Holborn and Oxford Street. Crowds of up to 200,000 people lined the streets, a third of London's population at the time! After a pause at the City of Oxford Tavern, where Sheppard enjoyed a last drink, the cortège arrived at Tyburn. He was then strung up on the three-legged gallows – its tree-like appearance designed for simultaneous multiple executions – and left hanging for the prescribed 15 minutes.

The former site of the Tyburn Tree gallows can be found today on a traffic island at the corner of Bayswater Road and Edgware Road (W1) next to Marble Arch, which was relocated here when Buckingham Palace received its east front in 1847. Marked by an inscribed stone in the pavement it is difficult to imagine the huge crowds that once jostled to get a good view of the grisly proceedings. It has been estimated that up to 60,000 people were hung here although none of are commemorated. They included Oliver Cromwell, whose remains were disinterred from Westminster Abbey after the Restoration and hung in a posthumous execution.

Nearby at 8 Hyde Park Place is the little-known Tyburn Convent. Home to two dozen cloistered Benedictine nuns it was founded in 1901 as a shrine to the 105 Roman Catholics hung at Tyburn during the Reformation. The nuns maintain a round-the-clock prayer virgil in the ground-floor chapel, and can be glimpsed beyond a metal grille. The sign outside the convent depicts the three-legged gallows and a model of it is housed in the chapel crypt, which also contains the martyrs' bones, hair and bloodstained clothes. It was complaints from Mayfair's well-to-do residents that saw the gallows relocated to Newgate in 1783.

54 A Hyde Park Odyssey

W1J 7NT (Mayfair), a walk around Hyde Park commencing at Hyde Park Corner
Piccadilly line to Hyde Park Corner

Hyde Park covers an area of 350 acres making it the largest of London's Royal Parks. Originally a manor belonging to Westminster Abbey its name comes from the Old English *hid* being the unit of land measurement of 60 to 120 acres that originally defined it. Commandeered during the Dissolution as a hunting ground by Henry VIII (1509–1547) it has served subsequently as a royal garden, battlefield, place of protest, and people's park.

A glimpse of the Hyde Park pet cemetery from Bayswater Road

This clockwise walk begins at the park's ceremonial entrance on Hyde Park Corner installed by garden architect Decimus Burton (1800–1881), as part of a makeover commissioned by George IV (1820–1830). Burton also designed the nearby Wellington Arch, which provided a grand entrance into central London via Constitution Hill. Apsley House to the right of the entrance, which was acquired by the Duke of Wellington after his victory over Napoleon at Waterloo, was accordingly dubbed "No. 1, London".

Inside the park the sand-covered Rotten Row leads off to the left. This dead straight ceremonial route was laid out by William and Mary (1689–1694) to connect their home, Kensington Palace, with Westminster. A corruption of *Route du Roi* it was once illuminated by 300 lanterns making it the first road in England to be artificially lit.

Just before the Serpentine a path on the right-hand side leads to the Holocaust Memorial Garden. The Serpentine itself was created in 1728 when the wife of George II (1727–1760) had the River Westbourne dammed. Hardy swimmers can be seen taking a dip here each Christmas morning. Of Joseph Paxton's Crystal Palace constructed along the left-hand side of Rotten Row for the Great Exhibition of 1851 nothing remains.

At the far end of Rotten Row on the right-hand side is the memorial fountain to Diana, Princess of Wales. Turn right just beyond here onto West Carriage Drive. This broad thoroughfare is part of the so-called Ring, a circular carriageway created by Charles I (1625–1649) when he made the park public in 1637. It passes the Serpentine Gallery, which occupies a former 1930s tea pavilion, and then crosses the Serpentine by means of a bridge designed by John Rennie (1794–1874). Around this time Hyde Park was formally separated from Kensington Gardens to the west.

On the other side of the bridge is the Serpentine Sackler Gallery, which occupies a former gunpowder magazine built in 1805, when England feared invasion from France. Continuing northwards, West Carriage Drive passes a sculpture on the right-hand side called *Rima*, which is a memorial to ornithologist William Henry Hudson by pioneering modern sculptor Jacob Epstein (1880–1959).

West Carriage Drive turns eastwards onto North Carriage Drive at Victoria Gate. Visible here through the railings on Bayswater Road are the tiny headstones of a pet cemetery opened in 1880. Continue now all the way to Speaker's Corner, where members of the public have been free to voice their opinions since 1872.

The return south to Hyde Park Corner is made along Broad Walk passing the *Animals in War Memorial* (opposite the refreshment kiosk), the *Joy of Life Fountain*, and the stark *7th July Memorial* recalling those killed in the London bombings of 2005. The low embankment between Broad Walk and Park Lane is a remnant of the earthwork raised by Parliamentarians during the English Civil War (1642–1651) to protect the City of Westminster from Royalist attack.

The tour finishes with *Achilles*, London's first naked statue cast from cannon captured during Wellington's campaigns, and the Queen Elizabeth Gate celebrating the life of the Queen Mother.

At noon on the penultimate Sunday of September the Church of St. John's on Hyde Park Crescent (W2) hosts Horseman's Sunday, a service celebrating horse riding in central London. It is given by a priest on horseback!

55 Of Feedback and Fugue

**W1K 4HB (Mayfair), the Handel House Museum
at 25 Brook Street
Central, Jubilee lines to Bond Street; Bakerloo, Central,
Victoria lines to Oxford Circus**

Many London addresses boast former celebrity occupants but fewer can lay claim to two. An example is 37 Fitzroy Street (W1) in Fitzrovia, which for a year during the 1880s was home to Irish playwright George Bernard Shaw (1856–1950). A quarter of a century later the Scientologist and science fiction writer L. Ron Hubbard (1911–1986) occupied the same premises, which function now as a shrine to his work.

An equally unlikely pair lived at different times as neighbours on Brook Street (W1) in Mayfair. During the 18th century the German classical composer George Frideric Handel (1685–1759) was drawn to Number 25 by the property's proximity to St. James's Palace and the King's Theatre in Haymarket. Some 250 years later the area's music venues attracted American rock guitarist Jimi Hendrix (1942–1970) to an upstairs flat at Number 23. The Handel House Museum today bears witness to the achievements of both these remarkable musicians.

Handel was born in Halle in Saxony, where aged 17 he was appointed organist in the city's cathedral. He then travelled to Italy to hone his skills further and was noticed by representatives of the court of Han-

The restored Rehearsal and Performance Room at the Handel House Museum over. As a result in 1710 he was appointed Kapellmeister to the Elector of Hanover and shortly afterwards granted permission to travel to London, where he found immediate success with his opera *Rinaldo*. Handel is credited not only with introducing Italian opera to England but also developing English oratorio, which revolutionised English music.

Handel's popularity in England can be gauged from the fact that in 1713 Queen Anne (1702–1714) granted him a Royal pension, which was extended a year later when the Elector of Hanover became George I of England (1714–1727). Handel decided to stay on in London and secured the lease on Brook Street after penning his famous *Water Music* for a royal party on the Thames.

Were Handel alive today he would still recognise his old home. The Handel House Trust has gone to great lengths to restore the building's early Georgian interiors, which helps visitors imagine Handel composing some of his greatest works here, including *Messiah*, *Music for the Royal Fireworks*, and *Zadok the Priest*. The latter was commissioned as the coronation anthem for George II (1727–1760) and has been performed at every coronation since. Although Handel died in one of the upstairs rooms, regular rehearsals and a programme of concerts keeps his spirit very much alive.

The Handel House Museum will become even livelier once plans are realised to integrate the Jimi Hendrix flat into it. The guitarist first arrived in London in 1966 and formed the Jimi Hendrix Experience, which quickly established a reputation for incendiary live performances. The success of their early record releases cemented Hendrix's European status before he returned home to conquer America. It was after an American tour in 1968 that he moved into Brook Street with his girlfriend, Kathy Etchingham, who furnished the flat with carpets and curtains from John Lewis on Oxford Street. Hendrix remained there for three months whilst preparing for a series of sell-out concerts at the Royal Albert Hall. On learning that Handel had lived next door he visited the One Stop Record Shop on nearby South Molton Street and bought some of Handel's music.

The Jimi Hendrix Experience first played in public on 25th November 1966 at the Bag o'Nails Club on Kingly Street (W1). They also played at the Marquee Club at 90 Wardour Street (W1) and recorded at the Regent Sound Studio at 4 Denmark Street (WC2). Jimi's last public appearance was at Ronnie Scott's Jazz Club at 47 Frith Street (W1) just days before his untimely death in a Notting Hill hotel.

Other places of interest nearby: 56, 66, 67

56 A Lost London River

W1K 5AB (Mayfair), a journey tracing the course of the 'lost' River Tyburn including Grays Antiques at 58 Davies Street
Central, Jubilee lines to Bond Street

In September 1854 more than 500 Soho residents died during an outbreak of cholera. A local doctor, John Snow (1813–1858), correctly identified the cause as a public water pump on Broadwick Street (W1) tainted by human effluent (its former site is marked by a pink granite kerbstone outside the John Snow pub). At the time much of London's drinking water was taken from the Thames into which the city's raw sewage flowed freely. Snow's explanation, however, went largely unheeded until the 'Great Stink' of 1858, when the smell was enough to close Parliament. By this time thousands more had died forcing the authorities to commission the Metropolitan Board of Works' engineer, Joseph Bazalgette (1819–1891), to install London's first modern sewer system.

Between 1859 and 1865 Bazalgette constructed six main sewers totalling almost 160 kilometres in length, one of which was incorporated into the newly-built Thames Embankment. These were fed by 725 kilometres of smaller sewers, which in turn conveyed the contents of 21,000 kilometres of local sewers. Between them they collected London's sewage and deposited it safely downstream.

Bazagette's brick-built sewers are things of considerable beauty and still remain at the heart of London's sewerage system – but few

The former site of a River Tyburn conduit on Marylebone Lane

ever get to see them. Instead, why not follow the course of one of London's 'lost' rivers? These Thames tributaries wound their way across central London until the 18th century, when they were canalised due to pollution and development. Stretches of them are today incorporated into Bazalgette's system, where they serve as storm drains.

The River Tyburn is a good example rising near Fitzjohns Avenue (NW3) in Hampstead and discharging into the Thames at Vauxhall Bridge. Along the way it makes its watery presence felt in a number of surprising ways. After running under Swiss Cottage, for example, it crosses Regent's Canal by means of a combined footbridge and aqueduct at the end of Charlbert Street (NW8). Then, after bypassing the lake in Regent's Park, which it has not fed since the 19th century, it traverses the lines of the Baker Street Tube station through an iron duct just inside the Paddington-bound tunnel.

South from here the river once watered the village of Tyburn, where the gallows known as the Tyburn Tree was located (see no. 53). Since the 17th century the village has been called Marylebone ('bourne' meaning stream) after a church dedicated to St. Mary that stood on the riverbank at the top of Marylebone High Street (W1). It has been replaced by the Church of St. Marylebone around the corner at 17 Marylebone Road (NW1), where the Victorian poets Elizabeth Barrett and Robert Browning married in 1846 (the church has a considerable musical pedigree, a theme picked up in the Royal Academy of Music Museum directly opposite). Farther south the winding course of Blandford Street and Marylebone Lane mimics exactly that of the ancient river below. An inscribed stone at 50 Marylebone Lane marks where drinking water was siphoned off during the 18th century.

After crossing Oxford Street into Mayfair the Tyburn makes its only real appearance in the basement of Gray's Antiques at 58 Davies Street (W1). The proprietors insist this is the real river and have adorned it with miniature footbridges! From here it flows down South Molton Lane, across the aptly-named Brook Street, and down Avery Row, where it can be heard gurgling beneath the manhole covers. Beyond Conduit Street, where water was piped eastwards into the City, it flows down Hay Hill and exits Mayfair near Shepherd Market. It was here on the riverbank that the original May Fair was held until the area was developed in the mid-18th century.

Now the river flows beneath Green Park and Buckingham Palace, where it originally split into three, with two branches flowing eastwards to form Thorney Island on which Westminster Abbey was built (see no. 85). Today it only continues southwards along King's Scholars' Passage (SW1), where schoolboys once bathed, and then down

The Tyburn makes a rare appearance in Gray's Antiques on Davies Street

Tachbrook Street to its outfall beneath Tyburn House at 140c Grosvenor Road.

London's other 'lost' rivers include the Fleet, Walbrook, Westbourne, Effra, and Neckinger. As with the Tyburn, the course of these rivers can still be traced in the modern landscape.

Other places of interest nearby: 55, 67

57 This is the BBC!

W1A 1AA (Fitzrovia), a tour of BBC Broadcasting House
at 2–22 Portland Place
Circle, Hammersmith & City, Metropolitan lines to Great
Portland Street; Bakerloo, Central, Victoria lines to Oxford
Circus; Bakerloo line to Regent's Park (note: visitors' bags will
be checked upon entry)

The BBC was the world's first national broadcasting organisation. Founded on 18th October 1922 by the General Post Office and the wireless industry, its aim was to educate the masses through independent public service broadcasts. Its nickname of Auntie was coined to distinguish its 'serious' approach financed by the sale of licenses from that of its commercial rival, ITV.

The BBC's first ever broadcast was transmitted on 14th November 1922 from the seventh floor of Marconi House on the Strand (WC2). To avoid competition with newspapers, however, the government banned the transmission of news programmes before 7pm and then only permitted the use of secondhand news from wire services. A year later the BBC relocated its broadcasting studios to nearby Savoy Hill House, where in 1929 John Logie Baird demonstrated his newly-invented television. In 1932 the company moved again only this time to the purpose-built Broadcasting House at 2–22 Portland Place (W1). It was in the basement here that Baird refined his invention in Britain's first dedicated television studio. This led to the world's first regularly scheduled television service broadcast on 2nd November 1936 from the BBC's transmitter at Alexandra Palace.

From the outside Broadcasting House is an imposing edifice. Designed by George Val Myer (1883–1959) its streamlined façade and *Art Deco* flourishes have often been compared to a 1930s ocean liner. The use of Portland stone to face the building's steel frame links it to the traditional architecture of Regent Street. The inclusion of sculptures by Eric Gill (1882–1940), however, most notably the statues of *Ariel* and *Prospero* from Shakespeare's *The Tempest*, introduce an altogether more Modernist element.

Since 2013 visitors have been able to take tours of Broadcasting House. Originally the interior layout was such that office accommodation around the outside of the building acted as sound insulation for the twenty or so broadcast studios within. War damage, technological advances, and the inflexibility of the original design, however, have meant that most of these original studios have now been replaced.

Despite this a tour of Broadcasting House is still fascinating. As well as learning the history of the BBC, visitors are given the chance to watch the new state-of-the-art studios at work, including the all-important newsroom. And if schedules permit they can also visit the Radio Theatre, where concerts and comedy shows are recorded. Budding presenters can have a go at reading the news and weather on a special interactive set.

At the end of the tour be sure to look up at the roof of the building's new east wing. Mirroring the old building's radio mast is an inverted cone-shaped glass memorial to journalists killed in the line of duty. Called *Breathing* it glows gently at night and projects a beam of light vertically into the sky when the *BBC News at Ten* is broadcast. The memo-

Broadcasting House on Portland Place is the home of the BBC

rial was designed by Catalan Spanish artist Jaume Plensa (b. 1955) and unveiled in 2008 by UN Secretary-General Ban Ki-Moon.

Near the BBC at 309 Regent Street (W1) is London's oldest cinema. Part of the University of Westminster, the Regent Street Cinema is where the Lumière brothers demonstrated their moving pictures in 1896.

In front of Broadcasting House stands All Souls' Church. The only surviving church designed by Regency architect John Nash (1752–1835) it cleverly masks an awkward bend where Nash's Regent Street joins the earlier Portland Place (see no. 33).

Other places of interest nearby: 58, 59, 60

58 Sustenance in Strange Places

W1W 6DY (Fitzrovia), a selection of unusual places to eat and
drink including the Attendant at 27a Foley Street
Bakerloo, Central, Victoria lines to Oxford Circus; Circle,
Hammersmith & City, Metropolitan lines to Great
Portland Street

Some of London's cultural institutions offer places to eat and drink
that are visitor attractions in their own right. They include the magnificent King's Library in the British Library at 96 Euston Road (NW1), the
light-filled RIBA in the Royal Institute of British Architects at 66 Portland Place (W1), and the 19th century Keeper's House in the Royal
Academy of Arts on Piccadilly (W1). There are others, however, that
revel in their comparative obscurity.

The Attendant at 27a Foley Street (W1) is a case in point. Identified
only by ornate iron railings at street level this unusual café occupies
a former underground gents' toilet! Built in 1890 and abandoned half
a century ago it has been lovingly transformed. The original porcelain
urinals now support tables, with green stools to match the Victorian
floor tiles, and a tiny kitchen in the former attendant's office. Whilst
enjoying a coffee here spare a thought for English sanitary engineer
George Jennings (1810–1882), who originally pioneered these underground public conveniences.

Another Victorian space that has been ingeniously reused is the
Coal Vaults at 187b Wardour Street (W1). This former subterranean
coal bunker has been given a high quality makeover and low level
lighting, where diners are seated in intimate brick-built vaults. No less
post-industrial is the former boiler house at the Old Truman Brewery at
91 Brick Lane (E1), which now serves as a food hall, and the undercroft
at St. Pancras Station, where barrels of beer have been replaced by a
bustling shopping mall (see nos. 7 & 48). There is even a Starbucks at
6A Vigo Street (W1) with a carved mahogany ceiling from Damascus
installed in 1903 when the premises served as an oriental carpet shop!

Elsewhere several of London's religious buildings have been
pressed into service as cafés. The Cloister Café in the Church of
St. Bartholomew the Great on West Smithfield (EC1) occupies one of
only two ecclesiastical cloisters in London (see no. 19). Stained-glass
windows and a hushed atmosphere make it the perfect place for a
quiet lunch, with Trappist beers a reminder that the building was once
part of a monastery. London's other cloister is at Westminster Abbey

(SW1), where the Cellarium Café occupies a vaulted space in which Benedictine monks once stored their bread and ale.

The ecclesiastical theme continues with three cafés in church crypts. The aptly-named Café Below is located under the famous Church of St. Mary-le-Bow on Cheapside (EC2), which is named for the sturdy bow-shaped vaults used in the Norman crypt's construction (see no. 19). The coffee here is roasted in Hackney and the beer brewed in the East End. The Neo-Classical Church of St. Martin-in-the-Fields built in the 1720s in Trafalgar Square (WC2) is equally famous on account of its orchestra and has a café in its brick-built crypt. The most recent example is the Café in the Crypt, which lies beneath the Church of St. John in Smith Square (SW1). A masterpiece

The Attendant on Foley Street is a Victorian gents' toilet turned into a café!

of 18th century English Baroque by Thomas Archer (1668–1743) the church was converted into a concert hall after being damaged during the Second World War.

Most famous of all is St. Paul's Cathedral, which also has a café in its crypt. Where else can one take tea alongside the remains of Nelson, Wellington and Christopher Wren?

On the subject of public conveniences the streets of Victorian London once boasted Parisian-style cast iron urinals. A solitary example stands abandoned in Star Yard off Carey Street (WC2), where it features in London's only walking tour of public toilets (www.lootours.com)!

Other places of interest nearby: 57, 59, 60

59 The World of Charles Dickens

W1W 6DL (Fitzrovia), a tour of locations associated with Charles Dickens beginning with the former Cleveland Street Workhouse
Northern line to Goodge Street

Few writers have so successfully evoked the spirit of a place at a particular time as Charles Dickens (1812–1870) did with Victorian London. As much a social commentator as a novelist his keenly-observed characters set against a living backdrop enabled him to draw attention to the failings of society and the need for improvement. Little wonder fellow writers from Tolstoy to Orwell praised him not only for his prose style but also his realism.

Armed with his books and a handful of addresses it is possible to recreate something of Dickens' world. Before setting out, however, one should set the scene by visiting the Charles Dickens Museum at 48 Doughty Street (WC1), where the author lived in the 1830s after finding fame with *The Pickwick Papers*. Decorated as it would have been in his day the museum contains not only the writing desk where he wrote *Great Expectations* but also examples of the pioneering way in which his novels were first published in affordable instalments.

First stop thereafter is the former Cleveland Street Workhouse (W1) in the shadow of the BT Tower. The horrors of the Victorian workhouse, where the neediest toiled to earn a pittance, pervade Dickens' works. This one was built in the mid-1770s, when Fitzrovia was still semi-rural, and offered shared beds in rooms smaller than those in London's prisons. As a child and again as a teenager Dickens lived at 22 Cleveland Street – today the suitably old-fashioned Taylors Buttons shop – so the workhouse inevitably coloured his writing of *Oliver Twist* (the original manuscript is displayed in the Victoria and Albert Museum).

Neighbouring Covent Garden is an area rich in Dickensian locales. As well as running his *All the Year Round* newspaper from 26 Wellington Street (WC2) and having David Copperfield bathe in the so-called Roman Bath (actually an 18th century plunge pool) on Strand Lane, Dickens used the Seven Dials area in *Sketches by Boz*. It is hard to believe that a place defined today by upmarket shops and restaurants was once part of the Victorian St. Giles' Rookery (or slum), where the poor lived "like maggots in cheese".

Dickens set much of the legal action in *Bleak House* in Lincoln's

Inn Fields, where his menacing lawyer Mr. Tulkinghorn lives, one of many unsavoury characters to flow from his pen (see no. 39). Whether the 16th century building on nearby Portsmouth Street really inspired *The Old Curiosity Shop* is a moot point but Dickens certainly frequented the 17th century Ye Olde Chesire Cheese at 145 Fleet Street (EC4), which he alludes to in *A Tale of Two Cities*.

Moving up to Farringdon, the sinister name of Bleeding Heart Yard (EC1) recalls a 16th century inn sign depicting the heart of the Virgin Mary. In *Little Dorrit*, however, Dickens alludes to a more colourful legend concerning the gruesome murder of Lady Elizabeth Hatton (1578–1646). The working-class community that

The BT Tower looms over the former Cleveland Street Workhouse

lived here in Dickens' day inspired the poor but cheerful Plornish family in the same book. Nearby, on the opposite side of Greville Street, is Saffron Hill, which in Victorian times was another slum. Dickens uses it to good effect by locating Fagin's den in *Oliver Twist* here, its "filthy odours" referencing the nearby River Fleet, which by Dickens' day had become a noxious covered sewer.

Bleeding Heart Yard is one of several locations associated with Charles Dickens

This tour concludes south of the river on Tabard Street (SE1), where a brick wall in the churchyard of St. George the Martyr is all that remains of Marshalsea Debtors' Prison. When his father was incarcerated here in 1824 the 12 year old Dickens was forced out of school to work in a boot blacking factory. The traumatic experience lies at the heart of *Little Dorrit* and provided the impetus for Dickens' lifelong interest in social reform.

Other places of interest nearby: 45, 58, 60

60 A Buddhist Temple in Fitzrovia

W1W 8TD (Fitzrovia), the London Fo Guang Shan Temple at 84 Margaret Street
Bakerloo, Central, Victoria lines to Oxford Circus; Central line to Tottenham Court Road

Fitzrovia is still remembered fondly for its Bohemian reputation between the wars, when the likes of Dylan Thomas and George Orwell drank at the Fitzroy Tavern at 16 Charlotte Street (W1). These days it should be better known for its diverse places of worship, three of which can be found in close proximity around Margaret Street (W1).

The first is the Church of All Saints at 7 Margaret Street completed in 1859 to a design by the Gothic Revivalist, William Butterfield (1814–1900). Unlike other churches in the same idiom, which were entirely nostalgic in their design, All Saints took the Gothic Revival to a new level, with the use of banded brickwork and London's first polychrome spire. The building inside is gloriously over-decorated, too, with every inch covered in marble, tiles, and paintwork. Of special interest are the chancel paintings by fellow Revivalist Ninian Comper (1864–1960), whose work also appears in Westminster Abbey. The pulpit made from a variety of inlaid stones is astonishing.

Across the road at Number 84 is something very different. The London Fo Guang Shan Temple is a Chinese Buddhist centre housed inside a former Protestant priests' training institute. Opened in 1992 it

The Buddha on the walls of the London Fo Guang Shan Temple

is one of 200 branches worldwide of the Fo Guang Shan Monastery in Taiwan founded in 1967 by the Venerable Master Hsing Yun (b. 1927). Yun is considered a leading light in the modern reformation of Buddhism, and so it comes as no surprise to learn that the Fo Guang Shan order (meaning 'Buddha's Light Mountain') promotes Humanistic Buddhism, with the stated aim of making the religion relevant beyond the monastery walls.

It is a memorable experience to visit this tranquil place, especially when one considers its proximity to busy Oxford Street. Visitors should announce their arrival at the reception after which a member of staff will gladly conduct a short tour of the temple complex. The main shrine is located on the first floor and shoes must be removed before entering. It is dedicated to Siddhārtha Gautama, as the Buddha is known, and contains three large statues. The walls are covered with ceramic plaques depicting the Five *Dhyani* or Wisdom Buddhas, representing the five qualities of the Buddha. The panels on the ceiling each comprise the Eight *Tathāgatas* or designations used by the Buddha when referring to himself. The numbered tags attached to all the effigies identify the individuals who have sponsored them.

On the second floor of the temple is a meditation hall, which also contains a small stage and multimedia system. Together with the dining hall and tea house in the basement it is a reminder that the Fo Guang Shan approach to Buddhism is not only about welcoming strangers but also enlightening them. Chanting, tea ceremonies, meditation classes, and children's activities take place here. All are aimed squarely at promoting Hsing Yun's four worthy principles: propagating *Dharma* through cultural activities, fostering talent by education, benefitting society through philanthropy, and purifying human minds. The temple also celebrates the Buddha's birthday each year in Leicester Square.

Around the corner on Eastcastle Street a third distinctive place of worship stands at Number 30. This is the Welsh Church of Central London, which was built as a Baptist chapel in 1888 and is fronted by a distinctive colonnaded façade. Behind it is an elegant galleried interior replete with a perfectly preserved preaching box.

London's Buddhist experience continues at the Jamyang Buddhist Centre at 43 Renfrew Road (SE11), where a garden with a reclining Buddha occupies the former prisoners' exercise yard of the Victorian Old Kennington Courthouse.

Other places of interest nearby: 58, 59, 61, 62, 63

61 Signs of the Times

W1D 4AT (Soho), a selection of old trade signs including
the goldbeater's arm on Manette Street
Central, Northern lines to Tottenham Court Road

In the days when few people could read, London's inns, shops and workplaces were identified by figurative trade signs. As literacy improved so their number diminished although enough remain today to make for an unusual thematic journey.

A fine example is the gilded arm clutching a mallet on Manette Street (W1) marking the former premises of a goldbeater's workshop. Among the customers for its goldleaf would have been the manufacturer of carriage ornaments known to have existed nearby. Manette Street itself was named after the fictional doctor of the same name, who lived here in Charles

This goldbeater's trade sign can be found on Manette Street

Dickens' *A Tale of Two Cities* (1859). Indeed Dickens mentions the "golden arm starting out of the wall of the front hall" as if some mysterious giant "had beaten himself precious"!

A street retaining multiple trade signs is Lombard Street (EC3) in the financial heart of the City. They are not that old though having been re-hung here to mark the coronation of Edward VII (1901–1910).

Of the original twenty those remaining include a portcullis outside the Trustees Savings Bank, a cat-a-fiddling over the Commercial Bank of Scotland, and an anchor on the London & County Bank. Another is a gilded grasshopper over Martins Bank founded in 1563 by the merchant Sir Thomas Gresham (1519–1579). The grasshopper was the badge of the Gresham family being both a symbol of industry and a *rebus* (a visual pun) since *gres* is Middle English for grass. Gresham also founded the nearby Royal Exchange, Britain's first specialist commercial building, which features a grasshopper on its weathervane.

During Victorian and Edwardian times trade signs took many different forms. Mass-produced tin signs were especially popular and a wonderful example promoting "Elastic glue, leather, grindery, and general ironmonger" survives over the door of the former F. W. Collins hardware store at 14 Earlham Street (WC2). Others were rendered in paint, including Donovan Brothers' on Crispin Street (E1), who once supplied wrapping papers to the florists of Spitalfields, the saddle and harness maker B. Flegg at 67 Monmouth Street (WC2), and Fribourg & Treyer "Tobacconists to His Majesty" on a window pane at 34 Haymarket (SW1). Advertisements for particular products survive, too, including "Bate's Salve for wounds and sores" in Regent Square (WC1) and another for "Bonsoir Pyjamas" on Turnmill Street (EC1).

But paint and tin weren't the only media available for advertising. The name of the former Royal Waterloo Hospital for Children and Women at 51–55 Waterloo Road (SE1) is rendered in green Doultonware lettering. Lambeth's Royal Doulton factory also created the hospital's nursery-themed friezes, which can now be found in St. Thomas's Hospital.

The largest trade sign of all is the OXO Tower on the South Bank (SE1). Erected in the 1920s by the Liebig Extract of Meat Company – manufacturers of the famous stock cube – the tower's vertically-aligned windows contain the letters O-X-O thereby circumventing a council ban on trade signs being placed so high!

London's oldest street advertisement is dated 1680 and can be seen embedded in a much later building at 63 King's Cross Road (WC1). It marked the entrance to Bagnigge House, one of Georgian London's most popular tea gardens, frequented by the courtesan and actress Nell Gwyn (1650–1687).
London's oldest street sign inscribed 'Yorke Street 1636' is also now part of a much later building at 34 Tavistock Street (WC2).

Other places of interest nearby: 35

62 Hotels with History

W1F 7HL (Soho), a tour of some historic hotels including
the Courthouse Hotel at 19–21 Great Marlborough Street
Bakerloo, Central, Victoria lines to Oxford Circus

Until the arrival of the railways, visitors to London
rented rooms or stayed in
coaching inns. London's first
hotel, Brown's at 33 Albemarle
Street (W1), only opened in
1837 attracting guests such as
Theodore Roosevelt and Rud-
yard Kipling, who completed
his *Jungle Book* there. In 1876
Alexander Graham Bell also
visited and made Britain's first
successful telephone call. The
shopping arcade connecting
the hotel with Bond Street was
added in 1879 and re-named
Royal Arcade after a visit by
Queen Victoria.

London's original 'Grand
Hotel' was the Langham farther north at 1C Portland
Place. When it opened in 1865
the sprawling building boasted
a hundred water closets and
the country's first hydraulic
lifts. Guests included Napoleon III and Noël Coward, and

Mick Jagger's prison cell is now part of the Courthouse Hotel
in Soho

a wall plaque recalls a meeting
convened at the hotel in 1889 during which Oscar Wilde was commissioned to write his *Picture of Dorian Gray*.

Wilde's story continues not far away in the Courthouse Hotel at
19–21 Great Marlborough Street. The name reminds patrons that the
hotel occupies the former Great Marlborough Street Magistrates Court,
which was converted into a hotel in the 1980s. Wilde came here in
1895 for his ill-fated libel case against the Marquess of Queensberry,

Eclectic furnishings in the Zetter Townhouse in Clerkenwell

who had accused him of being a "posing Sodomite" (Room 118 of the Cadogan at 75 Sloane Street (SW1) is where Wilde was later arrested). More recent celebrity trials have featured Mick Jagger and Johnny Rotten. Today the hotel restaurant occupies the old Number One court, where the Judge's bench, witness stand and dock take centre stage, whilst the bar incorporates the former prison cells.

The district of St. James's farther south was developed in the 18th century as a residential area for the aristocracy because of its proximity to the Royal Court. It has subsequently gained a reputation for members' clubs and classic hotel bars, including the American Bar in the Stafford at 16–18 St. James's Place (SW1), which opened in the early 1930s to lure American tourists with American-style cocktails. During the Second World War it became a club for American and Canadian officers, and patriotic visitors have been leaving mementoes here ever since. The cocktail theme continues in the intimate bar of Duke's at Numbers 35–36. Author Ian Fleming (1908–1964) was a regular here and this is where he first conjured up the Vodka Martini – shaken not stirred – for his character James Bond.

The royal connection continues behind Buckingham Palace at the Goring on Beeston Place (SW1). Once the Queen Mother's favourite hotel and the place where Catherine Middleton stayed before her wedding to Prince William, it was the first hotel to offer central heating and an en-suite bath in every room. To this day it remains in the hands of the family that built it in 1910.

Farther east stands the Savoy on the Strand (WC2) opened in 1889 by impresario Richard D'Oyly Carte using profits from his theatre next door. The world's first hotel lit by electricity its forecourt is Britain's only public street where vehicles are required to drive on the right. This dates from when hackney carriage drivers would reach out of their windows to open the passenger door, which had the handle at the front and opened backwards.

This tour finishes with the Zetter Townhouse at 49–50 St. John's Square (EC1), where each room is quirky take on British home comforts and cocktails are served against a Georgian backdrop, and the Andaz at 40 Liverpool Street (EC2), opened in 1884 by the Great Eastern Railway. An unusual feature here is an ornate Masonic Temple installed in 1912 by the Freemasons who helped finance the hotel's construction (visits by appointment www.andaz.com).

Central London's most secretive residential address is the Albany on Albany Place (W1), just off bustling Piccadilly. Few passers-by are aware how many colourful characters have sought refuge behind the converted mansion's Georgian façade. They include Lord Byron, Aldous Huxley, J. B. Priestley, Greta Garbo, Terence Stamp, Bruce Chatwin, and Bryan Ferry.

Other places of interest nearby: 60, 63, 64, 66

63 Shrines to Shopping

W1B 5AH (Soho), some classic London department stores including Liberty on Great Marlborough Street
Bakerloo, Central, Victoria lines to Oxford Circus

London's West End has been a magnet for shoppers ever since the well-to-do began gravitating here in the mid-17th century. Although their elegant Mayfair town houses are now mostly commercial properties some of the shops established to service them remain in St. James's (see no. 78). These have now been supplemented by famous-name department stores along nearby Oxford Street, Regent Street and Piccadilly, with their eyecatching façades and newsworthy window displays. What follows is a selection of them.

London's oldest department store is Fortnum & Mason at 181 Piccadilly (W1). It was founded as a grocery store in 1707 by William Fortnum, a footman to the household of Queen Anne (1702–1707), and his landlord, Hugh Mason. Fortnum financed the project using money made by selling unburned candle stubs removed from St. James's Palace! When Fortnum's grandson entered the service of Queen Charlotte, wife of George III (1760–1820), the store began its longstanding association with the Royal Family and garnered the first of many Royal Warrants. It later became famous for its worldwide deliveries, including supplies for H. M. Stanley during his search for Dr. Livingstone in Africa and beef tea for Florence Nightingale in the Crimea (see no. 92).

Having made a name selling luxury goods Fortnum's has never been averse to finding new ways of delighting its customers. In 1886 it became the first store in Britain to stock tins of Heinz baked beans and since 2008 it has offered honey from beehives on its roof. The present building was erected in the 1920s and the clock over the main entrance added in 1964. On the hour two immaculately-dressed figures representing Messrs. Fortnum and Mason emerge and bow to each other as a carillon plays an 18th century tune.

Across the road from Fortnum's is Burlington Arcade (W1), Britain's oldest covered shopping arcade. A precursor of the modern mall it was created in 1819 by Lord George Cavendish (1754–1834), later Earl of Burlington, down one side of his London home, Burlington House. Uniformed Beadles recruited by Cavendish to ensure his wife's safety are still employed to curtail rowdy behaviour.

Another idiosyncratic department store is Liberty established in 1875 by Arthur Liberty (1843–1917) at 218a Regent Street (W1). Ini-

Liberty on Great Marlborough Street still retains the feel of an old-fashioned emporium

tially it sold household ornaments, fabrics, and Japanese *objets d'art* but quickly expanded to include furniture, carpets and clothing. Quick to embrace the Arts and Crafts movement, Liberty forged relations with many contemporary designers and helped establish *Art Nouveau* in Britain. The building's attic frieze depicts the transport of exotic goods from the Orient and this nautical theme is picked up by the galleon weathervane around the corner on Great Marlborough Street.

Smart shops and a red carpet define Burlington Arcade

Liberty opened this Mock Tudor extension in 1924 using timbers salvaged from the warships *HMS Impregnable* and *HMS Hindustan*. Don't miss the galleried atrium, which gives the impression of being inside a medieval house, and the Decorative Arts and Carpets department on the 4th floor, which retains the old-fashioned feel of the original emporium.

Different again is Selfridges at 400 Oxford Street (W1). The enormous building was opened in stages from 1909 onwards by American-born retail magnate Harry Gordon Selfridge (1858–1947), and was one of the first buildings in London built on a steel frame. Ever the innovator Selfridge hosted entertainments on the roof, mounted striking window displays for which the store is still famous, and was the first department store owner to position the profitable perfume counter just inside the main entrance. He even exhibited the monoplane flown by Louis Blériot across the Channel and invited John Logie Baird to give the first public demonstration of television. Don't miss the bronze *Queen of Time* statue by Gilbert Bayes (1872–1953) over the main door trimmed with blue faience and Doulton stoneware.

Only in size did Selfridges take second place to Harrods at 87–135 Brompton Road (SW1). Built between 1894 and 1912 and containing over 300 separate departments it remains the largest shop in Britain. The first to install escalators Harrods also boasts a world famous food hall and a façade illuminated by 12,000 lightbulbs. Such features would undoubtedly have pleased Charles Henry Harrod (1799–1885), who relocated his grocery store here in 1849 with a turnover of £20 a week!

Other places of interest nearby: 62, 64, 66, 67

64 Eros and the Rebus Myth

W1J 0DA (St. James's), the statue of Eros in Piccadilly Circus
Bakerloo, Piccadilly lines to Piccadilly

A popular heraldic device used during the Middle Ages was the *rebus*. A visual pun it rendered a person's name visually rather than with words. Examples in London include that of Abbot John Islip in Westminster Abbey (a boy slipping out of a tree = I-slip), Prior Robert Bolton in the Church of St. Bartholomew the Great (a crossbow bolt piercing a barrel (or tun) = Bolt-tun), and the Blessed Thomas Abel (1497–1540) in the Tower of London (the letter 'A' on a bell = A-bel).

Some guidebooks suggest that the well-known statue of *Eros* unveiled in 1893 in Piccadilly Circus is also a *rebus*. Designed by English sculptor Sir Albert Gilbert (1854–1934) in the form of a naked winged archer it has been claimed that were its arrow to be fired the

Few realise that the statue of *Eros* in Piccadilly is misnamed

'shaft' would 'bury' itself in Shaftesbury Avenue! Others have claimed that the archer faces towards the Earl's country seat in Dorset so the 'shaft' would 'bury' itself there instead. Both theories are ill-founded, however, since an early photograph of the statue shows clearly that it has always faced Lower Regent Street.

Of greater interest is the material the statue is made from and the ongoing confusion surrounding the statue's name. Sir Albert Gilbert was a goldsmith by profession and was fascinated by metallurgical innovation. It is therefore no surprise that *Eros* was one of the first large-scale statues to be cast in lightweight aluminium, which facilitated its distinctive one-legged pose (the model was Gilbert's 16-year-old studio assistant, Angelo Colarossi).

Although the statue is commonly known as *Eros*, the Greek god of sensual love, it actually represents his twin brother, *Anteros*, the god of selfless love. Whilst *Eros* perhaps befits the carnal pleasures traditionally associated with nearby Soho, it is the less frivolous *Anteros* who Gilbert had in mind. After all, the statue was erected as a monument to the philanthropy of the 7th Earl of Shaftesbury (1801–1885), who did so much to improve the wretched lot of Victorian child labourers.

Not surprisingly the naked statue raised eyebrows when it was first unveiled and for a while objections were tempered by renaming it *The Angel of Christian Charity*. It never stuck though and it soon reverted to plain old *Eros*. These days no-one seems to care.

The name Piccadilly is derived from the word *pickadil*, a stiff disposable collar with scalloped edges and a broad lace or perforated border popular during the 17th century. One tailor who made his fortune selling *pickadils* was George Baker. His large house was dubbed Pickadilly Hall by detractors and the name eventually lent its name to the street on which it stood. Piccadilly Circus was created in 1819 to connect Piccadilly with Regent Street. Described by Dickens as the nearest thing London had to a Parisian boulevard, visitors are drawn here today not only by *Eros* but also the famous illuminated advertisements.

Another of Sir Albert Gilbert's public works is his bronze memorial to Queen Alexandria, the long-suffering wife of Edward VII (1901–1910), on Marlborough Road (SW1). Commissioned in 1926 it is set into the garden wall of Marlborough House, which was once the Queen's London home. She is shown seated behind allegorical figures of Faith, Hope and Charity.

Other places of interest nearby: 33, 34, 35, 63, 65, 66, 79

65 A 20th Century Icon

W1J 0BD (Mayfair), the prototype K2 telephone kiosk inside the entrance to the Royal Academy of Arts at Burlington House on Piccadilly
Bakerloo, Piccadilly lines to Piccadilly Circus; Jubilee, Piccadilly, Victoria lines to Green Park

For climbers K2 means the second highest mountain after Everest. For the London explorer, however, it is short for Kiosk 2, the second of eight types of public telephone kiosks installed across Britain during the 20th century. Historically associated with London they are as much an icon of the capital as red double deckers and black cabs.

Alexander Graham Bell (1847–1922) patented his revolutionary new telephone in 1876. Three years later the world's first public telephone exchange opened in London at 36 Coleman Street (EC2), where it served just eight customers. Progress was swift though and by the turn of the century telephone cables were snaking their way across the capital alongside existing telegraph cables. By the time

The very first red telephone kiosk is preserved at Burlington House

London's Central Telegraph Office closed in 1962 the telephone was commonplace albeit still dependant on manual exchanges. Following the introduction of automatic exchanges at the end of the decade the telephone then went from strength to strength.

Although public telephone kiosks had appeared in Britain in the 1900s the first *national* kiosk was not unveiled until 1921. Designated K1 by the General Post Office and manufactured in pre-cast concrete the Victorian-looking kiosk was painted white with a red door and window frames. Considered old-fashioned for 1920s Britain the design proved especially unpopular in London. As a result the Royal Fine Art Commission announced a competition to design a more modern-looking kiosk. The winning design by British architect Sir Giles Gilbert Scott (1880–1960), which was designated K2, is said to have been inspired by the tomb of architect Sir John Soane (1753–1837) in Old St. Pancras Churchyard.

Unveiled in 1926 in Kensington and Holborn the K2 was constructed of cast-iron panels. It was tall enough to accommodate a gentleman's top hat and featured a domed and pedimented roof containing a pierced Tudor crown to ventilate cigar smoke. Three sides of the kiosk each contain 18 individual windows, the fourth side being a door made of teak with a metal cup-shaped handle. Although Scott originally proposed the K2 be painted silver with a bluish-green interior, the General Post Office decided on bright red for maximum visibility.

Due to the high manufacturing cost of the K2 most were installed in London, where 200 or so are still standing. There is one K2 kiosk, however, that is unique. Secreted inside the entrance to the Royal Academy of Arts at Burlington House on Piccadilly (W1) is Gilbert Scott's original wooden prototype. Like all K2s it is now protected as a structure of national historical importance making it the smallest listed building in London.

Outside London a more cost-effective concrete version of the K2 – called the K3 – was prevalent. Two further versions followed until 1935, when the K6 was launched to celebrate the Silver Jubilee of George V (1910–1936). The introduction of the St. Edward's Crown in the pediment in 1952 to mark the accession of Queen Elisabeth II resulted in the K7, which continued in production until it was replaced by the glass-sided K8. Only when British Telecom was privatised in 1984 was a purely utilitarian design introduced that finally consigned the K series to the history books.

As much a part of London's street scene as telephone kiosks are its post boxes. Introduced in 1853 they too have been painted red since 1874, with the ruling monarch's cipher a reliable sign of their age.

Other places of interest nearby: 64, 66, 67, 78, 79

66 For Members Only!

W1S 3RF (Mayfair), a tour of London's historic private members' clubs finishing with Buck's Club at 18 Clifford Street
Jubilee, Piccadilly, Victoria lines to Green Park; Bakerloo, Piccadilly lines to Piccadilly Circus (note: only members can enter club premises)

It is probably true to say that relatively few readers will ever cross the hallowed thresholds of London's 50 or so historic private members' clubs – and that includes the author. But this is not to say one can't tarry awhile on their doorsteps and imagine the goings-on inside. What follows is a selection of a few of them.

The classical notion of a London club is of an elegantly-appointed mansion, where well-heeled gents are fed, watered and entertained. That notion hasn't really changed in the three centuries since the first clubs were established as boltholes for young aristocrats passing their time before attending St. James's Palace. The only real difference is that women are now admitted to many of them.

Boodle's on St. James's Street is a classic London club

The oldest club in St. James's is White's at 37–38 St. James's Street (SW1). With a restricted male-only membership and a nine-year waiting list it has been in business since 1693. The dandy Beau Brummel (1778–1840) used to parade himself in the bay window here, and when in the late 19th century an anxious member enquired if the bar was still open he was told "Bless my soul, sir, it has been open for 200 years"! A few doors away at Number 28 is the slightly younger Boodle's, with its open fires, red leather armchairs, and a revered Orange Fool for pudding.

Such stories abound in London's Clubland. Take, for example, the Oxford and Cambridge at 71–77 Pall Mall, where two Guards' officers were relaxing whilst their own club was being refurbished. "These middle class fellows know how to do themselves well," one of them observed, as slowly an elderly member lowered his newspaper to reveal himself as the Duke of Wellington!

Probably the largest London club is the National Liberal Club on Whitehall Place (SW1), with an outdoor riverside terrace where on hot days members are permitted to remove their jackets. Decidedly more intimate is Pratt's at 14 Park Place, established in 1841 as a dining club for the 7th Duke of Beaufort in his steward's basement. Despite a 600-strong membership today just 14 can be seated around the single dining table.

Other clubs are known for their distinctive interiors. The Travellers Club at 106 Pall Mall, for example, was founded in 1819 as a meeting place for gentlemen who had ventured "at least 500 miles from London". It boasts a superb colonnaded library decorated with a cast of a Greek temple frieze. The dining facilities are said to be top notch, too, with *The Times* describing it as "heavy on fish and game (partridges to potted shrimps) with echoes of school food (bread pudding) and a superb wine cellar".

This tour concludes with a relatively young club in Mayfair. The idea for Buck's at 18 Clifford Street (W1) was conceived in 1918 by Captain Herbert Buckmaster, who vowed to open a club if he survived the war in France. He envisaged somewhere less stuffy than the well-established clubs of St. James's, with the added novelty of an American-style cocktail bar. Within a couple of years of opening in 1919 the club's bartender had created the Buck's Fizz cocktail in his honour.

London is also home to many open clubs for people with particular interests. They include the Tall Persons' Club (www.tallclub.co.uk), the London Philosophy Club (www.londonphilosophyclub.com), the Letter Box Study Group (www.lbsg.org), and the Pie & Mash Club (www.pie-n-mash.com). Stitch London (www.stitchldn.com) serves the needs of those crazy about crochet, whilst the Handlebar Moustache Club (www.handlebar-club.co.uk) attracts men with "hirsute appendages of the upper lip, with graspable extremities"!

Other places of interest nearby: 55, 63, 65, 67, 79

67 Banksy's Falling Shopper

W1J 6JH (Mayfair), some street art including Banksy's
Falling Shopper on Bruton Lane
Jubilee, Piccadilly, Victoria lines to Green Park; Bakerloo,
Piccadilly lines to Piccadilly Circus

The street art phenomenon is nothing new. Writing and drawings known collectively as *graffiti* have been scribbled, scratched and daubed illicitly in public places since ancient times. These days the spray can is the street artist's weapon of choice, and in the hands of an expert it can produce truly eyecatching results.

London has become one of the most pro-*graffiti* cities in the world. Although legally forbidden outside officially sanctioned areas it has a huge following amongst both practitioners and members of the public. At best it is both provocative and intriguing in a way that sometimes eludes traditional commissioned art.

Banksy's *Falling Shopper* is sprayed onto a wall in Mayfair

One of the street artists whose work is easily recognisable is London-based graffitist Stik. Now working around the world his distinctively quirky stick figures first appeared in Shoreditch. Before gaining celebrity status, however, he lived in a hostel for the homeless and gave away poster copies of his art with *The Big Issue*. These days it's more likely he's selling his work for thousands and donating the proceeds to his favourite charities.

The problem in putting together a tour of street art is the necessarily ephemeral nature of the genre. Intervention both human and elemental means that few installations can be considered permanent. To avoid disappointment it is therefore best to take a dedicated street art tour hosted by a specialist walking company (see no. 11).

Works by Stik feature prominently on such tours, as do those of the legendary Banksy, one of the most celebrated contemporary graffitists. Both artists are fiercely protective of their identities allowing their work to represent their opinions. Fortunately in the case of Banksy his is now considered so important that several of his installations have been preserved for posterity beneath Perspex sheets. These include *Choose Your Weapon* at the corner of Grange Road and The Grange (SE1), depicting a realistic-looking young man wearing a hoodie with an abstract dog, and *If Graffiti Changed Anything* at the corner of Clipstone Street and Cleveland Street (W1). In the latter a rat creating its own graffiti breaks off to look at the sub-title: *It Would be Illegal*.

Banksy's work is typified by the use of elaborate hand-cut stencils which when sprayed imbue a three-dimensional quality to his figures. Whilst his work has traditionally been associated with the grungier parts of London, notably South Bank underpasses and East End back streets, it sometimes appears in more unexpected locales. A fine example is his *Falling Shopper* (also known as *Shop 'Til You Drop*) on the side of an office building on Bruton Street in Mayfair (W1). Perhaps inspired by the tragic images of September 11th it depicts a woman reluctant to lose hold of her shopping trolley as she plunges headlong towards earth, a wine bottle, purse and string of pearls clearly visible. Choosing such an upmarket location renowned for its luxury stores is a necessary part of the message, namely the folly and inhumanity of unfettered commercialism.

Not strictly *graffiti* but worth mentioning here is *Memoir of the Century* by Polish expressionist painter Feliks Topolski (1907–1989). This enormous mural on a series of hardboard panels was created in the artist's studio beneath the viaduct on Concert Hall Approach (SE1). Painted in fits and starts between 1953 and 1979 it records the personalities and political upheavals of the 20th century – from Mao's China and the Second World War to Elvis Presley and the British Royal family. Some of the panels are preserved in the nearby Topolski Bar and Café at 150–152 Hungerford Arches.

Other places of interest nearby: 55, 63, 65, 66

68 A Wayside Miscellany

SW7 1JY (Knightsbridge), a collection of street furniture
including coal hole covers in Montpelier Square
Circle, District, Piccadilly lines to South Kensington;
Piccadilly line to Knightsbridge

Coal plates in Montpelier Square

Street furniture is a catch-all term for wayside objects installed for the benefit of the general public. It encompasses everything from bollards and coal hole covers to drinking fountains and street lamps. What connects them all is a craftsmanship and elegance that raises them above mere function. Some have been discussed elsewhere, for example phone kiosks, police call posts, road signs, and public conveniences (see nos. 58, 61, 65 & 83). What follows is a miscellany of the rest.

We begin with a few rare items. Until recently the bus stop opposite 128 Piccadilly (W1) was accompanied by what looked like an oversized wooden bench. A helpful inscription explained that it was erected in 1861 "for the benefit of porters and others carrying burdens." Presumed stolen by Westminster City Council it is now in the process of being replaced. Until this happens this tour begins with the similarly philanthropic stone mounting block on Waterloo Place (SW1). It was installed at the request of the Duke of Wellington so that gentlemen could more comfortably mount their horses outside the Athenaeum Club. Decidedly more prosaic but no less useful is the 19th century sand bin on Temple Place (WC2) used to give traction to horsedrawn carts in winter. Most modest of all is a hook at the corner of Great Newport Street and Upper St. Martin's Lane used by Metropolitan

A public drinking fountain on Holborn Viaduct

policemen in the 1930s to hang their capes whilst directing traffic!

More common items of street furniture include coal hole covers (known as coal plates) and pavement skylights. Both were manufactured by Hayward Brothers in Borough, a family firm of glass cutters that branched out into ironmongery in 1848. They took out profitable patents on both circular self-locking coal plates, through which merchants delivered coal directly into cellars, and the glass prisms in pavement skylights used to illuminate them. A veritable gallery of coal plates embossed with various company names can be found in the lovely late Georgian Montpelier Square (SW7).

Parish boundary markers are far older and date from a time when the City's churches were built so close that it was often unclear where one parish ended and another began. One of the oldest examples consists of a pair of stones at 55 Carey Street (WC2), one carved with an anchor representing St. Clement Danes and the other with 'SDW' for St. Dunstan-in-the-West. Around the corner on Chancery Lane two wall-mounted markers are inscribed 'SDW' and 'SAH' (for St. Andrew Holborn). By contrast purely utilitarian boundaries were once demarcated with redundant cannon barrels upended in the pavement as seen outside the Church of St. Helen Bishopsgate (EC3). Their muzzles were sometimes stoppered with cannonballs and modern pavement bollards still mimic this form.

A most important item of street furniture was the drinking fountain. Many were erected by the Metropolitan Drinking Fountain Association, which was established in 1859 to offer free potable water in the hope of discouraging alcohol and disease. The first can still be seen embedded in the railings of the Church of St. Sepulchre-without-Newgate on Holborn Viaduct (EC1) – directly opposite a pub! From 1867 onwards the Association also commissioned troughs to water horses.

Another category of street furniture is lighting. Before the introduction of gas lamps the well-to-do were escorted home by torch bearers known as 'linkmen'. Upon arrival the torch (or link) would be snuffed out in a metal cone outside the door. Link extinguishers can still be seen in upmarket areas such as Berkeley Square (W1), St. James's Square and Queen Anne's Gate (both SW1).

London's first public gas lamps appeared in 1807 on Pall Mall, when the route to St. James's Palace was illuminated to celebrate the birthday of George III (1760–1820). Between 1813 and 1937 the world's first public gasworks on Great Peter Street fuelled street lighting throughout Westminster, with lamp standards embossed with the familiar portcullis crest. A curiosity surviving from the time is the J.E. Webb Patent Sewer Gas Lamp at the bottom end of Carting Lane (WC2). Looking much like any other old-fashioned street lamp it features a separate pipe designed to remove potentially explosive methane gas from the sewer below and to burn it off harmlessly.

A link extinguisher preserved in Berkeley Square

Street furniture also manifests itself in novel sculptural decorations. Cherubs became popular during the 18th century, which explains the pair playing marbles over a doorway at 1 Laurence Pountney Hill (EC4). A single cherub on the façade of the Royal Automobile Club built in 1911 at 89–91 Pall Mall (SW1) is suitably depicted at the wheel of a car!

Equally cherubic is the relief of a young boy sitting on what appears to be a basket on Panyer Alley (EC4). It is thought to mark the place where bakers' boys once sold bread from woven baskets or panniers (the accompanying inscription dated 1688 identifies the spot as one of London's highest).

Other carved novelties include a pair of tiny mice scampering up a façade at 23–25 Eastcheap (EC3), a lifelike bust of William Shakespeare looking down from a pub window at 29 Great Marlborough Street (W1), and a Victorian frieze at 12 Poultry (EC2) commemorating visits to the City by four different monarchs: Edward VI, Elizabeth I, Charles II, and Victoria.

Other places of interest nearby: 70, 72

69 The Home of Geography

SW7 2AR (Kensington), the Royal Geographical Society
at 1 Kensington Gore
Circle, District, Piccadilly lines to South Kensington

Since the early 1800s Mayfair's fashionable Savile Row (W1) has been associated with men's tailoring (the dinner jacket, or tuxedo, was invented there in 1865). Less well known is the street's connection with travel and adventure. The opening sentence of Jules Verne's *Around the World in Eighty Days* (1873) has the book's principal character, Phileas Fogg, living at 7 Savile Row. It is no coincidence that at the same time the Geographical Society London was located just a few doors away at Number 1.

The society had been in existence for 40 years when in 1870 it arrived on Savile Row. Founded for the advancement of geographical science, like many learned societies it began as a gentlemen's dining club, where esteemed members such as Sir John Franklin (1786–1847) and Sir Francis Beaufort (1774–1857) debated current geographical issues. It became known as the Royal Geographical Society (RGS) in 1859, when Queen Victoria granted its Royal Charter.

The society's Savile Row premises were suitably fitted out with a glass-roofed map room in the courtyard and an astronomical observatory on the roof. Many famous British explorers set out from here into Africa, Asia and Antarctica. Those who failed to return included

The nameplate identifying the Royal Geographical Society on Kensington Gore

Captain Robert Falcon Scott (1868–1912), who died attempting to be first at the South Pole, and the missionary David Livingstone (1813–1873), who succumbed to malaria in what is now Zambia (his remains minus the heart, which remained in Africa, were laid out at 1 Savile Row before being interred in Westminster Abbey).

In 1911 a new direction was given to the RGS by the election to president of Earl Curzon (1859–1925), former Viceroy of India, who relocated the society to its present site at 1 Kensington Gore (SW7). Known as Lowther Lodge this imposing house was built in the 1870s by renowned domestic architect Norman Shaw (1831–1912) for the diplomat William Lowther and his wife, Alice (their initials are carved over the entrance). The new premises were inaugurated in 1913, the same year that women were admitted after the original decision to do so had been quickly revoked in 1893 (the globetrotting Isabella Bird (1831–1904) was amongst them). The building offered welcome potential for expansion and in 1929 a new east wing was added, including a new map room and a 750-seat lecture theatre.

The fabric of Lowther Lodge still reflects the colonial era of British exploration, with statues of Livingstone and polar explorer Ernest Shackleton (1874–1922) adorning the façade (London cabbies have nicknamed it 'Hot and Cold Corner'!). The journals, maps and photographs of such pioneers are what make the society's historical collections unique. However, whilst the RGS still actively supports its members' globetrotting expeditions, it is the way it has increasingly engaged with the general public that really impresses today. Now a registered charity, the society's membership has been opened up to include teachers, students and schoolchildren. Non-members, too, can make use of the Foyle Reading Room and attend exhibitions staged in the Pavilion on Exhibition Road (see www.rgs.org). The involvement of members and non-members alike helps support the society's ongoing mission to develop and promote geographical knowledge, and to apply it to the serious environmental challenges facing the planet today.

It seems fitting that the RGS numbers several foreign embassies amongst its neighbours, as well as the little-known Sikorski Museum at 20 Prince's Gate, which preserves the memory of Polish armed forces in the West since the time of the Napoleonic Wars. Those wishing to embark on their own expedition should visit Stanfords at 12–14 Long Acre (WC2), the world's largest map retailer, and Daunt Books at 83 Marylebone High Street (W1), an Edwardian-era bookshop with a magnificent galleried reading room lined with travel books and maps.

Other places of interest nearby: 70, 71, 72

70 Orthodoxy in Knightsbridge

SW7 1NH (Knightsbridge), the Russian Orthodox
Cathedral of the Dormition of the Mother of God
at 67 Ennismore Gardens
Circle, District, Piccadilly lines to South Kensington;
Piccadilly line to Knightsbridge

Ennismore Gardens is a pleasant corner of well-to-do Knightsbridge. One side of the street is lined with elegant porticoed town houses erected in the mid-19th century, the other with 1930s red-brick flats. Together they make up the Kingston House estate, named after a Palladian mansion that once occupied the site. Although the Ennismore Arms, the first element of the estate erected in 1847, is long gone, the Italianate All Saints Church built around the same time still stands. Only close scrutiny, however, will reveal it has changed denomination. Originally Anglican, the church now serves as London's Russian Orthodox Cathedral of the Dormition of the Mother of God.

The change to Orthodoxy came in 1956, when the Parish of the Dormition relocated here from a church on Buckingham Palace Road. Having served the Russian Embassy in London from 1716 it became part of the Diocese of Sourozh in 1962, named after an ancient episcopal see in the Crimea that no longer had a bishop. The founding of the diocese is recorded in Cyrillic on the wall plaques flanking the church entrance alongside the distinctive Russian Orthodox Cross, with its three horizontal crossbeams.

Until 2003 the new diocese was headed by Metropolitan Anthony Bloom, a man renowned for his cosmopolitan brand of Orthodoxy. With the fall of Communism, however, a new wave of Orthodox Christians began arriving into the diocese from Russia, and they demanded his 'wayward' habits be brought back into line. What they saw as normalisation was viewed by existing parishioners as Russification, the latter moreso since the parish had since 1931 been technically under the sway of the Patriarchate of Constantinople rather than Moscow. Tensions grew until 2006, when the cathedral was taken over by Moscow and several of Metropolitan Anthony's colleagues removed.

Politics aside, a visit to the church is a memorable experience. Built to a design by the architect Lewis Vulliamy (1791–1871) it is modelled on the 11th century basilica of San Zeno Maggiore in Verona. Noteworthy are the Biblical murals in *sgraffito*, a Renaissance technique by which a surface layer of plaster is scraped away to reveal underlying colours. The *iconostasis* (altar screen) installed after the church switched to Orthodoxy was removed from the chapel of the Russian Embassy in London following the 1917 revolution. Noteworthy, too, is the miraculous icon of St. Nicholas. Painted originally for a Russian warship it was thrown into the sea by an explosion during the Russo-Japanese War, where it helped save the lives of several sailors who clung to it before being rescued.

Although Divine Liturgy (Communion) is celebrated here every morning except Monday, for something really memorable attend Easter Matins, the Orthodox celebration of the Resurrection. Shortly after midnight on Easter Saturday the

Inside the Russian Orthodox Cathedral of the Dormition of the Mother of God

priests and choir enter the church with candles, icons, incense, and acclamations. As there are no pews there is standing room only and the service is sung in Old Church Slavonic. The Liturgy then continues until 4am!

Central London's other Orthodox places of worship include the Church of St. Dunstan-in-the-West at 186a Fleet Street (EC4), which is the only church in England to share its building with the Romanian Orthodox community (see no. 19). Their chapel to the left of the main altar is closed off by a richly decorated *iconostasis* removed in 1966 from Antim Monastery in Bucharest. The Church of St. Botolph-without-Bishopsgate on Bishopsgate (EC2) is similar in that it shares its premises with the Greek Orthodox Church of Antioch. London's only other Antiochian place of worship is St. George's Cathedral at 1a Redhill Street (NW1), which ceased being Anglican in 1989.

Other places of interest nearby: 68, 69, 71, 72

71   Quest for the First Computer

SW7 2DD (South Kensington), Charles Babbage's Difference
Engine in the Science Museum on Exhibition Road
Circle, District, Piccadilly lines to South Kensington

The Science Museum on Exhibition Road (SW7) is one of three great museums in South Kensington. Like the Victoria and Albert Museum it finds its origins in the Great Exhibition of 1851, and the desire to see permanent applied art and industry collections established in London.

For a while both masterpieces and machines found a home in the South Kensington Museum, a hotchpotch of buildings old and new straddling Exhibition Road, which opened in 1857. Including historical machinery removed from the Patent Office Museum it was the world's first museum to offer refreshments, with gas lighting so that the working classes could visit in the evenings. But as the collections grew so did the need for separation, and in 1909 the rebranded Science Museum became a separate entity. In the same year the South Kensington Museum's art holdings were relaunched as the Victoria and Albert Museum (see no. 72).

The present buildings housing the Science Museum opened in stages from 1919 onwards and today contain 300,000 items. They include the world's oldest surviving steam locomotive, *Puffing Billy* (1814), Britain's first jet engine (1941), the DNA model made by Francis Crick and James Watson (1953), and Britain's last typewriter (2012). Much to the delight of younger visitors the museum also includes over 50 interactive exhibits in its Launchpad Gallery and an IMAX cinema showing science documentaries in 3D. Since 2000 the Wellcome Wing has made the museum a world class centre for the presentation of contemporary science, too.

The *Making the Modern World Gallery* contains some of the museum's most iconic objects. Displayed as a timeline chronicling humankind's technological advance it includes an Apollo space capsule, a transgenic sheep called Tracy, and the so-called Difference Engine No. 1, the world's first automatic calculating machine and a milestone in the prehistory of programmable computers.

The Difference Engine was devised in 1812 by English mathematician and engineer Charles Babbage (1791–1871). Its function was to calculate and print error-free mathematical tables as an aid to computation in the workplace. Babbage commenced development after securing a government loan but politics and personality got in the way.

By the time the project collapsed in 1833 only the small part displayed had been built – and the government had invested the equivalent of the cost of two warships!

Part of the problem was Babbage's own brilliance since he was already envisaging a more powerful machine that could be programmed to calculate almost any mathematical function. Conceived in 1834 this new steam-powered machine – known as the Analytical Engine – also remained incomplete. A trial part completed before Babbage's death can be found in the museum's *History of Computing Gallery*.

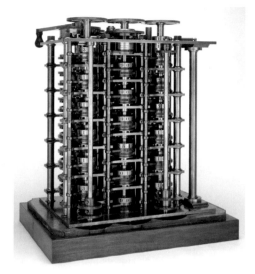

The Science Museum contains a piece of Charles Babbage's Difference Engine No. 1

Also displayed in this gallery is something Babbage never saw in his lifetime. It is a working replica of his Difference Engine No. 2, which he designed in the late 1840s to streamline his earlier machines (Difference Engine No. 1 would have required the manufacture of some 25,000 components!). Using Babbage's original plans it was constructed in 1991 by museum staff to mark the 200th anniversary of his birth. It is a masterpiece of engineering built to tolerances achievable in the 19th century. As such it is proof that had it been built in Babbage's day it would have fulfilled its function perfectly. Weighing in at over two tons, however, Difference Engine No. 2 is a far cry from the computing devices that would eventually follow in its wake.

A wall plaque on a modern block of flats at 1a Dorset Street (W1) marks the former site of the house where Charles Babbage lived between 1829 and 1871.

Other places of interest nearby: 69, 70, 72, 73

72 Building the V&A

SW7 2RL (South Kensington), an architectural tour of the
Victoria and Albert Museum on Cromwell Road
Circle, District, Piccadilly lines to South Kensington

A detail of the original main entrance to the Victoria and Albert Museum

The Victoria and Albert Museum on Cromwell Road (SW7) has been called many things. "An extremely capacious handbag" seems fair given that its 145 galleries make it the world's largest collection of decorative arts. But what about "a refuge for destitute collections"? This is credited to the museum's first director, Sir Henry Cole (1808–1882), who in 1857 relocated his Museum of Manufactures to Exhibition Road as part of the new South Kensington Museum, where it was displayed alongside the collections of the embryonic Science Museum (see no. 71). In 1909 the Science Museum became a separate entity and the art holdings of the South Kensington Museum were rebranded as the Victoria and Albert Museum. A decade earlier Queen Victoria (1837–1901) in her last official public appearance had laid the building's foundation stone.

The V&A today is a veritable palace of art filled to bursting with sculpture, ceramics, textiles, jewellery, furniture, paintings and books. Everything is here from Victorian pincushions to Leonardo da Vinci's journals. Amongst the many superlative items is the oldest photograph of London (a view down Whitehall taken in 1839), the world's first Christmas card (1843), the earliest surviving wedding suit (1673), and the world's oldest carpet woven in 1539 in Iran.

Sir Aston Webb designed the museum's magnificent Portland stone façade

Not surprisingly the buildings housing the V&A are worthy of a visit in their own right. Together with the nearby Science and Natural History Museums, as well as Imperial College, the Royal Colleges of Art and Music, and the Royal Albert Hall, they make up a cultural landscape dubbed *Albertopolis* because of the involvement of Prince Albert in its creation.

The oldest surviving part of the museum is the Sheepshanks Gallery erected in 1857 along the east side of what is now the John Madejski Garden. It was designed by Royal Engineer-turned-architect Captain Francis Fowke (1823–1865), who added the north and west ranges in brick and terracotta in the early 1860s. The north range served originally as the main entrance to the museum, which explains the mosaic of Queen Victoria in the pediment and the bronze doors decorated with figures representing science and the arts. It is worth remembering that until the construction of the south range there was only grass between here and Cromwell Road!

The north range today contains the V&A Café housed in the museum's original refreshment rooms, which were once divided according to class. Each decorated by a different Victorian interior designer they formed the world's first museum refreshment rooms and remain gloriously well preserved. Be sure not to miss the stunning Ceramic Staircase nearby, which is smothered with terracotta ornaments.

Before his premature death Fowke also completed the quadrangle behind the Sheepshanks Gallery, which he roofed over to form the North and South Courts. Thereafter the architectural baton was picked up by another military man, Colonel Henry Young Darracott Scott (1822–1883). Having co-designed the Royal Albert Hall with Fowke he expanded the museum in 1872 by adding what is now known as the Henry Cole Wing. He also installed the two huge skylit Cast Courts to the southeast of the garden, on land occupied previously by a series of temporary corrugated iron display halls nicknamed the 'Brompton Boilers' (Brompton was the original name of South Kensington before the museum authorities gave it a more fashionable-sounding name).

Scott's final work was the Art Library erected along the south side of the garden in 1883. This created another quadrangle with the garden at its centre but left the museum without a proper façade. The task of creating that fell to Sir Aston Webb (1849–1930) and it was the foundation stone for this part of the museum that Queen Victoria laid in 1899. Built predominantly from Portland stone it reaches right down to Cromwell Gardens, where the main façade stretches for 220 metres. Webb's extraordinary main entrance features a Romanesque arch, a Gothic tower and Classical detailing, with figures of Queen Victoria and Prince Albert worked into the design.

Other places of interest nearby: 68, 69, 70, 71, 73

73 In the Spirit of Darwin

SW7 5BD (South Kensington), the Natural History Museum
on Cromwell Road
Circle, District, Piccadilly lines to South Kensington

London's Natural History Museum is one of the greatest collections of its type in the world. More than 80 million life and earth specimens are deposited here from the oldest fossilised insect to a rare meteorite from Mars. A part of the British Museum until 1992 it has occupied its own magnificent premises on Cromwell Road (SW7) since 1881 (see nos. 71 & 72).

The influence of English naturalist Charles Darwin (1809–1882) pervades the museum throughout. Consider first the exterior. Designed by Gothic Revival architect Alfred Waterhouse (1830–1905) it is covered with smog-resistant terracotta moulded into flowers and animals, with living species on the west wing and extinct ones on the east. This deliberate separation is thought to have been at the request of museum superin-

A winged dinosaur on the façade of the Natural History Museum

tendant Richard Owen (1804–1892). An outstanding naturalist remembered for coining the term 'Dinosaur' he agreed with Darwin's groundbreaking theory of evolution but believed his attempt to link present species with past ones through the theory of natural selection was too simplistic. The decoration of the museum façade can thus be seen as Owen's rebuttal writ large!

Beyond the main door the visitor enters the imposing Hintze Hall named after a generous benefactor. One of the world's great museum entrance halls this cathedral-like space contains the replica skeleton of a Diplodocus (to be replaced in 2017 by the real skeleton of a Blue Whale) and a slice of a 1,300-year-old Giant Sequoia tree. Seated in a prominent position at the head of the grand staircase is a statue of Darwin installed in 1885. Although this would understandably have displeased Owen it should be noted that in 1927 his own statue replaced Darwin's for a while (Darwin returned in 2004 to mark the 200th anniversary of his birth).

To the right of the Hintze Hall is the museum's Green Zone. Here in the Cadogan Gallery is a display called *Treasures* containing 22 extraordinary objects. They include a rare first edition of Darwin's book *On the Origin of Species* (1859), as well as the pet pigeons that provided him with crucial evidence for his theory. The ceiling of the gallery is adorned with the artwork *TREE* inspired by the 'Tree of Life' sketch drawn by Darwin to help explain evolution. It is made from a wafer-thin 17-metre long section of a 200-year-old oak tree.

During his five-year round-the-world trip on HMS *Beagle* Darwin also wrote books about geology. Redolent of the age in which he travelled are the Victorian wooden display cabinets in the Green Zone's Mineral Gallery. The geological theme is continued in the Red Zone's Earth Hall, which features an earthquake simulator.

Darwin's presence also pervades the Blue Zone to the left of the Hintze Hall, with its animatronic Tyrannosaurus Rex. He did much theorising on the extinction of these great creatures and also wrote a book on corals of the type seen in the Marine Invertebrates Gallery. However, it is in the Orange Zone's Darwin Centre that he is best remembered. Opened in 2002 this combined museum and research facility houses 'dry' specimens in its so-called Cocoon building and 'wet' specimens preserved in alcohol in the Spirit Collection. The latter is displayed on 27 kilometres of shelving, a tiny part of which can be seen on the museum's daily guided tours. Highlights include specimens collected by Darwin himself and a giant squid called Archie!

The Natural History Museum runs a wide-ranging programme of events. Its *After Hours* programme includes night time safaris through the galleries and the opportunity to sleep in the Hintze Hall beneath the Diplodocus! For details visit www.nhm.ac.uk.

Other places of interest nearby: 71, 72, 74

74 Monument to the Michelin Man

SW3 6RD (Chelsea), Michelin House at 81 Fulham Road
Circle, District, Piccadilly lines to South Kensington

London is filled with historic buildings that have outlived their original function and been adapted for reuse (see nos. 7, 11 & 95). An extraordinary example is Michelin House at 81 Fulham Road (SW3), where the fitting of car tyres has been replaced by fine dining and interior design.

The pneumatic tyre was invented in 1887 by Scottish inventor John Boyd Dunlop (1840–1921). The expiry of its patent in 1904, however, created an opportunity for foreign companies to invest. Chief amongst them was French company Michelin, which opened Michelin House

A stained glass Monsieur Bibendum at Michelin House in Chelsea

as its British headquarters in 1911. In doing so they created one of London's most flamboyant buildings.

Michelin House was designed by François Espinasse (1880–1925) under the auspices of company co-directors Édouard and André Michelin. Although little is known about Espinasse – he worked in Michelin's construction department in Clermont-Ferrand – he managed to create something unique. Commentators are still undecided whether the building's style is late *Art Nouveau* (witness the decorative metalwork at the front of the building) or proto *Art Deco* (the use of external advertisements is very 1930s). All that can really be said is that it is the most completely French Edwardian building in London!

The front entrance facing what was one of the main routes into London looks much as it did originally. Three magnificent stained-glass windows feature *Monsieur Bibendum*, the rotund Michelin Man, separated by corner turrets topped off with piles of glazed ceramic tyres. At street level a series of decorative tiled panels by Edouard Montaut (1879–1909) depict racing cars and motorcycles using Michelin products (see page 4). The deliberate blurring of their wheels to evoke a sense of speed was influenced by early photography. Inside the building was the tyre-fitting bay, the floor of which still retains its mosaic of *Bibendum* holding up a glass of nuts and bolts proclaiming "Nunc est Bibendum" (Now is the time to drink). Whilst their cars were driven onto a weighbridge to ensure the exact tyre pressure was applied, waiting customers could retire to an adjacent touring office, where Michelin's own brand maps for journey planning were displayed.

Michelin House is an important early example of a type of reinforced-concrete construction pioneered by French engineer François Hennebique (1842–1921). The technique offered rapid construction time – in this case just five months – and fire proofing, which was important considering the fact that 30,000 tyres were once stored in the basement. When required these were brought up on a lift and rolled to the front of the building along a sloping floor.

When Michelin eventually vacated the building in 1985 it was bought by publisher Paul Hamlyn and restaurateur-cum-designer Sir Terence Conran. Between them they restored the outside of the building and converted the interior for use as offices, a shop, and restaurant. Conran's much-praised Bibendum Restaurant still occupies the front of the building, with the Conran Shop to the rear.

The golden age of motoring is also recalled at the Wolseley at 160 Piccadilly (W1). This smart café was once the showroom of Wolseley Motors Limited built in 1921 to a design by William Curtis Green (1875–1960). It retains its original magnificent interior with walls of polished Portland stone, black and white marble floors, and a domed ceiling supported by columns finished in black and gold Japanese lacquer. Dating from the same period the *Art Deco* Lex Garage on Brewer Street (W1) once offered a waiting area for chauffeurs and changing rooms for ladies!

Other places of interest nearby: 73

75 In Praise of the Humble Shed

SW1W 0RP (Belgravia), a tour of unusual sheds beginning in
Lower Grosvenor Gardens on Buckingham Palace Road
Circle, District lines to Victoria

Not long ago several news-papers ran an article entitled "An Englishman's Home is his Shed". It described how the humble shed provides modern man with a space in which to be himself, away from what some consider the feminine domain of the home. Be that as it may, the shed is no modern invention. Dotted around London are numerous historic examples, where men (and more recently women) have been keeping busy for a century or more.

One of a pair of shell sheds in Lower Grosvenor Gardens

This tour begins with a delightful pair of shell-encrusted sheds in Lower Grosvenor Gardens on Buckingham Palace Road (SW1). They were constructed in 1952 as part of a Gallic makeover of the gardens in honour of Anglo-French comradeship. The location is pertinent considering a statue of French First World War hero Marshall Ferdinand Foch (1851–1929) has stood here since 1930, and that the gardens contained an air raid shelter during the Second World War.

The sheds were designed by French architect Jean Moreux (1889–1956), who was also responsible for the library of the Institut Français in South Kensington (SW7). They take the form of small pavilions, or *Fabriques*, of a type used as eye-catchers in French landscape gardens of the 18th century. The shells themselves came from the shores of both Britain and France making the sheds a truly cross-cultural ef-

A cabmen's shelter on Northumberland Avenue

fort. Despite their whimsical appearance, however, they serve a practical purpose being used for storing tools and deckchairs.

A very different type of shed stands in Soho Square (W1). Rendered in the style of an octagonal Tudor market cross building it is not nearly as old as it looks. Now a combined garden shed and arbor it was built in the mid-1920s and served originally to hide an electricity substation! In this practical respect it resembles the much larger Neo-Baroque substation installed in 1905 in Brown Hart Gardens (W1). Soho Square itself was laid out in the late 17th century and was originally called King Square after Charles II (1660–1685). This explains the battered statue of the monarch standing there today. Before being remodelled in 1838 the smart townhouse at Number 21 was the high-class White House brothel, a reminder of Soho's red light reputation.

Different again is the tiny brick-built shed at Lincoln's Inn in Holborn (WC2). Built in 1860 this charming Mock Elizabethan structure once housed an *ostler*, whose job it was to look after horses belonging to visiting law students. His profession was made redundant by the arrival of the motor car since when the shed has been used to store tools. It is London's second smallest listed building after the city's iconic red telephone kiosks (see no. 65).

This tour finishes with the most common form of historic London shed, namely its cabmen's shelters. These green wooden sheds were financed in 1875 by the philanthropically-minded 7th Earl of Shaftesbury (1801–1885) to provide shelter for drivers of horse-drawn Hansom cabs – and to keep them out of the pubs! Each contains a kitchen and a rest room for ten drivers. Despite the arrival in 1908 of motorised Hackney cabs the dozen or so shelters still standing – including examples on Russell Square (WC1), Northumberland Avenue (WC2), Embankment Place (WC2), and Wellington Place (NW8) – continue to provide sustenance for cabbies and the general public.

Other places of interest nearby: 76

76   A Tour of Buck House

SW1A 1AA (Westminster), Buckingham Palace
on Buckingham Gate
Jubilee, Piccadilly and Victoria lines to Green Park; Piccadilly
line to Hyde Park Corner; Circle, District lines to St. James's
Park or Victoria

In 1607 James I (1603–1625) hatched a plan to seize control of the silk industry from the French. He instructed his gardener to plant mulberry trees where Buckingham Palace now stands. When the scheme failed a townhouse was built instead for the Duke of Buckingham (1647–1721). This was acquired in 1761 by George III (1760–1820), who extended it as a private retreat for his wife. His son, George IV (1820–1830), then set about transforming the house into a palace with the help of architect John Nash (1752–1835) but died before the work was complete, as did his brother William IV (1830–1837). Queen Victoria (1837–1901) was therefore the first monarch to occupy the palace,

A frosty morning on the way to Buckingham Palace

which has been the London residence and principal workplace of all Britain's monarchs ever since.

The most important change made subsequently to Buckingham Palace occurred in 1850, when architect Edward Blore (1787–1879) completed a new east wing. Sir Aston Webb (1849–1930) refaced it in 1913 with Portland stone creating the public face of the palace as seen today from The Mall. It contains the balcony from which the Royal Family acknowledge the crowds on momentous occasions (see no. 77).

'Buck House', as the palace is known colloquially, is owned by the

British state. The public have been allowed to visit for a fee since 1993, when funds were needed to repair fire damage at Windsor Castle. Revenue raised today is used for ongoing repairs to the palace itself. A tour of the State Rooms reveals the tastes of George IV to be remarkably intact, indeed the chandeliers and much of the furniture comes from Carlton House, his home while Prince Regent (see no. 33).

Each State Room has its specific function. The Throne Room, for example, is where the monarch receives loyal addresses on special occasions, such as Jubilees. The Music Room, with its bow window facing the garden, is where guests are presented during State visits. And in the White Drawing Room the Royal Family gathers prior to official occasions. One of the finest rooms is the Picture Gallery, where works from the Royal Collection are displayed. Note the four marble fireplaces, each adorned with a pair of female figures holding palettes and brushes and a medallion of a famous painter (Titian, Leonardo da Vinci, Dürer and Van Dyck). The room is also used as an assembly point for those awaiting investiture in the Ballroom.

A separate building to the rear of the palace contains the Queen's Gallery, where more works from the Royal Collection are exhibited. Opened in 1962 it occupies the site of the palace chapel, which was destroyed in an air raid during the Second World War. Next door on Buckingham Palace Road is the Royal Mews, where the royal carriages are kept. They include the Brougham used to convey post between Buckingham Palace and St. James's Palace, and the Golden State Coach used at every coronation since that of George IV. The Queen's Diamond Jubilee Coach is also displayed here.

A little father away on The Mall is Clarence House, the official London residence of the Prince of Wales. Built in the 1820s for George III's son, the Duke of Clarence, its most famous occupant was Queen Elizabeth, the Queen Mother (1900–2002).

Since 2002 thousands of invited guests have enjoyed summer parties in Buckingham Palace Gardens. The largest private garden in London it features a lake with its own flock of flamingos, a helipad, and a single surviving mulberry tree from the time of James I.

Other places of interest nearby: 75, 77

77 Septem juncta in uno

SW1E 6HQ (Westminster), the Household Guards at Wellington Barracks on Birdcage Walk
Jubilee, Piccadilly and Victoria lines to Green Park; Piccadilly
line to Hyde Park Corner; Circle, District lines to St. James's
Park or Victoria

Members of the Household Guards form up before marching to Buckingham Palace

Visitors revel in London's colourful pageantry. Whilst much of it is
preserved out of tradition, other facets still serve their original function. Chief amongst these are the activities of the Household Division,
seven regiments of the British Army tasked with the duty of providing
security and ceremony for the monarch. Their motto *Septem juncta in
uno* (Seven joined in one) could not be more appropriate.

Five of the seven regiments, known collectively as the Household
Guards, comprise foot soldiers from the Grenadier, Coldstream, Scots,
Irish and Welsh Guards. Those with good eyes can identify them by
the arrangement of buttons on their scarlet tunics: the Grenadiers' are
evenly spaced, the Coldstream have them in twos, the Scots in threes,
the Irish in fours, and the Welsh in fives.

The Grenadiers were the first to be established in 1656, as part
of the bodyguard of the exiled Charles II during the period known as
the Commonwealth. Originally called the 1st Regiment of Foot Guards
they were rebranded the Grenadiers in 1815 after defeating the French
at Waterloo, when they took to wearing their enemy's bearskin caps.
The Coldstream Guards followed in 1660 with the Restoration of the
Monarchy (although previously they fought for the Parliamentarians

in the New Model Army), then the Scots (1686), the Irish (1900), and the Welsh (1915).

The Household Guards can be seen in action in front of Buckingham Palace during Changing the Guard. Performed daily from May to July and on alternate days the rest of the year (www.royal.gov.uk) the ceremony begins at 11.30am and is accompanied by a Guards band (a separate detachment protects the Royal Court at St. James's Palace). Since 1833 they have been based at Wellington Barracks on nearby Birdcage Walk (SW1), where they can be seen forming up before leaving for the Palace. The barracks also contain the Guards Museum. Previously they were based on Wilton Row (SW1), where their former officers' mess is now the much storied Grenadier pub.

The other two regiments of the Household Division, known collectively as the Household Cavalry, comprise mounted soldiers from the Life Guards and the Blues and Royals. The former, who were also raised at the time of Charles II's restoration, wear scarlet tunics with a metal cuirass and white-plumed helmet. The latter wear blue tunics with a red plume and like the Coldstream Guards originated in the New Model Army. The story of both regiments is given in the Household Cavalry Museum inside Horse Guards on Whitehall. As the official entrance to Buckingham Palace this building witnesses its own daily Changing the Guard ceremony at 11am (10am Sundays), with a dismounting parade at 4pm.

The greatest spectacle of all occurs on a Saturday morning in June, when regiments of the Household Division assemble on Horse Guards Parade for Trooping the Colour. Originally a way of reminding troops of their regimental standard it now marks the monarch's official birthday. The monarch is in attendance to inspect the troops after which the King's Troop Royal Horse Artillery fires a 41-gun salute in Green Park. Almost as colourful is Beating the Retreat on two successive evenings in the same month, when the Household Division's massed bands recall the tradition of closing camp gates at sunset. Tickets for both events are available at www.householddivision.org.uk.

Other regimental museums in London include the Fusiliers Museum in the Tower of London (EC3), where the infantry regiment was raised in 1685, the Honourable Artillery Company Museum on City Road (EC1), which celebrates the British Army's oldest surviving regiment formed in 1537, and the London Scottish Regimental Museum at 95 Horseferry Road (SW1), which documents a volunteer corps established in 1859.

Other places of interest nearby: 75

78 London Made to Measure

SW1A 1EG (St. James's), a tour of specialist and bespoke retailers in St. James's beginning with Berry Bros. & Rudd at 3 St. James's Street

Bakerloo, Piccadilly lines to Piccadilly Circus; Jubilee, Piccadilly, Victoria lines to Green Park

Facing north up St. James's Street (SW1) is the Tudor gatehouse of St. James's Palace. Completed in 1536 for Henry VIII (1509-1547) the palace became the monarch's official principal residence after fire destroyed the Palace of Whitehall in 1698 (see nos. 33 & 81). Although Buckingham Palace has served as the monarch's main London residence since the reign of Queen Victoria (1837–1901), St. James's Palace remains the hub of the Royal Court, where foreign diplomatic missions are still formally received (it is therefore closed to the public except occasionally for visits to the Chapel Royal).

From the late 17th century onwards the presence of the Court made a patrician enclave of St. James's attracting

Berry Bros. & Rudd in St. James's supply wine and spirits to the Royal Family

specialist and bespoke retailers revelling in their Royal Warrants (see no. 63). What follows is a whistlestop tour of those still trading on St. James's Street and Jermyn Street.

Berry Bros. & Rudd at 3 St. James's Street is Britain's oldest wine and spirit merchants. Established in 1698 as a grocery store to service the area's newly-fashionable coffee houses, the firm's extensive wine cellars have since supplied the British Royal family, the luxury liner *Titanic*, and even smugglers running alcohol into Prohibition-era

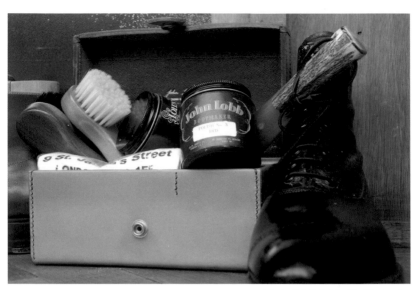
John Lobb is Britain's oldest bootmaker

America. A narrow passageway alongside the shop leads to a tiny gaslit Georgian square, Pickering Place, where duels were once fought and ministers from the independent Republic of Texas were based in 1842–1845 (see page 240).

Lock & Co. at Number 6 has been supplying headwear since 1676. They made the cocked hat worn by Nelson at Trafalgar, fitted the crown for Queen Elizabeth II's coronation, and even supplied Indiana Jones with his well-worn fedora. Lock's also lays claim to the bowler hat, which they commissioned for an aristocratic customer who wanted a compact hard hat for his gamekeepers that would not be knocked off by overhanging branches.

John Lobb at Number 9 is Britain's oldest bootmaker and since 1866 has provided handmade shoes for monarchs, politicians and celebrities. From its wood-panelled premises the firm continues a tradition established earlier by the St. James's bootmaker Hoby, who supplied the Duke of Wellington with his famous customised boots, the mass production of which made the duke a household name. Across the street at Number 71 is Truefit & Hill, the world's oldest barber, although it only arrived in St. James's in 1994.

James J. Fox at Number 19 has been supplying smoking accessories since 1787 making it the world's oldest cigar shop. It contains a smokers' lounge upstairs and a small museum in the basement, as well as the leather armchair used by Winston Churchill, who was a regular customer. Almost as old is D. R. Harris at Number 29, which has been chemist to the Court and its dignitaries since 1790 and retains many of its original fixtures.

Continuing around the corner onto Jermyn Street, shirtmaker, hosier and glover Turnbull & Asser at Numbers 71–72 has been dressing royalty, politicians and film stars since 1885 (one of Winston Churchill's famous 'Siren Suits' is displayed in the basement). The gents' hatmaker Bates is opposite at Number 37 and has provided bespoke homburgs and boaters since 1902. Even the shop mascot, a stuffed cat called Binks, wears a top hat!

Farther along at Number 89 is Floris the perfumer, where change is still given on velvet-covered mahogany change-pads. Paxton & Whitfield at Number 93 is Britain's oldest cheese shop founded in 1742, and the first place in London to sell Stilton. The tour concludes with the family-owned shirtmaker Harvie & Hudson at Numbers 96–97.

James J. Fox is where Churchill purchased his cigars

Central London's other specialist retailers include the long-established clerical outfitters J. Wippell & Co. at 11 Tufton Street (SW1), the barber Geo. F. Trumper at 9 Curzon Street (W1), the gunsmiths Holland & Holland at 34 Bruton Street (W1), and the walking stick and umbrella manufacturer James Smith & Sons at 53 New Oxford Street (WC1), where Prime Minister William Gladstone (1809–1898) purchased his brollies. Smith's Victorian premises are wonderfully well-preserved with painted glass advertisements promoting dagger canes and sword sticks!

Other places of interest nearby: 65, 76, 79

79 Bolt-holes for Bookworms

SW1Y 4LG (St. James's), a tour of bookshops and libraries including the London Library at 14 St. James's Square
Bakerloo, Piccadilly lines to Piccadilly Circus; Jubilee, Piccadilly, Victoria lines to Green Park (note: daily, weekly, or annual membership is necessary to visit the London Library)

London has many bolt-holes for bookworms and some are very special places indeed. Take, for example, Maggs Bros. at 50 Berkeley Square (W1). Located in a Georgian townhouse in the heart of Mayfair this firm has been purveying rare books and manuscripts since 1853. The historic premises retain their Robert Adam fireplaces, tiled pantries, and cast-iron kitchen range, so it's little wonder the place is said to be haunted.

Around the corner at 10 Curzon Street (W1) is another storied bookseller. G. Heywood Hill opened his eponymous shop in the 1930s only to face closure in 1942 when he was conscripted. Fortunately a group of loyal helpers kept the business running in his absence. They included the novelist Nancy Mitford (1904–1973), whose own books were inspired by the group of young bohemian aristocrats and socialites known as the Bright Young Things, with whom she kept company.

The oldest London bookshop is Hatchards not far away at 187 Piccadilly (W1). Trading here since 1797 the shop resembles a small country house, with six floors of rooms clustered around a grand central staircase. Lord Byron and Oscar Wilde were regulars and the shop boasts three Royal Warrants. Equally atmospheric is Sotheran's across the road at 2–5 Sackville Street (W1), the longest established antiquarian bookseller in the world. In the same area, too, are the original headquarters of Penguin Books at 8 Vigo Street (W1), where a plaque records how in 1935 founder Allen Lane published the world's first paperbacks and "changed reading habits throughout the English-speaking world."

Booklovers in need of respite from the busy West End should visit the London Library at 14 St. James's Square (SW1). This independent lending library was founded by the Scottish writer Thomas Carlyle (1795–1881) after he became frustrated at the lack of seating (not to mention the snoring and spitting!) at the British Museum Library. With its eccentric classifications, encouragement of browsing, and long loan periods it has been a haven for the city's literati since 1841. Famous faces scrutinising the shelves have included Tennyson, T. S. Eliot, and Tom Stoppard, and from the world of fiction, James Bond and Conan Doyle's Doctor Watson.

With men so prominent it seems only right that in 2002 the London Library got its first female librarian. Elsewhere in London, women and books have gone hand-in-hand for far longer. The Women's Library in the London School of Economics and Political Science at 10 Portugal Street (WC2) was established in 1926. It houses Europe's largest collection of books, photographs and other media charting the role of women throughout history. The location is a pertinent one being the former site of the headquarters of the Women's Social and Political Union – known popularly as the Suffragettes – which was founded in 1903 by Emmeline Pankhurst (1858–1928).

The London Library in St. James's Square is a paradise for booklovers

Someone who took a dim view of libraries was the playwright Joe Orton (1933–1967): he described them as having "endless shelves for rubbish and hardly any space for good books." Despite this he was not averse to stealing library books and removing pages to decorate his Islington bedsit! Orton and his partner Kenneth Halliwell enjoyed defacing library books, too, until they were arrested. The books retrieved by police are today the pride of Islington Local History Centre in Finsbury Library at 245 St. John Street (EC1), where samples can be viewed in the downstairs museum.

Other places of interest nearby: 65, 66, 78

80 History Ahoy!

SW1A 2HR (Westminster), a tour of historic ships on the
Thames beginning with the PS *Tattershall Castle* moored
on Victoria Embankment behind Whitehall
Bakerloo, Circle, District, Northern lines to Embankment

A novel way to enjoy the Thames is to tour the historic vessels moored along its banks. The most famous are HMS *Belfast*, a former Royal Navy light cruiser, and the *Golden Hinde II*, a replica of Sir Francis Drake's famous galleon, both at London Bridge (SE1). But there are others less well-known and a gentle stroll along Victoria Embankment – from Westminster Bridge downstream to Blackfriars Bridge – takes in several of them.

The first is the PS *Tattershall Castle* behind Whitehall (SW1). This paddle steamer built in Hartlepool in 1934 served as a ferry on the Humber between Hull and the village of New Holland in Lincolnshire. During the Second World War she doubled as a tether for barrage balloons and became the first civil vessel to carry radar. Decommissioned in 1974 prior to the inauguration of the Humber Bridge, which rendered the ferry service redundant, she was then towed to London and has served since 1981 as a floating bar and restaurant.

Another former ferry, the twin screw motor vessel *Hispaniola*, lies immediately astern. Launched in 1953 she was one of a quartet of vessels commissioned to modernise the Clyde fleet. As the MV *Maid of Ashton* she plied the Gourock to Holy Loch service for the Caledonian Steam Packet Company until 1971, when the car ferry revolution put her out of work. She was then sold and renamed *Hispaniola* and like the *Tattershall Castle* now serves as a bar and restaurant.

The third historic vessel on this tour is the former Thames cargo barge *Wilfred* moored at Temple Pier (WC2). Built in Greenwich and launched in 1926 to haul sand and ballast she was retired in 1970 and now serves as a party vessel. Also moored here is the former steamship *St. Katharine*. She was commissioned in 1927 by the Port of London Authority as a survey and inspection vessel, which explains the stained-glass window with the motto *Floreat Imperii Portus* (Let the imperial port flourish). Commandeered by the Admiralty during the Second World War she was sent to guard the Medway Channel, and in November 1939 became the first vessel to engage the enemy in the Port of London. After the war she was refitted as a cruise ship to entertain visiting Heads of State, including King Faisal, Benazir Bhutto, and

Leonid Brezhnev. Since her decommission in 1971 she has served as a floating restaurant and club called the Yacht.

Nearby is the HMS *Wellington*, a Grimsby-class Royal Navy sloop launched in 1934. Based initially in the Pacific she served during the Second World War as a convoy escort ship in the North Atlantic. She shared in the destruction of a U-Boat and helped with the evacuation of Allied troops from Dunkirk. In 1948 the Admiralty sold her to the Honourable Company of Master Mariners for use a floating livery company hall, a function she has served admirably ever since (for annual open days visit www.thewellingtontrust.com).

The final vessel on this tour is HMS *President* a little farther downstream. Built as HMS *Saxifrage* in 1918 she was a Flower-class Q-Ship, one of the first vessels built specifically for anti-submarine

HMS *Wellington* helped evacuate troops at Dunkirk, with the City's Walkie-Talkie Tower in the background

warfare. Today she is one of the last three surviving Royal navy warships built during the First World War and serves as an events venue (visits by appointment at www.hmspresident.com).

The view around the *St. Katharine* will change in 2017 if plans for the so-called Garden Bridge reach fruition, a pedestrian footbridge planted with trees and shrubs connecting Temple Tube station and the South Bank Centre.

Other places of interest nearby: 31, 32, 82, 83, 93

81 Whitehall Above and Below

SW1A 2ER (Westminster), Henry VIII's Wine Cellar and the
Banqueting House on Whitehall
Circle, District, Jubilee lines to Westminster

A stroll along Whitehall (SW1) reveals many of the buildings associated with British Government, including the Cabinet Office and the Ministry of Defence. The Treasury and the Foreign and Commonwealth Office are here, too, and can be visited during Open House London (www.openhouselondon.org.uk). The name 'Whitehall' recalls the Palace of Whitehall that once stood here, which from 1530 until 1698 served as the main London residence of the monarchy. With over 1500 rooms it was bigger than both the Vatican and Versailles and yet today only a few tantalising fragments remain.

From 1049 until the construction of the Palace of Whitehall the monarch resided at the Palace of Westminster. This made the surrounding area highly sought after and in 1240 the Archbishop of York, Walter de Grey (c.1180–1255), also built a home here, which he called York Place. It was so luxurious that Edward I (1272–1307) stayed there whenever work was being carried out at Westminster.

During the 15th century York Place was rebuilt by another Archbishop of York, Thomas Wolsey (1473–1530). As chief advisor to Henry VIII (1509–47) he was one of the most powerful men in England. By the time Wolsey had finished with York Place only Lambeth Palace – the Archbishop of Canterbury's London residence – rivalled it (see no. 88). Not surprisingly when Henry removed Wolsey from power in 1530, following his refusal to annul his marriage to Catherine of Aragon, he acquired York Place for himself. He renamed it the Palace of Whitehall on account of the white stone used in its construction, and set about extending it at great expense. The Palace of Westminster, whilst remaining a royal palace, was used henceforth as the Houses of Parliament (see no. 86).

Of Henry's palace little remains. His tiltyard stood on what is now Horse Guards Parade and his cockpit is today the Cabinet Office, where the gable wall of his indoor tennis court still stands. The most significant survival, however, is the Tudor brick-vaulted undercroft from Wolsey's Great Chamber preserved beneath the Ministry of Defence. Known as Henry VIII's Wine Cellar it would have been lost to redevelopment in the 1930s had it not been carefully encased within a steel frame and painstakingly relocated to the basement of the

Henry VIII's wine cellar is hidden beneath the Ministry of Defence

present building (visits by special arrangement only at www.helm.org. uk, tel. 0044 (0)870 607 4455).

After the reign of Henry further changes were made to the palace by James I (1603–1625). In 1622 he commissioned the Banqueting House on the corner of Whitehall and Horse Guards Avenue to an Italianate design by Inigo Jones (1573–1652). By 1650 the palace was the largest in Europe stretching from Northumberland Avenue all the way to Downing Street, and from Horse Guards Road to the Thames. Two disastrous fires, however, in 1691 and 1698 destroyed it and financial restraints meant it was never rebuilt. Only the Banqueting House survived intact and it can easily be visited today. It includes a vaulted undercroft used by the king as a private drinking den and a ceiling in the Main Hall commissioned from Rubens by Charles I (1625–1649). A bust outside the building marks where Charles was beheaded during the English Civil War, the only king to be publically executed in Britain. The Society of King Charles the Martyr marks the event each 30th January at 11.40am by laying a wreath followed by Mass in the Banqueting House itself (www.skcm.org).

Whitehall is known for its war memorials. They include the Cenotaph, Britain's primary war memorial, and the Monument to the Women of World War II, which was funded in part using money raised by Baroness Boothroyd during an appearance on the television game show *Who Wants to Be a Millionaire?*

Other places of interest nearby: 80, 82, 83, 84

82 A World Famous Front Door

SW1A 2AA (Westminster), the Prime Minister's office and
residence at 10 Downing Street
Circle, District lines to Westminster (note: the property
can only be visited occasionally with places allocated by
public ballot)

Until the 1980s it was possible to stroll along Downing Street and pose
for a photograph outside the Prime Minister's office and residence at
Number 10. These days the threat of terrorism means that sturdy gates
and policemen bar the way. The famous front door has consequently
disappeared from view only increasing curiosity about its history and
what it conceals.

The first house constructed on the site was leased by Elizabeth I
(1558–1603) to the nobleman Sir Thomas Knyvet (1545–1622). He
made his name in 1605 by arresting Guy Fawkes in the cellars of the
Houses of Parliament. After Knyvet's death the house passed to his
niece, Elizabeth Hampden, whose son was a leading Parliamentarian
and opponent of Charles I (1625–1649). Whilst living at the house
she witnessed not only the ensuing English Civil War (1641–1651) and
execution of the king but also the Protectorship of Oliver Cromwell
(1653–1658) and the eventual Restoration of the monarchy in 1660.

Another witness to these events was the statesman Sir George
Downing (1623–1684). A canny political survivor he worked under
both Cromwell and Charles II (1660–1685). He was also interested in
making money and in 1682, when the royal lease expired on Knyvet's
old home, he purchased the land and erected a terrace of modest,
brick-built houses. It was known thereafter as Downing Street.

The new houses attracted a variety of occupants, including James
Boswell (1740–1795), who penned the biography of Samuel Johnson,
and the Scottish author Tobias Smollett (1721–1771). Then in 1732
George II (1727–1760) purchased the property at Number 10 and presented it to Sir Robert Walpole (1676–1745) in gratitude for his services
as First Lord of the Treasury. It was Walpole who had it connected to an
older and larger house at the rear, which in part explains why the inside
of the property is so much bigger than it appears externally. That and
the fact that these days Number 10 is also connected to Numbers 11 and
12, which serve as the official residence of the Chancellor of the Ex-
chequer and the Prime Minister's Press Office respectively. As a result
the modest front door of Number 10 now leads to around 160 rooms!

The front door of Number 10 is today made of blast-proof steel

The door itself has quite a history. Executed in the Georgian style with a semicircular fanlight it dates from renovations carried out in the 1770s. The door leaf was originally of oak with the number "10" in white numerals. After the IRA launched a mortar attack on the building in 1991 it was replaced by a blast-proof steel door, although it retains the skewed zero dating back to a botched repainting of the original door in 1963 (the original door is now displayed in the Churchill Museum at the Cabinet War Rooms).

Although Number 10 is normally off-limits to the public it can be visited during Open House London (www.openhouselondon.org.uk) with places allocated strictly by public ballot and subject to a background security check.

Escorted tours of the garden at Number 10 created in 1736 by Robert Walpole are also available occasionally as part of London Open Square Weekend. Again places are allocated by public ballot (www.opensquares.org).

Other places of interest nearby: 80, 81, 83, 84

83 Scotland Yard on the Move

SW1A 2JL (Westminster), Scotland Yard in the Curtis Green Building on Victoria Embankment
Circle, District, Jubilee lines to Westminster (note: Scotland Yard is not open to the public)

Scotland Yard has for so long been synonymous with the Met – London's Metropolitan Police Service – that many people have forgotten how it got its name. Similarly the etymology of the various nicknames given to the Met – Cops, Peelers, Bobbies, Old Bill – is also subject to conjecture. With the service in the process of changing address for the third time in its history it seems timely to set the record straight.

London's first professional police force was founded in 1749 by novelist and magistrate Henry Fielding (1707–1754). Dubbed the Bow Street Runners they were attached to Fielding's courthouse at 4 Bow Street (WC2), which paid them to serve writs and arrest offenders. At the time their activities were supplemented by those of unofficial thief-takers, private individuals paid by victims to bring criminals to justice. The term Cop, from the Latin *capere* meaning 'to capture', dates from this period.

By the early 19th century shortcomings in London's policing were causing public concern. A parliamentary committee was appointed and the Home Secretary Sir Robert Peel (1788–1850) was tasked with acting on its findings. He believed in making policing an official paid profession answerable to the public, as a result of which in 1929 the Metropolitan Police Service was created. At the same time blue-coloured uniforms were introduced to distinguish the police from the British military, who at the time wore red and white.

Peel now looked for a suitable headquarters for his force, inevitably nicknamed Peelers or Bobbies in his honour, and settled on a row of houses in Whitehall Place (SW1). They occupied the former site of Great Scotland Yard, where Scottish kings lodged when they visited their English counterparts in London. Although the practice had been discontinued since 1603, when James VI of Scotland (1567–1625) became James I of England (1603–1625), the name stuck.

In 1890 Great Scotland Yard moved to new purpose-built premises in Westminster on land created by the building of Victoria Embankment. The plot was originally earmarked for an opera house but when funds were not forthcoming the Met took it instead. Renamed New Scotland Yard its red brick buildings were designed by the architect

The famous revolving sign outside New Scotland Yard

Norman Shaw (1831–1912), with foundations of Dartmoor granite hewn by convict labour.

In 1967 New Scotland Yard moved to a building on Victoria Street. The famous revolving sign outside the building dates from this time, as probably does the nickname Old Bill, although no-one really knows its etymology (the website of the Met (www.met.police.uk) gives 13 possible explanations!).

Fast forward to 2015 and the Met is returning again to Whitehall to occupy the neo-Classical Curtis Green Building alongside the Norman Shaw building. To avoid confusion the name will now simply be Scotland Yard. They will be accompanied by their grisly collection of crime-related artefacts known as the Black Museum, which is normally only open to the police and associated bodies. It includes execution ropes and death masks of convicts hanged at Newgate, personal possessions belonging to the Great Train Robbery gang, gallstones which failed to dissolve in a 1940s acid bath murder, and the poison pellet used in 1978 to kill Bulgarian dissident Georgi Markov.

To find out more about policing visit the City of London Police Museum at 37 Wood Street (EC2). Exhibits include homemade bombs manufactured by the Suffragettes and a blue-painted call post of a type once common in the City (the streets were considered too narrow for the full-sized boxes made famous in the television series *Doctor Who*).

Other places of interest nearby: 80, 81, 82, 84, 85, 86

84 Bombs and Bunkers

SW1A 2AQ (Westminster), a tour of locations associated with
the First and Second World Wars including the Churchill War
Rooms alongside Clive Steps on King Charles Street
Circle, District lines to St. James's Park; Circle, District,
Jubilee lines to Westminster

Londoners first experienced the horrors of aerial warfare in the First
World War, when German airships made a series of nightime raids that
claimed several hundred lives. During one of them on 9th September
1915 the airship L-13 dropped bombs in a line from Euston to Liverpool
Street. Their impact is recalled today by commemorative plaques in
Queen Square (WC1) and at 59–61 Farringdon Road (EC1), as well as
shrapnel damage outside St. Bartholomew's Hospital on West Smithfield (EC1). More poignant is the rebuilt Dolphin Tavern at 44 Red Lion
Street (WC1), where a battered wall clock pulled from the rubble of the
original building shows the exact time the building was hit.

Twenty five years later the threat of air raids returned to London
with the start of the Second World War. The first bomb fell in August
1940 at the corner of Fore Street and Wood Street (EC2) just prior to
the London Blitz. Between September 1940 and May the following year
the capital would be targeted 71 more times by the German Luftwaffe
killing 20,000 civilians in the process.

The Home Office knew the potential for loss of life was far greater
this time. Accordingly they began constructing London's first purpose-
built air raid shelters. The public initially made do with cramped
surface shelters and strengthened cellars, a reminder being the signs
identifying "Public shelters in vaults under pavements in this street"
stencilled onto houses at Numbers 8 and 16 Lord North Street (SW1).
Civilians were prevented from sheltering in the London Underground,
however, for fear they would not return to work. But as the raids inten-
sified, and civil disobedience spread, so the government was obliged
to open many stations as shelters.

Even the Underground was no guarantee of safety though as demonstrated by an incident at Marble Arch, where a bomb penetrated the
station roof killing 20 people. Such events prompted the decision in
October 1940 to build ten deep-level shelters, five north of the Thames
and five to the south, providing secure accommodation for 80,000 people. Each was to comprise two parallel tunnels up to 430 metres long
containing two levels of bunk accommodation. Access was possible

A sign pointing the way to an air raid shelter in Lord North Street

from adjacent Underground stations or else spiral staircases from the surface, where sturdy concrete block-houses protected the entrances.

By August 1942 eight of the ten deep-level shelters were ready, although the threat of intensive Luftwaffe bombing had by then diminished. Instead those at Chancery Lane (WC2) and Goodge Street (W1) found an alternative use as communications and command posts. Goodge Street was requisitioned by General Dwight D. Eisenhower (1890–1969) in his role as Supreme Allied Commander and used to help coordinate the Normandy Landings in 1944. After the war it served as a troop hostel and later a secure archive, its fortified entrances still visible on Chenies Street and Tottenham Court Road. The Chancery Lane shelter became a Cold War-era international telephone exchange called Kingsway, the freight entrance to which is still marked with an external hoist on Furnival Street.

In addition to civilian shelters there were others created for important personnel, most notably the Prime Minister and his War Cabinet beneath what is now the Treasury on King Charles Street (SW1) in Whitehall. Known as the Cabinet War Rooms this shelter was made operational in August 1939, just days before Britain declared war on Nazi Germany and was just one element in an elaborate network of tunnels and bunkers (today they contain the crisis command centre known as Pindar and the Cabinet Office Briefing Centre COBRA). The shelter lay at the heart of a city-wide network of fortified government

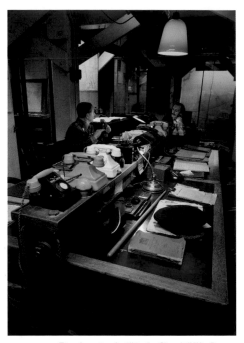
Time has stood still in the Churchill War Rooms

and military centres dubbed 'citadels', with the ivy-clad Admiralty citadel still standing on The Mall.

The Cabinet War Rooms remained in use throughout the Second World War and were only abandoned in August 1945 following the surrender of Japan. Under the auspices of the Imperial War Museum they were reopened in 1984 as a museum known today as the Churchill War Rooms. The key rooms remain much as they were and include the Map Room, where members of the armed forces produced a daily intelligence summary for the King, the Prime Minister and the military Chiefs of Staff, and the Cabinet Room, where Winston Churchill as Prime Minister convened a total of 115 Cabinet meetings. Other important rooms include the Translatlantic telephone Room, where Churchill could speak securely with President Roosevelt in Washington, and Churchill's office-bedroom from where he made several wartime broadcasts.

There are many types of war memorial in London. Best known are the impressive bronzes around Wellington Arch, along Whitehall, and outside the Ministry of Defence on Victoria Embankment. Others are more intimate, including a bust on Albert Embankment (SW1) to Violette Szabo (1921–1945), the former Brixton shop assistant executed by the Germans for spying in occupied France, and the Kindertransport memorial outside Liverpool Street Station (EC2), recalling the Jewish children who found a safe haven in Britain away from Nazi persecution. London's sole Nazi-era memorial is the gravestone of German ambassador Leopold von Hoesch's dog, Giro, alongside the former German embassy at 7 Carlton House Terrace (SW1).

Other places of interest nearby: 81, 82, 83, 85, 86

85 The Abbey on Thorney Island

SW1P 3PA (Westminster), Westminster Abbey in Dean's Yard
Circle, District, Jubilee lines to Westminster

On 7th January 1928 central London suffered its last major flood. Melting snow in the Cotswolds, where the Thames finds its source, combined with an unusually high spring tide caused the river to pour over the top of Victoria Embankment. One of the unexpected consequences of the flooding was the reappearance in Westminster of the 'lost' River Tyburn, which had been culverted several centuries earlier (see no. 56). It was a graphic reminder that Westminster Abbey, Britain's largest church, once stood on an island!

Despite persistent legends to the contrary the Abbey finds its origins in the 960s, when King Edgar (959–975) installed a community of Benedictine monks on Thorn Ey, a bramble-covered islet in a delta formed

Nicholas Hawksmoor's towers were a late addition to Westminster Abbey

where the Tyburn flowed into the Thames. The monks subsequently tamed and drained the land sufficiently to allow England's penultimate Saxon king, Edward the Confessor (1042–1066), to rebuild the Abbey, together with Westminster Palace nearby. At the prompting of the pope he named it in honour of Saint Peter and he was buried there shortly after its consecration (the only English monarch ever canonised his tomb sits behind the altar). In 1066 the first Norman king of England, William the Conqueror (1066–1087), was crowned at the Abbey, setting a precedent that continues to this day (since 1308 all monarchs have been crowned on the Abbey's Coronation Chair, which until 1996 contained the much-travelled Stone of Scone).

In the cloisters at Westminster Abbey

Construction of the present building was initiated by Henry III (1216–1272), with work on the 31-metre high nave completed during the following century. Note the *Triforium* beneath the rose window, a high-level arcade running around the nave providing what John Betjeman called "the greatest view in Europe" (plans are afoot to open it to visitors in 2017). Today the nave contains many of the Abbey's 600 or so memorials, including Poets Corner in the south transept, a clutch of politicians inside the north porch, and the Unknown Warrior by the west door (the painting of Richard II (1377–1399) facing the door is the earliest known portrait of a living monarch). Many visitors are surprised to learn that the two towers fronting the nave were only completed in 1745 to designs by Nicholas Hawksmoor (1661–1736).

The Chapter House completed in 1259 boasts the country's finest medieval tiled floor, with Britain's oldest door displayed near its entrance, and is where the early House of Commons convened before relocating to Westminster Palace (see no. 86). The addition in 1512 of Henry VII's Lady Chapel completed the main structure of the Abbey seen today, its superb fan vaulted ceiling representing the climax of English Gothic. It has been described as having the "wonderful minuteness and airy security of a cobweb".

Monastic life at Westminster ended when Henry VIII (1509–1547) dissolved the monastery and declared the building a cathedral. Later in 1560 Elizabeth I (1558–1603) established the Collegiate Church of St Peter at Westminster – to give the Abbey its correct name – and made it a Royal Peculiar, namely a church falling under the jurisdiction of the monarch rather than a bishop, whilst remaining within the Church of England.

Away from the main building lie the Abbey cloisters. They provide access to an 11th-century vaulted undercroft containing an extraordinary collection of royal funerary effigies. Dressed in actual clothes taken from the monarch's Great Wardrobe they demonstrate how much smaller people were in medieval times. The delightful Little Cloister leads to College Garden, which was laid out by the original Benedictine monks. As such it is the oldest garden in England.

Amongst the Abbey's traditions is the distribution by the monarch of specially-minted Maundy Money to as many elderly people as the monarch's age. The ceremony takes place on the Thursday before Easter once every ten years and can be attended by prior arrangement (www.westminster-abbey.org). In intervening years the ceremony takes place in other English cathedrals.

Westminster Abbey may hold the record for Britain's loftiest church nave but that of widest goes to Westminster Cathedral (18 metres) on Ambrosden Avenue (SW1). As London's Catholic cathedral it was built between 1895 and 1903 and features Byzantine-style copper roof domes and striped brickwork. A lift takes visitors up the 83-metre high belfry at the top of which is a bell named Big Edward.

Other places of interest nearby: 84, 86

86 The First Parliament

SW1A 0AA (Westminster), the Houses of Parliament on
St. Margaret Street (Cromwell Green entrance)
Circle, District, Jubilee lines to Westminster (note: guided
tours are by appointment only)

England has a long tradition of monarchs discussing important matters with their subjects. Anglo-Saxon kings consulted the *Witenagemot* (Meeting of Wise Men), the Normans the *Curia Regis* (King's Council), and post-Conquest kings the *Magnum Concilium* (Great Council). Membership of these bodies, however, was restricted to nobles and church leaders. The emergence of a more broad-based Parliament – from the French *Parlement* meaning 'discussion' – only emerged in 1295, when Edward I (1272–1307) admitted elected representatives from the country's counties and boroughs.

By the reign of Edward III (1327–1377) Parliament had separated into two distinct chambers: the House of Lords (nobles and clergy) and the House of Commons (shire and borough representatives). Gradually assuming its modern form it sought progressively to limit the power of the monarchy. This process culminated in the English Civil War (1642–1651) and the execution of Charles I (1625–1649). With the Restoration of the monarchy under Charles II (1660–1685) the supremacy of Parliament was established and the role of monarch reduced to one of reigning rather than ruling.

Parliament has always convened in the Palace of Westminster. Built in the 11th century by Edward the Confessor (1042–1066) the palace remained a royal residence until its destruction by fire in 1512, after which Henry VIII (1509–1547) relocated the Court to the Palace of Whitehall (see no. 81). Whilst the Lords met in various chambers in the palace, the Commons made do with the Chapter House in Westminster Abbey, only moving to St. Stephen's Chapel in the palace after it was secularised in 1547. All was lost when another fire destroyed the palace in 1834 leaving only the crypt beneath St. Stephen's (known as the Chapel of St. Mary Undercroft), the Jewel Tower and Westminster Hall intact. With its superb hammerbeam roof installed in 1393, Westminster Hall served as the Royal Courts of Justice from the time of Henry II (1154–1189) until the late 19th century, when they were relocated to the Strand (WC2).

These remains (with the exception of the detached Jewel Tower) were incorporated into the New Palace of Westminster (SW1) built

Big Ben is the defining element of the Houses of Parliament

on the same site between 1840 and 1870. Commonly known as the Houses of Parliament, and containing over a thousand rooms, it was designed by Charles Barry (1795–1860), with Neo-Gothic interiors by Augustus Pugin (1812–1852). It is punctuated at either end by a tower: the Victoria Tower contains a record of every law passed since the 11th century and the Elizabeth Tower contains a clock reached by 334 spiral steps. Although the clock is known by most as Big Ben, this name actually refers specifically to the clock's hour bell.

A third tower at the centre of the building rises above the Central Lobby, which separates the chambers of the Lords and Commons. Both chambers feature on the official tour of the Houses of Parliament, which also takes in the remains of the Old Palace, as well as the Robing Room, where the monarch dresses for the annual State Opening of Parliament. Traditions associated with this important event include the Yeoman of the Guard searching the cellars for would-be Guy Fawkeses, the summoning of MPs from the Commons by an usher called Black Rod, and the delivery of a Parliamentary hostage to Buckingham Palace to ensure the monarch's safe return!

The Chapel of St. Mary Undercroft was restored to its medieval splendour in 1860 by Charles Barry's son, Edward (1830–1880). He was also responsible for the equally glitzy Neo-Byzantine St. Christopher's Chapel at Great Ormond Street Hospital (WC1).

Other places of interest nearby: 84, 85

87 A Celebration of English Gardening

SE1 7LB (Lambeth), the Garden Museum on Lambeth
Palace Road
Bakerloo line to Lambeth North; Victoria line to Vauxhall;
Bakerloo, Jubilee, Northern and Waterloo & City line to
Waterloo; Circle, District, Jubilee lines to Westminster

London's green spaces come in all shapes and sizes, and many of them
have ancient origins. From the intimate squares of Bloomsbury to the
sprawling Royal Parks they help make London the greenest major city
in Europe. To dig deeper into Britain's unique love affair with gardening visit the Garden Museum on Lambeth Palace Road (SE1).

The museum is located in the former parish Church of St Mary-at-
Lambeth, constructed originally in the 12th century to serve nearby
Lambeth Palace, the London residence of the Archbishop of Canterbury (see no. 88). After the church was deconsecrated in 1972 because
of depopulation it was visited by the museum's founder, Rosemary
Nicholson, who came looking for the tomb of the renowned garden-
ers and plant hunters, John Tradescant the Elder (c. 1570–1638) and
Younger (1608–1662). Appalled to find the church thereatened with
demolition she established the Tradescant Trust, which was awarded
a 99-year lease on the building from the Diocese of Southwark. Following the Trust's repair of the church it was reopened in 1977 as the
world's first museum of garden history.

Visiting the museum is a delightful experience, and the old churchyard provides the perfect setting. In 1983 a garden in memory of the
Tradescants was unveiled here by HM Queen Elizabeth, the Queen
Mother. Designed by then museum president, the Dowager Marchion-
ess of Salisbury, it takes the form of an Elizabethan Knot garden, with
the Tradescants' ornately carved tomb alongside it (note also the grave
of William Bligh (1754–1815) of *Bounty* fame, who lived nearby). Out-
lined with clipped box hedges, the garden is planted with species introduced by the Tradescants including the scarlet runner bean, red maple
and tulip tree.

The church tower is the oldest extant structure in the Borough
of Lambeth other than the crypt of Lambeth Palace. The rest of the
church, however, was rebuilt in Victorian times, and includes a rare
total immersion font and various ornaments donated by Sir Henry

This Knot Garden is a lovely feature of the Garden Museum in Lambeth

Doulton (the remains of his ceramic factory can be found nearby on Black Prince Road). Against this historic backdrop the museum and an exhibition space have been installed. On display are items of antique gardening equipment (including a Victorian cucumber straightener and a Sweet Pea seed counter), an important early 20th century painting of an unknown black gardener, and a rare copy of the 17th century catalogue of the Tradescants' cabinet of curiosities – the Musaeum Tradescantianum – which they installed in their now demolished Lambeth home. It was in the garden there that they are first thought to have hybridised the now ubiquitous London plane tree four centuries ago.

Two little-known London gardens can be mentioned here. The tiny Red Cross Garden on Redcross Way (SE1) was laid out in 1887 by Victorian philanthropist Octavia Hill (1838–1912) on the site of a derelict paper factory. She designed it as an open-air sitting room for those living in Southwark's insanitary slums (the Guinness Trust Buildings not far away on Snowsfields were erected a decade later to re-house such people and offered outside toilets, shared bathrooms and gas lighting). The gate bedecked with ribbons at the northern end of Redcross Way marks the site of Cross Bones Graveyard, where 15,000 of the area's paupers and prostitutes – the so-called 'Winchester Geese' – were buried on unconsecrated land from medieval until Victorian times (see page 2).
Sharing a similarly philanthropic ethos is the Phoenix Garden in St. Giles Passage, off New Compton Street (WC2). This community garden was created by local volunteers in 1984 on the site of a former car park and provides a green retreat for those with nerves frayed by London's West End.

Other places of interest nearby: 88

At Home with the Archbishop

SE1 7JU (Lambeth), Lambeth Palace on Lambeth Palace Road
Waterloo & City line to Waterloo; Circle, District, Jubilee lines
to Westminster (note: guided tours by appointment only)

Morton's Tower guards the entrance to Lambeth Palace

Lambeth Palace on the southern bank of the Thames is one of London's great unsung attractions. What a shame that people sometimes cross to this side of the river only to get a better view of the Houses of Parliament on the other (see no. 86)! As the official London residence since the late 12th century of the Archbishops of Canterbury, Lambeth Palace offers some equally fascinating history and architecture, which makes a visit here an unexpected delight.

The palace is entered through Morton's Tower, one of London's few surviving Tudor buildings. Built in 1490 by Archbishop Morton (1420–1500) it is regarded as the finest early Tudor brick gatehouse in England. In the courtyard beyond is the Great Hall rebuilt in 1663 by Archbishop Juxon (1582–1663) after being ransacked by Cromwellian troops during the English Civil War (1642–1651). Featuring a superb hammerbeam roof it contains the Lambeth Palace Library, with Church of England records stretching back to the 12th century. Its treasures include the Norman illuminated *Lambeth Bible*, a rare *Gutenberg Bible* printed in the 1450s, and a first edition of Thomas More's *Utopia* illustrated by

Holbein. Also exhibited here are the gloves given to Archbishop Juxon by Charles I (1625–1649) before his execution.

Alongside the Great Hall is the 14th century Guard Room, which reflects an age when the powerful and wealthy Archbishops required protection. The palace has been attacked numerous times in its history, including during the Peasants' Revolt of 1381, when Archbishop Sudbury (1316–1381) was executed for raising taxes. It was in the Guard Room that Thomas More (1478–1535) was arrested and later executed for refusing to deny the authority of the Pope in favour of Henry VIII (1509–1547) as head of the Church of England. Light relief is provided here by the shell of Archbishop Laud's tortoise, which lived in the palace garden from 1633 until 1753!

Beyond the Guard Room is a corridor leading to the Neo-Gothic Blore Building of 1833 containing the incumbent Archbishop's State Rooms. It also leads to the Chapel, which dates from the 13th century, although it is heavily restored. It was here in 1378 that the theologian John Wycliffe (1320–1384) was detained on charges of opposing papal authority. His translation of the *Bible* into vernacular English spawned the Lollardy movement, a precursor to the Protestant Reformation, which preached in favour of clerical reform. Several Lollardists were imprisoned in Lollard's Tower at the north-west corner of the palace, where the iron rings to which they were chained are still in place.

The only burial at Lambeth is that of Archbishop Parker (1504–1575) in front of the chapel altar. He was allegedly dubbed Nosey Parker by Elizabeth I (1558–1603) on account of his inquisitive nature. In 1559 in a small room overlooking the altar Archbishop Cranmer (1489–1556) authored his *Book of Common Prayer*.

Beneath the Chapel is the Crypt, the oldest part of the palace constructed around 1220, with a superbly vaulted ceiling supported on three columns of Purbeck marble. Now also serving as a chapel it was used originally to store beer and wine.

The tour concludes with a brief visit to the palace garden, where Archbishop Parker's remains were unceremoniously dumped during the period of the Commonwealth (1649–1660). It is the oldest continuously cultivated garden in London and the second largest private garden after that of Buckingham Palace. Don't miss Britain's oldest fig tree growing against the outside of the Great Hall. It is said to have been planted by Cardinal Pole (1500–1558), the last Roman Catholic Archbishop of Canterbury.

Other places of interest nearby: 87, 91

89 War and a Little Peace

SE1 6HZ (Lambeth), the Imperial War Museum
on Lambeth Road
Bakerloo line to Lambeth North; Bakerloo, Northern lines
to Elephant & Castle

Positioned in front of the Imperial War Museum on Lambeth Road (SE1) are two huge naval guns. Looking up at them incites mixed emotions. Whilst such weaponry has been used to bring down totalitarian regimes it is difficult not to have some sympathy with the Liberal MP Joseph Kenworthy (1886–1953), who opposed the museum's creation by refusing "to vote a penny of public money to commemorate such suicidal madness of civilisation".

Despite Kenworthy's protestations the Imperial War Museum opened in 1920 in the Crystal Palace at Sydenham. It moved to its present site in Lambeth in 1936. Kenworthy would undoubtedly have found it ironic, however, that the museum occupies the former premises of the Bethlem Royal Hospital, Europe's first mental asylum, whence the name 'Bedlam' is derived.

Founded originally to document the British Empire's involvement in the First World War, the museum's remit has since expanded to include all subsequent conflicts in which British or Commonwealth forces have been involved, and to encourage an understanding of the history and experience of modern warfare. Fulfilling this remit has meant overhauling the collections as Britain's military role in the world has evolved.

Nowhere is this more apparent than in the Atrium, which until recently contained a miscellany of military hardware described by one onlooker as "the biggest boys' bedroom in London". In 2013 the space was decluttered and now features what the museum calls its *Witnesses to War*. These include a Supermarine Spitfire and a V-2 rocket, as well as objects from more recent conflicts, notably the wreckage of a car destroyed during the Iraq War and a Reuters Land Rover damaged during a rocket attack in Gaza.

Ranged around the Atrium are four floors' worth of objects and associated media illustrating themes such as espionage, terrorism, and the family in wartime. Here it is often the mundane things that prove the most poignant: the sick bag issued to British troops on D-Day 6th June 1944, the George Cross given to the man who saved St. Paul's Cathedral by removing a German bomb, and a frag-

Military hardware displayed in the Atrium of the Imperial War Museum

ment of twisted steel retrieved from the rubble of the World Trade Center.

Two displays warrant special attention. The First World War Galleries are the most comprehensive in the world and at their heart is a recreated trench conveying what it was like to fight at the Front. Meanwhile the horrors of the Second World War are nowhere better illustrated than in the Holocaust Exhibition. Tracing the Nazi persecution of Europe's Jews from 1933 to 1945 it is impossible not to be moved by the discarded shoes, torn clothes, and children's toys.

After so much war a little peace is necessary, so it is entirely fitting that in 1999 the 14th Dalai Lama opened the Tibetan Peace Garden in the museum grounds. Its purpose is to provide a sanctuary for those wishing to reflect on the need for non-violent solutions to the world's problems. It also serves to promulgate the virtues of Buddhism, which explains the bronze *Mandala* at the centre of the garden. An inscribed pillar based on one in Lhasa acknowledges the rights of both Tibet and China to co-exist peacefully.

The Bethlem Royal Hospital occupied two previous locations before it moved in 1815 to Lambeth. Originally it stood on the site of Liverpool Street Station (EC2), where tunnelling for Crossrail in 2013 revealed skeletons from one of London's first extra parochial cemeteries, which replaced the hospital when it moved in the 17th century to nearby Moorfields. The hospital is today based at Monks Orchard near Croydon.

Other places of interest nearby: 91

90 Goldfinger's Crowning Glory

SE1 6BB (Elephant & Castle), Metro Central Heights
at 119 Newington Causeway
Bakerloo, Northern lines to Elephant & Castle

It's been a long time since the notoriously busy Elephant and Castle roundabout was part of rural Surrey, its rents supplying the monks of Canterbury with clothing. The curious name is derived from an 18th century tavern built on the site of a cutler's workshop. Cutlery handles were made of elephant ivory, and the 'castle' was probably the carriage or *howdah* used on an elephant's back The coat of arms of London's Worshipful Company of Cutlers features the same device.

At the time of writing plans are afoot to make the much-maligned roundabout a more people friendly place, which is good news for motorists since it has long boasted the greatest number of traffic collisions of any London junction. Pedestrians are pleased because they will be able to negotiate the roundabout *overground* rather than by means of gloomy subways. Plans also envisage restoring the Elephant as a major urban hub, a role it fulfilled before the Second World War, when it was a vibrant shopping and entertainment centre known as the Piccadilly of South London. What wasn't destroyed by German bombs was mostly swept away during wholesale redevelopment in the early 1960s.

The buildings that replaced the old department stores and cinema houses were typical of 1960s concrete Brutalism, with the Elephant and Castle Shopping Centre unveiled in 1965 a case in point. Despite being Europe's first American-style shopping mall it eventually had to be painted bright pink to lure in customers. Its critics consider it an example of London's failed postwar social projects and welcome its impending demolition to make way for housing, a fate already suffered by the nearby Heygate Estate. Others, however, will mourn the loss of community this will bring, the centre's various cafés, pubs, bingo hall and bowling alley each boasting a loyal clientele.

The Michael Faraday Memorial installed on the roundabout in 1961 has fared better, indeed it was listed in 1996. Consisting of a large stainless steel box it contains an electrical substation for the Northern and Bakerloo Tube lines. What better way to remember the local son who discovered electromagnetism (see no. 52).

Overlooking the memorial is another survivor from the sixties. Bounded by Newington Causeway and New Kent Road, Alexander

Fleming House was one of the largest and most lauded office complexes in Europe when it was completed in 1967. Consisting of four main blocks with linking bridges it was designed by the Hungarian modernist architect Ernő Goldfinger (1902–1997). The complex originally housed the Ministry of Health (hence it being named after the discoverer of Penicillin) and was considered by the architect to be his crowning glory (see no. 52). For others, however, it was an example of the soulless high-rise developments that blighted South London in the postwar period. Ironically Goldfinger preferred to live in his low-rise Modernist home in Hampstead. One of his neighbours there was the author Ian Fleming, who so disliked Goldfinger's work that he named a James Bond villain after him!

This office block by Ernő Goldfinger is now called Metro Central Heights

When Alexander Fleming House was vacated in 1989 it was reinvented as a fashionable residential address for young urbanites. As Metro Central Heights its subsequent Grade II listing has gone some way to endorsing Goldfinger's controversial vision for postwar London. As an émigré he would have approved of the ethnic diversity for which the area is now also gaining a reputation.

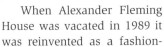

The Pullens Estate on nearby Amelia Street represents some of the last surviving Victorian tenements in London. After narrowly avoiding demolition in the 1980s it is now protected and was used in the film *The King's Speech*.

91 The Necropolis Railway

SE1 7HR (Waterloo), the former London Necropolis Railway
station at 121 Westminster Bridge Road
Bakerloo line to Lambeth North; Bakerloo, Jubilee, Northern,
Waterloo & City lines to Waterloo (note: the building is not
open to the public)

A curious building stands at 121 Westminster Bridge Road (SE1) not far from Waterloo Station. Rising four storeys with an elaborate façade it features an unusually wide entrance. There is nothing to suggest why this should be and only a trawl through the history books provides an answer. It once gave access to the London Necropolis Railway.

The origins of the London Necropolis Railway date back to the early Victorian period, when the city's population more than doubled, and with it the demand for burial space. Existing medieval parish churchyards were becoming so congested that bodies were often buried one on top of another. The churchyard of St. Botolph's-without-Aldersgate, for example, eventually rose several metres above the surrounding streets! The potential health hazards were highlighted by an outbreak of cholera in 1848, as a result of which a Royal Commission was established to investigate the problem. It was revealed that each year 20,000 adults and 30,000 children were being buried in barely a square kilometre of existing burial grounds. Gravediggers were forced to dismember old bodies in order to cram new ones into what little space remained.

In the wake of these findings the Burials Act of 1852 was passed. Under its terms further burials in the built-up areas of London were prohibited and seven new cemeteries were to be created in the suburbs, including Highgate, Nunhead, and Kensal Green. The London Necropolis Company (LNC), however, looked further ahead envisaging a time when all burials could be made in a single out-of-town cemetery. Accordingly in 1854 they opened Brookwood Cemetery in the Surrey countryside, where land was cheap and plentiful, and connected it to London by means of the Necropolis Railway. With little chance of it ever being affected by urban growth, the LNC believed that Brookwood could accommodate 50,000 funerals a year – and would continue doing so forever.

As the starting point for its railway the LNC selected a site near Waterloo Station. Corpses could easily be brought here by road and river, the existing lines of the London & South Western Railway (LSWR) could be used, and the anxieties of mourners eased since at the time the outward journey was largely through scenic open country. All that was needed was a private station at either end.

The station in London was constructed off York Road, abutting the arches of an LSWR viaduct. Coffins were hoisted by steam lift to the elevated platform, where they were then loaded onto waiting funeral trains bound for Brookwood. When Waterloo Station was enlarged in the 1890s this station was demolished and replaced by the one on Westminster Bridge Road. First class mourners arrived through the wide entrance still visible today and reached the platform by lift. Third class mourners entered through a rear entrance on Newnham Terrace and used stairs. Glass screens and distinct waiting areas ensured the classes remained segregated.

Passers-by ignore the former entrance to the London Necropolis Railway

The new station continued to service funeral traffic until it was badly damaged during an air raid in 1941. By this time usage of Brookwood had fallen far short of the LNC's original projections. The London Necropolis Railway was never used again and what had been touted as London's foremost cemetery went into terminal decline. The old station entrance on Westminster Bridge Road now serves as offices with part of the elevated track still visible on Newnham Terrace to the rear.

At the junction of Westminster Bridge Road and Kennington Road is the Lincoln Memorial Tower, a church spire erected in 1876 to mark the anniversary of American independence. The red and white stonework echoes the 'stars and stripes' of the American flag.

Other places of interest nearby: 88, 89, 92

92 The Lady with the Lamp

SE1 7EW (Lambeth), the Florence Nightingale Museum at 2 Lambeth Palace Road
Bakerloo, Jubilee, Northern, Waterloo & City lines to Waterloo; Circle, District, Jubilee lines to Westminster

To witness London's habit of aggrandising its heroes visit Waterloo Place (W1). Set against a Regency backdrop by architect John Nash (1752–1835) are imposing monuments to the Duke of York, Edward VII, several explorers, and sundry half-forgotten lords. Particularly impressive is the Guards' Memorial recalling the fallen of the Crimean War (1854–56). It is fronted by statues of then Secretary at War, Sidney Herbert (1810–1861), and the nurse Florence Nightingale (1820–1910). Unusually Florence is depicted clutching an oil lamp rather than the Turkish-style lantern or *Fanoos* with which she actually tended soldiers wounded in the war against Russia. The sculptor's error may have arisen because she was known in contemporary media as the Lady with the Lamp. Whatever the truth, her real lantern is now exhibited in the Florence Nightingale Museum at 2 Lambeth Palace Road (SE1).

Florence Nightingale was born into a wealthy British family in a villa in Florence. Named after her place of birth she was just a year old when her parents relocated to England, where she was raised a devout Anglican. It was there aged 17 that she first sensed a calling to devote her life to helping others.

Initially Florence honoured her mother's wishes for her not to pursue a career at all. However, in 1844 she revealed her determination to enter nursing. Three years later she met Sidney Herbert in Rome and it was through him that she and a staff of 38 other female nurses were permitted to go to the Crimea to help the war effort. Under difficult conditions Florence quickly made a name for herself as a compassionate and diligent nurse, renowned for making her ward rounds at night with her famous lantern.

If Florence had any failing at all it was wrongly citing malnutrition and cramped living conditions as the reason for the high mortality rates in military hospitals. Following her return to England, however, she came to understand that the real cause was poor sanitation. Sanitary design was therefore uppermost in her mind when in 1860 she founded the Nightingale School for Nurses at the Old St. Thomas's Hospital in Southwark (see no. 97). The world's first secular nursing school it enabled her to lay the foundations of the nursing profession as it exists today.

It was on Florence's recommendation that St. Thomas's was relocated to Lambeth, where it still operates as a major teaching hospital. The Florence Nightingale Museum is located there, too, and illustrates not only the many contributions Florence made to improving healthcare at home and abroad but also to improving the lot of working women. Alongside Florence's lantern can be seen the slate she used as a child, her stuffed pet owl Athena, and examples of the many medical tracts she wrote in simple English so they could be understood by nurses with poor literary skills.

The Turkish-style lantern used by Florence Nightingale in the Crimea

Outside the museum at the end of Westminster Bridge is a stone lion that once adorned a nearby brewery. Close scrutiny reveals it is not carved but rather cast using a man-made material called Coade's Artificial Stone. Perfected in 1769 by a firm operating where the Royal Festival Hall now stands it was designed to withstand London's corrosive atmosphere. Other examples of the use of Coade Stone include the sculptures on the Royal Opera House in Covent Garden and the statues on the front of Sir John Soane's house in Holborn (see no. 38).

Other places of interest nearby: 91

93 A Tonic for the Nation

SE1 8XX (Waterloo), the Royal Festival Hall
on Belvedere Road
Bakerloo, Circle, District, Northern lines to Embankment;
Bakerloo, Jubilee, Northern, Waterloo & City lines to Waterloo
(note: access to the auditorium is by ticket only)

During the summer of 1951 the Festival of Britain was staged by the Labour government of Clement Attlee (1883–1967). Its aim was to give the nation a feeling of recovery in the aftermath of war and to showcase the new principles of urban design that would be used to rebuild the country. The Festival's centrepiece was the South Bank Exhibition on a swathe of former industrial land between County Hall and Waterloo Bridge. Here British advances in science, technology and industrial design were demonstrated in a series of Modernist structures the likes of which had never been seen in London.

Described at the time as "a tonic for the nation" the South Bank Exhibition drew 8.5 million visitors in five months. Popular highlights included the Dome of Discovery, the 90-metre high Skylon, the Telecinema, and the Royal Festival Hall. Unfortunately the Festival became a party political issue too and any thoughts Labour had of benefitting from its success were dashed when Winston Churchill's Conservatives were returned to power at the end of the year. His first act as Prime Minister was to dismantle the exhibition, which he deemed Socialist propaganda!

Only the Royal Festival Hall on Belvedere Road (SE1) was spared. Its architectural importance was recognised in 1988, when it became Britain's first post-war building to receive Grade I listing. The building is unashamedly modern, which is not surprising considering only young architects were tasked with designing it. Chief amongst them was 39 year old Leslie Martin (1908–2000), who designed the building as an "egg in a box", a term he used to describe the separation of the 2,900-seat auditorium from the surrounding building so as to insulate it from the noise and vibration of the adjacent railway line. The conductor Sir Thomas Beecham (1879–1961) used a similar but less favourable analogy when he compared it to a "giant chicken coop"!

During the 1960s the building was altered substantially by the addition of various foyers, riverside terraces, and raised concrete walkways serving the newly-built Queen Elizabeth Hall, Purcell Room, and Hayward Gallery. Like the Royal Festival Hall these facilities are also constructed of reinforced concrete and glass. Loved and loathed in equal measure there is no escaping the fact that together they form Europe's largest centre for the arts, which since the 1980s has been known as the Southbank Centre.

The Royal Festival Hall underwent further alterations in 2007, when the acoustics of its auditorium were improved and a glass lift installed. Popular with those taking advantage of the hall's 'open foyers' policy, the lift can be used to reach not only the auditorium but also the Skylon Bar & Restaurant on Level 3 and the Poetry Library on Level 5, which contains all Britain's poetry published since 1912.

After leaving the Royal Festival Hall don't forget to visit the undercroft beneath Queen Elizabeth Hall, which

British skateboarding was born here beneath Queen Elizabeth Hall

has been hailed as the birthplace of British skateboarding. Also worth visiting is the BFI Southbank beneath Waterloo Bridge, where more than 2,000 films are screened each year. Beyond on Upper Ground is the National Theatre, an example of 1970s *Béton brut* at its best, with backstage tours available by appointment.

Much of the former site of the Festival of Britain is now covered by Jubilee Gardens, where the London Eye opened in 2000. Reaching a height of 135 metres and supported by an A-frame on one side it is the world's tallest cantilevered Ferris wheel. A trip in one of the 32 glass capsules takes 30 minutes and provides passengers with some breathtaking views.

Other places of interest nearby: 31, 80

94 Mr. Kirkaldy's Testing Works

SE1 0JF (Southwark), the Kirkaldy Testing Museum
at 99 Southwark Street
Jubilee line to Southwark

An old hoist at the Leather Exchange recalls a lost
Bermondsey industry

Victorian South London was once an area packed with different industries. Although long since abandoned they have left some fascinating remains. The former Leather Exchange (1879) at 15 Leathermarket Street (SE1), for example, with its intact external hoists, recalls Bermondsey's leatherworking trade established here because of the area's plentiful running water. The Alaska Factory at 61 Grange Road (SW1), erected in 1869 and rebuilt in the 1930s, housed a seal fur factory, whilst the magnificent Hop Exchange (1868) at 24 Southwark Street is a reminder that Borough was once the centre of London's brewing industry (it is adorned with the white horse of Kent, whence London's hops originated). All three buildings have subsequently been redeveloped as offices, event spaces and accommodation.

Not far from the Hop Exchange is a unique industrial-era location. The Kirkaldy Testing Works at 99 Southwark Street (SE1) was once a global centre for measuring the tensile strength of construction materials. It was founded by the Scottish engineer David Kirkaldy (1820–1897), who as a young man was apprenticed at an iron

The large tensometer at the Kirkaldy Testing Museum

foundry in Glasgow. He quickly moved from factory floor to drawing office, where between 1858 and 1861 he undertook a ground-breaking series of tensile load tests. With the Industrial Revolution in full swing, steel was fast replacing wrought iron, and tests were necessary to better understand the new material's strengths and limitations.

In 1863 and by now an expert in his field Kirkaldy left Glasgow and relocated to London to establish his own testing works. He designed and patented a large hydraulic tensile test machine, or tensometer, which was manufactured in Leeds and sent down to Southwark in 1865. The machine was moved to its present custom-built location in 1874, where visitors can still see it operating today.

Over 14 metres in length and weighing in at 116 tons the tensometer is designed to work horizontally, with the desired load applied by a hydraulic cylinder and ram. With a load capacity of around 450 tons it can test samples up to six metres in length in either tension or compression, and up to eight metres in bending. Crushing, shearing and torsion tests are also possible. Powered originally by high pressure water from the London Hydraulic Power Company the tensometer is now worked by electricity. In deference to the machine's antiquity a load

The inscription over the entrance to Kirkaldy's Testing Works

not exceeding 20 tons is used when breaking specimens for visitors.

Until its closure in the 1960s the Kirkaldy Testing Works tested materials sent from all over the world. Locally they tested parts used in the construction of the Empire Stadium at Wembley (1923) and the Skylon at the Festival of Britain (1951) (see no. 93). Metals suspected of failing were also tested, including the remains of a de Havilland Comet aircraft that crashed off Elba in 1954. Most famously the works tested samples for the official inquiry into the Tay Bridge disaster. The bridge had collapsed during a storm in 1879 claiming the lives of all 75 passengers in a train crossing over it at the time. Using his tensometer Kirkaldy demonstrated categorically that the cast iron lugs used to connect the framework of the bridge to the columns supporting it had failed. Little wonder the phrase "Facts not opinions" is inscribed over the works' entrance!

Members of the Greater London Industrial Archaeology Society first visited the abandoned works in 1974, as a result of which the building and its contents were listed for preservation (the first time in Britain such a joint listing had occurred). The ground floor and basement of the works were subsequently converted into a self-financing museum and the upper floors turned over to offices. Since its opening the museum has become a resting place for numerous other testing machines making it a one-of-a-kind collection.

Around the corner from the old Leather Exchange is the Fashion and Textile Museum at 83 Bermondsey Street (SE1). This cutting edge centre for contemporary fashion, textiles and jewellery is housed in a striking building designed by Mexican architect Ricardo Legorreta (1931–2011).

Other places of interest nearby: 95

95 A Powerful Centre for the Arts

SE1 9TG (Bankside), Tate Modern on Bankside
Central line to St. Paul's; Circle, District lines to Blackfriars;
Jubilee line to Southwark

The cavernous former turbine hall at Tate Modern

Since 2000 Tate Modern on Bankside (SE1) has been home to Britain's national gallery of international modern and contemporary art dating from 1900 onwards. Welcoming 5.2 million visitors in its inaugural year it is the most visited gallery of its type in the world. This combined with the fact that it is housed inside a former power station makes Tate Modern truly a powerful centre for the arts!

Getting to Tate Modern can be an adventure in itself. The best way to arrive is by means of the Millennium Bridge connecting the City with Bankside. This pedestrian-only suspension bridge follows the route once taken by Thames watermen in their skiffs, who until the early 19th century were paid to convey fun-seeking Londoners to and from the theatres, brothels and bear-baiting rings of Bankside (a stone seat, where waterman would await their return customers, is still preserved in a wall on Bear Gardens). It is a far cry from the high-speed Thames Clipper catamarans that dock at Bankside Pier today.

As the Musée d'Orsay in Paris recycles a former railway station, so Tate Modern recycles the former Bankside Power Station. The original steel-framed and brick-clad building was designed in the 1940s by architect Sir Giles Gilbert Scott (1880–1960), who also designed Battersea Power Station, Waterloo Bridge, and London's iconic red telephone kiosks (see no. 65). With its 99-metre high chimney the station generated electricity from 1952 until 1981, when rising oil prices brought about its closure.

A decade later the site was earmarked by the Tate Gallery as premises for its expanding collection of modern art. Originally the plan was to demolish the power station but then the Swiss firm chosen to design the new building, Herzog & de Meuron, decided to rework the existing building instead. This was a good decision since the stark minimalist appearance of the old power station, now emptied of much of its redundant plant, sets off perfectly the sort of art displayed here. The narrow vertical windows piercing the brick façade, for example, admit dramatic shafts of light into the cavernous former turbine hall, where the original taupe walls, concrete floors and overhead crane enhance the post-industrial feel. The architects displayed particular courage in deciding to leave many of the building's vast internal spaces wide open, as they had originally been designed.

There have been some significant changes made to the old building though. One of the most obvious external changes is the bold two-storey glass extension covering the front half of the roof. It contains the Tate Modern Restaurant featuring specially-commissioned artworks and a view towards St. Paul's Cathedral that is one of the finest in London. To the rear is an 11-storey gallery extension containing social and learning spaces beneath which lie the power station's three former oil storage chambers. These have been transformed into a live performance and installation art space called the Tanks.

Contemporary art can also be enjoyed at the Institute of Contemporary Arts on The Mall (SW1). Founded in a cinema basement in 1946 to provide an alternative to the Royal Academy, the ICA hosted exhibitions of Braque, Pollock and Picasso in its early years. Its success facilitated the move to its present location, where in 1991 it staged the first gallery exhibition by Damien Hirst (b. 1965).

Other places of interest nearby: 94

96 The Cathedral across the Water

SE1 9DA (London Bridge), Southwark Cathedral
on Cathedral Street
Jubilee, Northern lines to London Bridge

Southwark Cathedral stands where London Bridge makes landfall on the southern bank of the Thames. Unlike St. Paul's Cathedral, its more famous counterpart, it is hemmed in by tower blocks, railway lines and the bustling Borough Market. But it is no less historic for that and has long served as a place of worship and refuge to everyone from prelates to prostitutes. The quiet cathedral churchyard is an ideal place to reflect on the building's eventful career.

According to oral tradition Southwark Cathedral began life as a convent founded in AD 606 by a young woman named Mary, using profits from her family's ferry business. The tradition goes on to

The gloriously-vaulted nave of Southwark Cathedral

record that during the 9th century the convent was converted into a monastery by St. Swithun. Whilst none of this has been proven, the building does significantly stand at the oldest crossing point of the Thames.

The earliest documented reference to the cathedral is in the Domesday Book survey of 1086, when a "Minster of Southwark" is recorded under the aegis of William the Conqueror's half-brother, Bishop Odo of Bayeux. It was then refounded in 1106 by the Bishops of Winchester as an Augustinian priory. They dedicated it to St. Mary with the added sobriquet of *Overie* meaning 'across the water'. The foundation also included a hospital named in honour of Thomas à Beckett, which still operates today as St. Thomas's in Lambeth (see no. 97).

It's worth pausing here to consider briefly the powerful Bishops of Winchester, who built their London palace alongside the priory (a glorious fragment of their Great Hall still stands on Pickfords Wharf). From 1107 they owned the so-called Liberty of the Clink, a 70-acre swathe of the south bank subject to their private jurisdiction rather than that of the City. The unusual name is probably derived from the sound of rattling chains in the bishop's commercially-run prison, which is recreated in the Clink Prison Museum at 1 Clink Street. Additionally the bishops owned and derived an income from the notorious Bankside 'stews' as brothels were known. It could therefore be said that punishment and pleasure were two of medieval Southwark's biggest industries.

Of the 12th century priory only an arch or two remains since the rest burned in 1212. The present building dates from between 1220 and 1420 making it London's first Gothic church. Step inside now to see the glorious vaulting of the nave and choir, and then take a pew to consider the rest of the cathedral's story.

After the Dissolution the church became the property of Henry VIII (1509–1547), who rented it to the congregation. They eventually bought it for £800 and renamed it St. Saviour's. As such it ministered to its parish until the 19th century, when the rebuilding of London Bridge brought the threat of demolition. Fortunately the cathedral was saved and in 1895 its nave rebuilt in readiness for the creation of a new and ultimately wealthier diocese. This occurred in 1905 when St. Saviour's became Southwark Cathedral.

A stroll around the interior reveals numerous interesting memorials. They include the oak effigy of a knight dated 1275, the recumbent figure of quack doctor Lionell Lockyer (1600–1672), the painted medieval canopied tomb of John Gower (1380–1408), one of the fathers of English poetry, and an alabaster figure of William Shakespeare (1564–1616), who worshipped here. The Harvard Chapel commemorates John Harvard (1607–1638), a local innkeeper's son, whose benefactions for a school in Massachusetts resulted in the famous university that now bears his name.

Other places of interest nearby: 97, 98, 99

97 History under the Knife

SE1 9RY (London Bridge), a tour of medical museums
beginning with the Old Operating Theatre and Herb Garret
at 9a St. Thomas Street
Jubilee, Northern lines to London Bridge

Students once witnessed surgical procedures at the Old Operating Theatre

As a great city of learning London lays claim to several medical firsts.
The Royal Hospital of St. Bartholomew, for example, opened in 1123
is Europe's oldest hospital still occupying the same site. In 1995 it
merged with the London Hospital Medical College – itself the country's
first medical school (1785) – to create Barts and The London School
of Medicine and Dentistry, one of Britain's leading medical and dental
schools.

It is less well known that London is also home to Europe's oldest
operating theatre. As the Old Operating Theatre Museum and Herb Garret it is located at 9a St. Thomas Street (SE1). The name reflects the fact
that the theatre is located in the garret (or attic) of St. Thomas' Church,
alongside which the 12th century St. Thomas' Hospital once stood (see
nos. 92 & 96). Installed when the church was reworked around 1700,
the attic was fitted out with wooden racks on which the hospital's
apothecary stored medicinal herbs. Indeed dried poppy heads were
found among the rafters when the attic was rediscovered in 1957.

The wood-pannelled operating theatre was installed in the garret in 1822 in response to a law requiring that student doctors witness operations in public hospitals. Since well-to-do citizens paid for surgical procedures in their own homes, it was inevitably poorer patients who were brought to the theatre. In the days before anaesthetics it must have been traumatic for those undergoing amputations here, whilst students in the tiered auditorium looked on in amazement.

London offers several other fascinating medical museums, including Bart's Pathology Museum in the Robin Brook Centre on West Smithfield (EC1). Purpose-built in 1879 it consists of a large skylit gallery with triple balconies connected by a spiral staircase. The walls are lined with hundreds of pathological 'pots' containing all manner of anatomical specimens. Also displayed is the skull of John Bellingham, who in 1812 became the only person to assassinate a British Prime Minister.

A rather similar experience is proffered by the Hunterian Museum in the Royal College of Surgeons at 35–43 Lincoln's Inn Fields (WC2). Created by the eccentric yet pioneering comparative anatomist John Hunter (1728–93) it contains a world class collection of pickled and other specimens. Pride of place goes to the skeleton of the Irish giant, Charles Byrne (1761–1783), who was 2.31 metres high.

The Hunterian Museum also contains a set of Winston Churchill's dentures although for that sort of thing one should really visit the British Dental Association Museum at 64 Wimpole Street (W1). This small collection dates back to 1919, when Lilian Lindsay, the country's first qualified female dentist, donated a collection of old dental instruments. The display of early dental drills is enough to make the onlooker wince!

This round-up of London's medical museums concludes with the Anaesthesia Heritage Centre at 21 Portland Place (W1), where the history of anaesthetics is given beginning with the first draft of ether administered in 1846, and the British Optical Association Museum at 41–42 Craven Street (WC2), which includes an antique artificial eye fitting set and a pair of Eskimo snow goggles.

Two little-known gardens with medical connections are the British Medical Association Council Garden on Tavistock Square (WC1) and the Royal College of Physicians' Medicinal Garden on St. Andrews Place (NW1). Both contain collections of physic plants used in pharmacology and are open as part of Open Garden Squares Weekend (www.opensquares.org).

Other places of interest nearby: 96, 98, 99

98 A Pint and a Play with Shakespeare

SE1 1NH (London Bridge), a visit to the George Inn
at 75–77 Borough High Street followed by Shakespeare's
Globe at 21 New Globe Walk
Jubilee, Northern lines to London Bridge

One way to explore Elizabethan London is to follow in the footsteps of the playwright William Shakespeare (1564–1616). Entire guidebooks have been written on the subject and all concur that the Bard left his greatest mark in the form of the Globe Theatre in Bankside. But before paying a visit why not pause in one of Shakespeare's preferred watering holes nearby? Although there is no hard evidence that Shakespeare frequented the George Inn at 75–77 Borough High Street it would seem highly likely on two counts. First of all he lived and worked in the area having relocated here from Bishopsgate in 1599. Secondly the George served not only as a coaching inn but also as a prototype Elizabethan theatre.

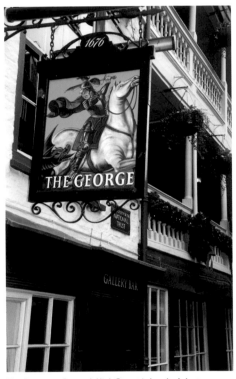

The George on Borough High Street is London's last galleried coaching inn

The George is first recorded during the 16th century, when Southwark became a busy terminus for coaches travelling the old Roman road between London, Canterbury and Dover. Since London Bridge, the only Thames crossing at the time, was locked each night the demand for accommodation here was high. Although the inn from Shakespeare's time was destroyed by fire in 1676 it was rebuilt to

The reconstructed Shakespeare's Globe theatre features a thatched roof

the original design. Like other coaching inns of the period it consisted of a large cobbled yard overlooked by colonnaded galleries. These provided a good vantage point when plays and other entertainments occurred below. With the arrival of the railways, however, coaching inns went into decline and today the George is the last of its kind in London.

In Elizabethan times the area surrounding the George would have been a bustling and bawdy place, especially in the so-called Liberty of the Clink. Falling outside the jurisdiction of the City this 'suburb of sin' was where pleasure-seeking Londoners came for their gambling, animal baiting, brothels and plays. Plays had been banned in the City since 1572, as a precaution against the spread of plague, but the Bishops of Winchester, who administered the Clink, were less scrupulous.

Before arriving in Bankside, Shakespeare and his company of players, the Lord Chamberlain's Men, were based at the Theatre in Shoreditch. Opened in 1576 it was England's first successful purpose-built playhouse. A dispute with the landlord in 1596, however, forced its closure and the troupe moved temporarily to the nearby Curtain Theatre (the remains of both venues have been unearthed by archaeologists on Curtain Road (EC2), where above ground can be seen numerous converted Victorian-era warehouses erected when Shoreditch was a centre for the furniture trade). The timbers of the Theatre were then

The thrust stage inside the Shakespeare's Globe theatre

dismantled and reused in the building of the Globe, which opened on what is now Park Street (SE1) in 1599. Soon joined by other theatres such as the Rose, the Swan and the Hope, Bankside became London's new Theatreland.

Like the George, the Globe today is not the original, which burned in 1613 after a theatre cannon misfired. No-one was hurt except a man whose breeches had to be extinguished with a bottle of ale! Rebuilt a year later it remained open until 1642, when the Puritans banned plays and had the theatre demolished to make way for houses.

Today's Globe opened in 1997 close to the site of the original with a production of Shakespeare's *Henry V*. This was apt since the play's prologue immortalises the building as "this wooden O" reflecting how the enclosed design of the galleried coaching inns influenced the lay-out of Elizabethan theatres. Based on documentary and archaeological evidence the rebuilt Globe takes the form of a polygonal wooden structure, with three-storey galleries surrounding an open yard and thrust stage. Using traditional materials it was the first thatched building erected in London since the Great Fire of 1666. Guided tours of the theatre are available daily.

Other places of interest nearby: 96, 97, 99

99 The View from the Shard

SE1 9SG (London Bridge), the View from the Shard
on Joiner Street
Jubilee, Northern lines to London Bridge (note: advance
booking is advisable)

The Shard is currently the tallest building in Western Europe

London is currently home to the tallest building in Western Europe. The Shard at 32 London Bridge Street rises an impressive 309 metres above the streets of Southwark. Whilst it's not cheap to take the lift up to the building's vertiginous outdoor observation deck, the view from the top is certainly a memorable one.

Standing at the heart of the regenerated London Bridge Quarter, the Shard was unveiled in 2013 to a design by Italian architect Renzo Piano (b. 1937). It takes the form of a tapering glass pyramid, which Piano envisaged as a vertical city, containing offices, restaurants, retail outlets and London's highest hotel. It is also home to the innovative View from the Shard visitor attraction.

Visitors enter on Joiner Street, where they are greeted by images of 140 famous Londoners in odd juxtapositions – Kate Moss marrying Henry VIII, for example! – and multimedia presentations showing the surrounding area past and present. They then board a lift and are whisked up to Level 33 in barely 40 seconds (the lift itself contains video screens designed to enhance the upward sensation). After transferring to another lift, passing a graffiti map of London in the process, the journey then continues up to Level 68.

The main viewing gallery is on Level 69 and offers 360 degree views for up to 65 kilometres in clear weather. Digital telescopes help identify 250 landmarks and even offer pre-recorded nighttime views. Those with a head for heights can then ascend further to an outdoor observation deck on Level 72 located a dizzying 244 metres above the ground. Overhead are a further 15 uninhabited storeys topped off with the jagged pinnacle that gives the building its name.

Looking out across London from the Shard it is fun looking out for the city's other highpoints, old and new. From west to east they include the headquarters of the British Secret Intelligence Service (MI6) at Vauxhall Bridge and the chimney of the Tate Modern on the South Bank. North of the river they include the dome of St. Paul's Cathedral, the three residential towers of the Barbican Estate, and the Tower of London, whilst back on the south side can be seen the wobbly-looking City Hall (see nos. 2, 15 & 103).

Another easily recognised structure is 30 St. Mary Axe (EC3). Dubbed the Gherkin because of its "stretched egg" wind resistant profile, it was designed by architect Norman Foster (b. 1935) and is 180 metres high (see front cover). Despite its appearance, however, the only curved piece of glass used in its construction is the lens-shaped cap at the very top. It can be visited during Open House London (www.openhouselondon.org.uk).

Alongside the Gherkin are several other City highpoints. The Heron Tower at 110 Bishopsgate (EC2) is 230 metres high making it London's third tallest structure after the Shard and One Canada Square (235 metres) at Canary Wharf. It boasts a lobby containing the country's largest private aquarium and a restaurant on the 39th floor (it will slip to fourth place, however, when the 288-metre high Pinnacle at 22–24 Bishopsgate is completed in 2017). Next highest is the so-called Cheese Grater at 122 Leadenhall Street (225 metres), with the Scalpel (190 metres) at 52–54 Lime Street also slated for completion in 2017. Tower 42 at 25 Old Broad Street is 183 metres high, with a decent view from its 42nd floor bar. The so-called Walkie-Talkie Tower at 20 Fenchurch Street (EC3) is 160 metres high and contains the Sky Garden, London's highest green space (visits by appointment at www.skygarden.london). The Lloyd's Building (95 metres) at nearby 1 Lime Street features external glass lifts and can also be visited during Open House London (www.openhouselondon.org.uk).

Other places of interest nearby: 96, 97, 98

100   A Plate of Pie'n'Mash

**SE1 4TW (Bermondsey), M. Manze's Eel and Pie Shop
at 87 Tower Bridge Road
Jubilee, Northern lines to London Bridge, then bus or walk
down Bermondsey Street**

For many years Britain's national dish was considered to be either roast beef or fish and chips. These days, however, it is just as likely to be Chicken Tikka Masala, a dry and spicy Indian dish with added sauce to satisfy the nation's craving for gravy. Curry is a good illustration of the way in which Britain has absorbed and adapted external culinary influences since the days of empire and it has been available in London since 1926, when Veeraswamy, Britain's first Indian restaurant, was established at 99 Regent Street (W1).

That's not to say roasts and fried fish have disappeared from London's culinary map. Far from it. Simpson's Tavern at 38 Ball Court (EC3), London's first chophouse, has been serving perfect pies and roasts since 1757. Rules at 35 Maiden Lane (WC2) has specialised in game since opening in 1798 and Sweetings at 39 Queen Victoria Street (EC4) has been bracketting its fresh fish lunches with the likes of potted shrimps and Spotted Dick pudding since 1889. Modest by comparison is the family-run Golden Hind at 73 Marylebone Lane (W1), which has been serving excellent fish and chips since 1914, and don't forget the Regency Café at 17–19 Regency Street (SW1), which has provided the best full English breakfasts in London since 1946.

Two delicacies unique to London are pie'n'mash and eels. Steeped in Cockney culture these honest, no-frills dishes have been enjoyed since the mid-1800s and are still available in more than 80 eel and pie shops in and around the capital. One of the best – and certainly the oldest – is M. Manze at 87 Tower Bridge Road (SE1). It is considered important enough to warrant its very own Blue Plaque, which is displayed inside the shop rather than being fixed to the wall outside because of the building's Grade 2 listed status.

Established in 1892 and taken over in 1902 by the Italian Manze family, the premises and the recipes remain exactly as they were a century ago. Behind the old-fashioned façade and green awning there is a single dining room lined neatly with green and white tiles. To one side a row of booths contain dark wooden benches and marble-top tables, where customers can enjoy their food sitting down. Those with less time queue at the take-away counter and enjoy this most original

Pie'n'mash and liquor sauce at Manze's on Tower Bridge Road

of fast foods outside. Either way the product is the same: a traditional beef pie with mashed potatoes served with a topping of parsley sauce, known as *liquor*. A splash of vinegar with a side helping of jellied or stewed eels completes the experience (although a global shortage of eels has seen a hike in prices recently). For devotees of the dish there is the Pie & Mash Club, which meets regularly at different restaurants and grades them accordingly (www.pie-n-mash.com).

Those in need of a stroll after eating should head north from Manze's to Bermondsey Square (SE1), where the shadowy 11th century remains of Bermondsey Abbey can be seen beneath a glass floor in the Del'Aziz restaurant at Number 11. Even more surprising, around the corner at the junction of Mandela Way and Page's Walk, is a decommissioned Soviet T-34 tank! It was placed here in 1995 by local property developer Russell Gray after his plans to develop the site were refused by Southwark Council.

London's Blue Plaques mark places where those who excelled in their chosen profession were born, lived, worked or died – and there are hundreds of them. The idea originated at the Royal Society of Arts in 1864, with the now-distinctive blue-and-white design adopted in 1937. Entire books have been written about them.

101 Cayenne Court and Cinnamon Wharf

SE1 2YR (Bermondsey), old riverside warehouses at Shad Thames
Jubilee line to Bermondsey; Jubilee, Northern lines to London Bridge

In Victorian times the south bank of the Thames between London Bridge and Tower Bridge was filled with riverside warehouses. Despite being abandoned in the 1970s those along the unusually-named Shad Thames survived demolition and have been variously adapted for use as apartments, shops and restaurants. It is said that when they were converted they still exuded the smell of the exotic spices once stored in them. This explains the area's spice-inspired street names today, including Cayenne Court and Cinnamon Wharf.

Shad Thames is first mentioned in a 1747 map of London and may be a corruption of St. John-at-Thames, a church that once stood here. The name is used today to describe not only a specific street but also the surrounding area bounded by Tower Bridge Road, Tooley Street and St. Saviour's Dock (Mill Street).

During the 19th century the Shad Thames area was home to the largest warehouse complex in London, including the colossal Butler's Wharf. Completed in 1873 they were used to store enormous quantities of tea, coffee, spices, and other commodities arriving into London by boat. Grain was another of the products stored here explaining the presence of the former Anchor Brewhouse.

At the far end of Shad Thames is St. Saviour's Dock. Around 1080 the Cluniac monks of Bermondsey Abbey carved it out of what was originally a tidal inlet at the mouth of the River Neckinger, and named it after their patron saint. The Thames is particularly deep here and is known as the Pool of London. In time what began as a safe landing for bishops became the site of London's Victorian inland port (that and a place where pirates were hung in the 17th century, 'the Devil's Neckinger' or neckerchief being a popular term for the hangman's noose). The river itself, which rises near Walworth, flows underground today.

Beyond the dock lay Jacob's Island, a notorious rookery (or slum). Charles Dickens in his novel *Oliver Twist* (1838) uses the area to great effect as the home of villain Bill Sikes. When it came to filming *Oliver!*

in 1968 the then dilapidated cobbled streets of the area provided the perfect backdrop.

During the 20th century the wharves and warehouses of Shad Thames went into terminal decline, as congestion forced ships to offload their goods farther downstream. After the last of the warehouses closed in 1972 the area was left derelict. But the picturesque warehouses with their distinctive brickwork, cranes, and painted wall signs weren't empty for long. During the 1980s and 90s the area's regeneration was spearheaded by designer and restaurateur Terence Conran (b. 1931), who opened several riverside eateries here (notably Butler's Wharf Chop House) and founded the Design Museum in a former 1940s-era banana

These aerial walkways high above Shad Thames were once used to transfer goods between riverside warehouses

warehouse (it will relocate to west London in 2016). Smart shops and luxury apartments soon followed. Against this backdrop of gentrification, public access to the riverbank was maintained by some heroic activists, one of whom is remembered in the alleyway known as Maggie Blake's Cause.

One of the most striking features of the reinvented Shad Thames are the high-level wrought-iron walkways criss-crossing overhead. Used originally as a means of shifting goods between warehouses they now serve as balconies for the private apartments.

On the north bank opposite Shad Thames is St. Katharine's Dock. Excavated in 1828 by Thomas Telford (1757–1834) it was never able to accommodate large ships due to its lack of depth. Amongst the first of the docks to close in 1968 none of its warehouses remain and it functions today as a marina.

Other places of interest nearby: 102

102 Tower Subway, Tower Bridge

SE1 2UP (Tower), the Tower Bridge Exhibition and Victorian Engine Rooms on Tower Bridge Road Circle, District lines to Tower Hill; Jubilee, Northern lines to London Bridge

At the bottom of Tower Hill (EC3) beside the Tower of London ticket office there stands a solitary brick turret with a doorway. It was once matched by another on Vine Lane, off Tooley Street (SE1), on the opposite side of the river. Together they once gave access to the Tower Subway, which for a brief period contained one of the world's first underground passenger railways.

The subway was the brainchild of civil engineer Peter W. Barlow (1809–1885). Whilst driving iron cylinders into London's clay for the piers of Lambeth Bridge he began considering cylindrical devices for tunnelling. Consequently in 1864 he patented a circular tunnelling shield, which improved considerably the rectangular device used by Marc Isambard Brunel (1769–1849) to excavate the Thames Tunnel between Rotherhithe and Wapping.

Approval for the Tower Subway was granted in 1868 and the contract was picked up by Barlow's apprentice, James Henry Greathead (1844–1896). Greathead perfected the shield and took less than a year to excavate the 410-metre long tunnel, which he lined with iron hoops rather than bricks. Fare-paying passengers were then transferred by lift down to a 12-seat, cable-hauled carriage inside the tunnel. Inevitably this limited capacity soon bankrupted the project but the tunnelling shield proved longer lasting, and in 1890 it was used to excavate the first deep-level tunnels of the Tube. By that time Tower Subway had been converted to a more profitable pedestrian walkway but in 1894 this too was rendered redundant by the opening of the toll-free Tower Bridge (the tunnel is now used by utility companies).

Tower Bridge was built to ease road congestion whilst maintaining access to the busy Pool of London docks. Designed by City architect Horace Jones (1819–1887) it comprises two towers on massive piers reached by suspension bridges. Between the towers are two high-level pedestrian walkways and a bridge for vehicles, which can be raised to enable large ships to pass. Since 1982 the bridge has been a visitor attraction in its own right, with lifts inside the towers transporting visitors up to the walkways (originally open air and accessible only by stairs they were closed for many years after being frequented by pickpockets and prostitutes). Now fitted with glass floors offering spectacular views the walkways contain interactive touch screens providing interesting facts about the bridge. Who knew, for example, that the *bascules* of the bridge are always raised to their maximum angle of 86 degrees for a craft carrying the monarch? Or that a Port of London Authority bylaw demands a bale of straw be hung from the bridge whenever maintenance work restricts the height for river traffic?

The bridge is still raised about a thousand times a year to allow large ships to pass (for lift times see www.towerbridge.org.uk). Electrohydraulic motors have done the job since 1974 before which stationary steam engines were used. These can

Tower Bridge replaced one of the world's first underground passenger railways

still be seen in the Victorian Engine Rooms, where the bridge makes landfall on the south bank. This part of the tour also includes a virtual bridge lift projected onto a giant screen.

There is no truth in the claim that when London Bridge was sold in 1968 to an American businessman he thought he was buying Tower Bridge. What is true is that the present London Bridge, which opened to traffic in 1973, replaced a stone-arched bridge built in 1831 (now in Arizona), which in turn replaced a 600-year-old medieval structure that was preceded by a succession of timber bridges. The oldest of these was built by the Romans (see no. 1).

Other places of interest nearby: 2, 101, 103

103 Across London in Seconds

SE1 2AA (London Bridge), City Hall
at 110 The Queen's Walk
Jubilee, Northern lines to London Bridge
(note: visitors are subject to a security search)

City Hall is a confusing name for a building located in Southwark that is not involved in the governance of the City of London. So confusing in fact that the building was officially renamed London House for the duration of the London 2012 Olympics so as not to bewilder visitors! Nomenclature aside, a visit to City Hall reveals one of the most intriguing and controversial modern structures on the south bank of the Thames.

City Hall stands at 110 The Queen's Walk (SE1), where it serves as the administrative headquarters of the Greater London Authority (GLA). Established in 2000, the GLA comprises the Mayor of London and the London Assembly. By comparison the City of London Corporation is ancient dating back to the time of Edward the Confessor (1042–1066), which makes it the world's oldest continually elected local government body. The headquarters of the Lord Mayor of the City of London Corporation is in a suitably ancient building, too, namely the medieval Guildhall on Gresham Street (EC2) (see no. 3). No wonder visitors get confused!

For the first two years of its life the GLA was based on Marsham Street (SW1) in Westminster, while City Hall was being erected on a site once occupied by wharves serving the Pool of London (see no. 101). Opened in July 2002 the building's novel design is by renowned architect Norman Foster (b. 1935), who has done much to define London's modern skyline (see no. 99).

From the outside, Foster opted for a modified sphere, with no obvious front or rear. Onlookers inevitably compared it to a misshapen egg, a woodlouse, an onion, even a motorcycle helmet. Former mayor Ken Livingstone went further and dubbed it the "Glass Testicle", whilst his successor, Boris Johnson, followed suit in referring to it as the "Glass Gonad"!

Inside, a spiral interior ramp reminiscent of that in New York's Guggenheim Museum ascends the full height of the 10-storey building. The walkway provides views into the interior of the building intended to stress the notion of transparency of government, a device similar to that used by Foster in the restored Reichstag in Berlin. At the top is an exhibition and meeting space called "London's Living Room", which is periodically open to the public.

City Hall is undeniably a striking building but it has its detractors. Some claim it was a waste of money at a time when it might still have been possible to use the existing head-quarters of the GLA's predecessor, the Greater London Council (GLC), which had been based at County Hall in Lambeth (it is now occupied by various businesses and visitor attractions – notably the London Dungeon – although the former council chamber remains intact). Oth-ers rejected the claim that the building's shape would improve energy efficiency, noting that in reality the extensive use of glass exceeds any ecological benefit. It should be said, however, that the heat generated by the building's com-puters and lights is successfully recycled, and groundwater is used to keep the building cool.

The only way to walk across London in seconds is to visit City Hall

Controversy aside there is one feature of City Hall that has proved popular with all sides. Located in the base-ment is the *London Photomat*, a bird's eye view of Greater London covering an area of 1,600 square kilometres. A mosaic of 200,000 aerial photographs laid out across the floor it enables the visitor to walk across London in seconds!

A magnificent 1:2000 3-D printed model of central London highlighting recent and pro-posed planning permissions is displayed at New London Architecture in the Building Centre at 26 Store Street (WC1).

Other places of interest nearby: 2, 102

*   *   *

The *London Photomat* in City Hall is as good a place as any to finish this odyssey during which some of the capital's unique, hidden, and unusual aspects have been revealed. London is often described as a series of villages but here the whole can really be appreciated enabling the satisfied city explorer to reflect on the 2,000 years of history that have shaped this world class metropolis.

Opening Times

Correct at time of going to press but may be subject to change.
Several of the places listed below can be visited during Open House London (www.openhouselondon.org.uk) and Open Garden Squares Weekend (www.opensquares.org).

10 Downing Street (SW1), by public ballot only during Open House London www.openhouselondon.org.uk; garden by public ballot only during Open Garden Squares Weekend www.opensquares.org

19 Princelet Street (E1), group bookings by appointment only www.19princeletstreet.org.uk

Alexander Fleming Laboratory Museum (W2), St. Mary's Hospital, Praed Street, Mon–Thu 10am–1pm

Algerian Coffee Store (W1), 52 Old Compton Street, Mon–Wed 9am–7pm, Thu & Fri 9am–9pm, Sat 9am–8pm

All Souls' Church (W1), Langham Place, Mass Sun 9.30am

Anaesthesia Heritage Centre (W1), 21 Portland Place, Mon, Tue, Thu & Fri 10am–4pm

Apsley House (W1), 149 Piccadilly, Apr–Oct Wed–Sun 11am–5pm, Nov–Mar Sat & Sun 10am–4pm

Argyll Arms (W1), 18 Argyll Street, Mon–Thu 10am–11.30pm, Fri & Sat 10am–12pm, Sun 10am–11pm

Arthur Beale (WC2), 194 Shaftesbury Avenue, Mon–Wed 9am–6pm, Thu & Fri 9am–8pm, Sat 10am8pm, Sun 11am–5pm

Attendant (W1), 27a Foley Street, Mon–Fri 8am–6pm, Sat 9am–6pm, Sun 10am–5pm

Bank of England Museum (EC2), Bartholomew Lane, Mon–Fri 10am–5pm

Banqueting House (SW1), corner of Whitehall and Horse Guards Avenue, daily 10am–1pm (occasionally 5pm)

Bart's Pathology Museum (EC1), Robin Brook Centre, St. Bartholomew's Hospital, West Smithfield, guided tours by appointment only www.qmul.ac.uk/bartspathology

Barbican Centre (EC2), Silk Street, Mon–Sat 9am–11pm, Sun 10am–11pm (guided tours www.barbican-org.uk)

Bates (SW1), 37 Jermyn Street, Mon–Fri 9.30am–5.45pm, Sat 10am–5.45pm

BBC Broadcasting House (W1), 2–22 Portland Place, daily guided tours by appointment only www.bbc.co.uk/showsandtours/tours/

Benjamin Franklin House (WC2), 36 Craven Street, Wed–Mon 10.30am–5pm

Berry Bros. & Rudd (SW1), 3 St. James's Street, Mon–Fri 10am–6pm, Sat 10am–5pm

Bevis Marks Synagogue (EC3), Bevis Marks, Mon, Wed & Thu 10.30am–2pm, Tue & Fri 10.30am–1pm, Sun 10.30–12.30am

BFI Southbank (SE1), Belvedere Road, daily 11am–11pm (Fri & Sat 11.30pm)

Black Friar (EC4), 174 Queen Victoria Street, Mon–Sat 10am–11pm, Sun 12am–10.30pm

Borough Market (SE1), Stoney Street, Wed & Thu 10am–5pm, Fri 10am–6pm, Sat 8am–5pm

Brasserie Zédel (W1), 20 Sherwood Street, Mon–Sat 11.30am–12pm, Sun 11.30am–11pm; Bar Américain Mon–Wed 4.30–12pm, Thu & Fri 4.30pm–1am, Sat 2.30pm–1am, Sun 4.30–11pm

Brick Lane Market (E1), Brick Lane, Old Truman Brewery, various times www.trumanbrewery.com

British Dental Association Museum (W1), 64 Wimpole Street, Tue & Thu 1–4pm

British Library (NW1), 96 Euston Road, Reading Rooms & Treasures Gallery Mon & Fri 9.30am–6pm, Tue–Thu 9.30am–8pm, Sat 9.30am–5pm, Sun 11am–5pm; King's Library Mon–Fri 9.30am–5pm, Sat 9.30am–4pm

British Museum (WC1), Great Russell Street, daily 10am–5.30pm (Fri 8.30pm)

British Optical Association Museum (WC2), College of Optometrists, 41–42 Craven Street, guided tours Mon–Fri 9.30am–5pm by appointment only www.college-optometrists.org

Broadgate Ice Rink (EC2), Exchange Square, Nov–Feb 10am–5pm

Brown's Hotel (W1), 33 Albemarle Street, Afternoon Tea Mon–Thu 2–6.30pm, Fri–Sun 12am–6.30pm

Buckingham Palace (SW1), Buckingham Gate, State Rooms, Aug daily 9.30am–7.30pm, Sep daily 9.30am–6.30pm, for other times www.royalcollection.org.uk; Changing the Guard May–Jul daily 11.30am, Aug–Apr alternate days 11.30am, www.royal.gov.uk; Queen's Gallery, Buckingham Gate, daily 10am–5.30pm; Royal Mews, Buckingham Place Road, Feb, Mar & Nov Mon–Sat 10am–4pm, Apr–Oct daily 10am–5pm; Clarence House, The Mall, Aug Mon–Fri 10am–4.30pm, Sat & Sun 10am–5.30pm

Bunhill Fields Cemetery (EC1), 38 City Road, daily Mon–Fri 8am–7pm (Oct–Mar 4pm), Sat & Sun 9.30am–7pm (Oct–Mar 4pm)

Burlington Arcade (W1), Mon–Sat 9am–8pm, Sun 11am–6pm

Butler's Wharf Chop House (SE1), 36E Shad Thames, Mon–Sat 8am–3pm, 6–11pm, Sun 8am–3pm, 6–10pm

Cartoon Museum (WC1), 35 Little Russell Street, Mon–Sat 10.30am–5.30pm, Sun 12am–5.30pm

Central Criminal Court (EC4), Old Bailey, Mon–Fri 9.55–12.40am, 1.55–3.40pm

Charles Dickens Museum (WC1), 48 Doughty Street, Mon–Sun 10am–5pm (last admission 4pm)

Christ Church Spitalfields (E1), Commercial Street, Mon–Fri 10am–4pm, Sun 1–4pm

Church of All Hallows-by-the-Tower (EC3), Byward Street, Mon–Fri 8am–6pm, Sat & Sun 10am–5pm; Beating the Bounds on Ascension Day

Church of All Saints (W1), 7 Margaret Street, daily 7.30am–6.30pm

Church of Notre Dame de France (WC2), 5 Leicester Place, daily 9am–9pm

Church of St. Andrew Undershaft (EC3), St. Mary Axe, visits by appointment only www.st-helens.org.uk (foyer open Mon–Fri)

Church of St. Andrew Holborn (EC4), Holborn Viaduct, Mon–Fri 9am–5pm

Church of St. Bartholomew the Great (EC1), West Smithfield, Mon–Fri 8.30am–5pm, Sat 10.30am–4pm, Sun 8.30am–8pm; Cloister Café Mon–Fri 8.30am–5pm, Sun 9.30am–6pm

Church of St. Benet Paul's Wharf (EC4), Paul's Wharf, Thu 11am–3pm

Church of St. Botolph-without-Aldersgate (EC1), Aldersgate Street, Tue 1.45–4pm

Church of St. Botolph-without-Aldgate (EC3), Aldgate High Street, Mon–Fri 9am–3pm

Church of St. Botolph-without-Bishopsgate (EC2), Bishopsgate, Mon–Fri 8am–5.30pm

Church of St. Bride (EC4), Fleet Street, Mon–Fri 9am–6pm, Sat hours vary, Sun 10am–6.30pm

Church of St. Clement Danes (WC2), Strand, daily 9am–4pm; Oranges and Lemons Service 3rd week of Mar

Church of St. Clement Eastcheap (EC3), Clements Lane, Eastcheap, Mass Thu 12am

Church of St. Dunstan-in-the-West (EC4), 186a Fleet Street, Mon–Fri 9.30am–5pm

Church of St. Etheldreda (EC1), 14 Ely Place, Mon–Sat 8am–5pm, Sun 8–12.30am

Church of St. Ethelburga Bishopsgate (EC2), 78 Bishopsgate, Fri 11am–3pm

Church of St. George Bloomsbury (WC1), Bloomsbury Way, daily 1–4pm

Church of St. Giles-without-Cripplegate (EC2), Fore Street, Mon–Fri 11am–4pm

Church of St. Helen Bishopsgate (EC3), Great St. Helen's, Mon–Fri 9.30–12.30am

Church of St. James Garlickhythe (EC4), Garlick Hill, Thu 11am–3pm

Church of St. John (SW1), Smith Square, café & restaurant Mon–Fri 8am–5pm

Church of St. John's Hyde Park (W2), Hyde Park Crescent (W2), Horseman's Sunday service on third Sun in September at noon

Church of St. Katherine Cree (EC3), Leadenhall Street, Communion Thu 1pm

Church of St. Leonard Shoreditch (E1), 119 Shoreditch High Street, Mar–Oct Mon–Fri 12am–2pm

Church of St. Luke Old Street (EC1), Old Street, only during concerts www.lso.co.uk

Church of St. Magnus the Martyr (EC3), Lower Thames Street, Tue–Fri 10am–4pm

Church of St. Margaret Pattens (EC3), Eastcheap, Mon–Fri 7.30am–6pm

Church of St. Martin-in-the-Fields (WC2), Trafalgar Square, Mon, Tue, Thu & Fri 8.30am–1pm, 2–6pm, Wed 8.30am–1.15pm, 2–5pm, Sat 9.30am–6pm, Sun 3.30–5pm; Café in the Crypt Mon & Tue 8am–8pm, Wed 8am–10.30pm, Thu–Sat 8am–9pm, Sun 11am–6pm; Costermongers' Harvest Festival first Sun in Oct 3pm

Church of St. Mary Abchurch (EC4), Abchurch Lane, Mon–Fri 11am–3pm

Church of St. Mary Aldermary (EC4), Watling Street, Mon–Fri 9am–4pm

Church of St. Mary-le-Bow (EC2), Cheapside, Mon–Wed 7.30am–6.00pm, Thu 7.30am–6.30pm, Fri 7.30am–4.00pm; Café Below Mon–Fri 7.30am–2.30pm; Costermingers' Harvest Festival last Sun in Sep 3pm

Church of St. Mary Woolnoth (EC4), King William Street, Mon–Fri 7.15am–5.15pm

Church of St. Marylebone (NW1), 17 Marylebone Road, Mon–Fri 9am–5pm, Sat & Sun 8am–6pm

Church of St. Michael Paternoster Royal (EC4), College Hill, Mon–Fri 9am–5pm

Church of St. Olave Hart Street (EC3), 8 Hart Street, Mon–Fri 9am–5pm

Church of St. Paul Covent Garden (WC2), Bedford Street, Mon–Fri 8.30am–5pm, Sat variable, Sun 9am–1pm; Costermongers' Harvest Festival second Sun in Oct 10am

Church of St. Sepulchre-without-Newgate (EC1), Holborn Viaduct, Wed 11am–3pm

Church of St. Stephen Walbrook (EC4), 39 Walbrook, Mon–Fri 10am–4pm

Churchill War Rooms (SW1), Clive Steps, King Charles Street, daily 9.30am–6pm

Cinema Museum (SE11), The Master's House, 2 Dugard Way, off Renfrew Road, visits by appointment only www.cinemamuseum.org.uk

City Hall (SE1), 110 The Queen's Walk, Mon–Thu 8.30am–6pm, Fri 8.30am–5.30pm; details of exhibitions www.london.gov.uk/city-hall

City of London Cogers (EC4), Old Bank of England, 194 Fleet Street, 2nd Mon each month 7–9.15pm

City of London Police Museum (EC2), 37 Wood Street, times vary www.cityoflondon.police.uk/about-us/history/museum

Clink Prison Museum (SE1), 1 Clink Street, Jul–Sep daily 10am–9pm, Oct–Jun daily Mon–Fri 10am–6pm, Sat & Sun 10am–7.30pm

Coach & Horses (W1), 29 Greek Street, Afternoon Tea daily 12am–6pm

Coal Vaults (W1), 187b Wardour Street, Mon–Sat 5–12.30pm

Columbia Road Market (E2), Columbia Road, Sun 8am–2pm

Counting House (EC3), 50 Cornhill, on–Fri 12am–10pm

Courtauld Gallery (WC2), Somerset House, Strand, daily 10am–6pm

Danielle Arnaud (SE11), 123 Kennington Road, Fri, Sat & Sun 2–6pm; for details of exhibitions www.daniellearnaud.com

Daunt Books (W1), 83 Marylebone High Street, Mon–Sat 9am–7.30pm, Sun 11am–6pm

Davenports Magic Shop (WC2), 7 Charing Cross Underground Arcade, Mon–Fri 9.30am–5.30pm, Sat 10.30am–4.30pm

De Hems (W1), 11 Macclesfield Street, Mon–Sat 11am–12pm, Sun 12am–10.30pm

Del'Aziz (SE1), 11 Bermondsey Square, Sun–Thu 7am–11pm, Fri & Sat 7am–1am

Dennis Severs' House (E1), 18 Folgate Street, Sun 12am–4pm, Mon following the 1st and 3rd Sun 12am–2pm; 'Silent Night' tours Apr–Sep Mon 6–9pm, Oct–Mar Wed 6–9pm by appointment only www.dennissevershouse.co.uk

Design Museum (SE1), 28 Shad Thames, daily 10am–5.45pm

Dirty Dick's (EC2), 202 Bishopsgate, Mon–Sat 11am–9.30pm, Sun 11am–8.30pm

D. R. Harris (SW1), 29 St James's Street, Mon–Sat 10am–6pm

Dolphin Tavern (WC1), 44 Red Lion Street, Mon–Sat 11am–11pm, Sun 12am–10.30pm

Dorchester (W1), Park Lane, Afternoon Tea 1pm, 2pm, 3.15pm, 4.15pm & 5:30pm

Dr Johnson's House (EC4), 17 Gough Square, Oct–Apr Mon–Sat 11am–5pm, May–Sep Mon–Sat 11am–5.30pm

Dr. Williams' Library (WC1), 14 Gordon Square, Mon, Wed & Fri 10am–5pm, Tue & Thu 10am–6.30pm

Duke's (SW1), 35–36 St. James's Place, Duke's Bar Mon–Sat 2–11pm, Sun 4–10.30pm

Dutch Church (EC2), 7 Austin Friars, 2nd & 4th Tue each month 11am–3pm

Ede & Ravenscroft (WC2), 93 Chancery Lane, 8.45am–6pm, Sat 10am–3pm

Faraday Museum (W1), Royal Institution, 21 Albemarle Street, Mon–Fri 9am–6pm

Fashion and Textile Museum (SE1), 83 Bermondsey Street, Tue–Sat 11am–6pm

Fitzroy House (W1), 37 Fitzroy Street (W1), daily 11am–5pm by appointment only www.fitzroyhouse.org

Fitzroy Tavern (W1), 16 Charlotte Street, Mon–Sat 11am–11pm, Sun 12am–10.30pm

Florence Nightingale Museum (SE1), 2 Lambeth Palace Road, daily 10am–5pm

Floris (SW1), 89 Jermyn Street, Mon–Sat 9.30am–6pm

Fortnum & Mason (W1), 181 Piccadilly, Mon–Sat 10am–9pm, Sun 12am–6pm

Foundling Museum (WC1), 40 Brunswick Square, Tue–Sat 10am–5pm, Sun 11am–5pm

Freemasons' Hall (WC2), 60 Great Queen Street, Library and Museum of Freemasonry, Mon–Fri 10am–5pm; guided tours daily 11am, 12am, 2pm, 3pm, 4pm

French House (W1), 49 Dean Street, Mon–Sat 12am–11pm, Sun 12am–10.30pm

G. Heywood Hill (W1), 10 Curzon Street, Mon–Thu 9am–7pm, Fri 9am–5.30pm, Sat 9am–4.30pm

Garden Museum (SE1), Lambeth Palace Road, Sun–Fri 10.30am–5pm, Sat 10.30am–4pm

Geo. F. Trumper (W1), 9 Curzon Street, Mon–Fri 9am–5.30pm, Sat 9am–5pm

George Inn (SE1), 75–77 Borough High Street, daily 11am–11pm

Golden Hind (W1), 73 Marylebone Lane, Mon–Wed 12am–3pm, 6–10pm, Thu–Sat 6–10pm

Golden Hinde II (SE1), St. Mary Overie's Dock, Clink Street, daily 10am–5.30pm

Goldsmiths' Hall (EC2), Foster Lane, guided tours Oct–Mar by appointment only www.thegoldsmiths.co.uk, library Mon–Fri 10am–4.45pm

Gordon's (WC2), 47 Villiers Street, Mon–Sat 11am–11pm, Sun 12am–10pm

Grant Museum of Zoology (WC1), Rockefeller Building, 21 University Street, Mon–Sat 1–5pm

Grays Antiques (W1), 58 Davies Street, Mon–Fri 10am–6pm, Sat 11am–5pm

Gray's Inn Walks (WC1), High Holborn, Mon–Fri 12am–2.30pm

Grenadier (SW1), 18 Wilton Row, daily 12am–11pm

Guards Museum (SW1), Wellington Barracks, Birdcage Walk, daily 10am–4pm

Guildhall (EC2), Gresham Street, during Open House London www.openhouselondon.org.uk

Guildhall Art Gallery and Amphitheatre (EC2), Guildhall Yard off Gresham Street, Mon–Sat 10am–5pm, Sun 12am–4pm

Handel House Museum (W1), 25 Brook Street, Tue–Sat 10am–6pm (Thu 8pm), Sun 12am–6pm

Harrods (SW1), 87–135 Brompton Road, Mon–Sat 10am–9pm, Sun 11.30am–6pm

Harvie & Hudson (SW1), 96–97 Jermyn Street, Mon–Sat 9.30am–6pm, Sun 12am–5pm

Hatchards (W1), 187 Piccadilly, Mon–Sat 9.30am–7pm, Sun 12am–6pm

Henry VIII's Wine Cellar (SW1), Ministry of Defence, Whitehall, guided tours by appointment only www.helm.org.uk tel. 0044 (0)870 607 4455

Hispaniola (SW1), Victoria Embankment, Whitehall, daily 11am onwards

HMS Belfast (SE1), The Queen's Walk (SE1) between London Bridge and Tower Bridge, Nov–Feb daily 10am–5pm, Mar–Oct daily 10am–6pm

Holland & Holland (W1), 34 Bruton Street, Mon–Fri 9am–6pm, Sat 10am–5pm

Honourable Artillery Company Museum (EC1), Armoury House, City Road, by appointment only www.hac.org.uk

Hoop and Grapes pub (EC3), 47 Aldgate High Street, Mon–Fri 10am–11pm, Sat 9am–9pm

Horse Hospital (WC1), junction of Herbrand Street and Colonnade, during exhibitions Mon–Sat 10am–6pm, evening events daily 7.30am–11pm www.thehorsehospital.com

Houses of Parliament (SW1), St. Margaret Street (Cromwell Green entrance), guided tours Sat and selected weekdays during Parliamentary recess by appointment only www.parliament.uk; Elizabeth Tower and Big Ben (Portcullis House entrance) guided tours for permanent UK residents only Mon–Fri 9am, 11am, 2pm (May–Sep 4pm) by arrangement with a local MP or member of the House of Lords; Jewel Tower, Abingdon Street, Apr–Sep daily 10am–6pm, Oct daily 10am–5pm, Nov–Mar Sat & Sun 10am–4pm

Household Cavalry Museum (SW1), Horse Guards, Whitehall, Apr–Oct 10am–6pm, Nov–Mar 10am–5pm; Changing of the Life Guard, Horse Guards Parade, daily 11am (Sun 10am), Daily Inspection, Front Yard Whitehall, 4pm; Trooping the Colour and Beating the Retreat, Horse Guards Parade, Jun, www.householddivision.org.uk

Hunterian Museum (WC2), Royal College of Surgeons, 35–43 Lincoln's Inn Fields, Tue–Sun 10am–5pm

Imperial War Museum (SE1), Lambeth Road, daily 10am–6pm

Inns of Court and City Yeomanry Museum (WC2), 10 Stone Buildings, Lincoln's Inn, Mon–Fri 10am–4pm by appointment only www.iccy.org.uk

Institute of Contemporary Arts (SW1), The Mall, daily 11am–6pm (Thu 9pm)

Ironmonger Row Baths (EC1), 1 Norman Street, Mon–Fri 6.30am–9.30pm, Sat & Sun 9am–6pm; Turkish Bath Mon women only 11am–6pm, Tue men only 10am–9pm, Wed mixed 10am–9pm, Thu women only 10am–5.30pm, men only 6–9pm, Fri women only 10am–9pm, Sat & Sun mixed 9am–6pm

Islington Local History Centre (EC1), Finsbury Library, 245 St. John Street, Mon & Thu 9.30am–8pm, Tue, Fri & Sat 9.30am–5pm

Islington Museum (EC1), 245 St. John Street, Mon & Tue, Thu–Sat 10am–5pm

Ismaili Centre Roof Garden (SW7), Cromwell Gardens (SW7), occasional openings only www.opensquares.org

J. Wippell & Co. (SW1), 11 Tufton Street, Mon–Fri 9am–5pm

James J. Fox (SW1), 19 St. James's Street, Mon–Wed, Fri 9.30am–5.45pm, Thu 9.30am–9.30pm, Sat 9.30am–5pm; museum Mon–Sat 9.30am–5.30pm

James Smith & Sons (WC1), 53 New Oxford Street, Mon, Wed–Fri 10am–5.45pm, Tue 11am–5.45pm, Sat 10am–5.15pm

Jamyang Buddhist Centre (SE11), 43 Renfrew Road, Mon–Fri 10am–6pm; Sat & Sun times vary www.jamyang.co.uk

Jeremy Bentham Auto-Icon (WC1), University College London, South Cloisters, Gower Street, Mon–Fri 7.30am–6pm

Jerusalem Tavern (EC1), 55 Britton Street, Mon–Fri 11am–11pm

John Lobb (SW1), 9 St. James's Street, Mon–Fri 9am–5.30pm, Sat 9am–4.30pm

John Wesley's House & Chapel (EC1), 49 City Road, Mon–Sat 10am–4pm, Sun 12.30am–1.45pm

Kettner's (W1), 29 Romilly Street, Mon–Fri 12am–12pm, Sat 11.30am–12pm, Sun 11.30am–10pm

Kirkaldy Testing Museum (SE1), 99 Southwark Street, first Sun each month 10am–4pm, www.testingmuseum.org.uk and www.openhouselondon.org.uk

Lamb (WC1), 94 Lambs Conduit Street, Mon–Wed 12am–11pm, Thu–Sat 12am–12pm, Sun 12am–10.30pm

Lambeth Palace (SE1), Lambeth Palace Road, guided weekday tours by appointment www.archbishopofcanterbury.org

Langham (W1), 1C Portland Place, Afternoon Tea in the Palm Court 1pm, 3.15pm, 4.30pm

Leadenhall Market (EC3), Gracechurch Street, Mon–Fri 10am–6pm (public areas 24 hours)

Liberty (W1), Great Marlborough Street, Mon–Sat 10am–8pm, Sun 12am–6pm

Lillywhites (SW1), 24–36 Regent Street, Mon–Sat 9.30am–10pm, Sun 11.45am–6pm

Lock & Co. Hatters (SW1), 6 St. James's Street, Mon–Fri 9am–5.30pm, Sat 9.30am–5pm

London Central Mosque (NW8), 146 Park Road, tours Mon–Thu 10.30am–3pm by appointment visits@iccuk.org

London Charterhouse (EC1), Charterhouse Square, guided tours Apr–Sep by appointment only www.thecharterhouse.org; also open during Open House London weekend

London Eye (SE1), Jubilee Gardens, times vary www.londoneye.com

London Film Museum (WC2), 45 Wellington Street, Mon–Sat 10am–6pm, Sun 11am–6pm

London Fire Brigade Museum (SE1), Winchester House, 94a Southwark Bridge Road, guided tours Mon–Fri at 10.30am & 2pm by appointment only www.london-fire.gov.uk

London Fo Guang Shan Temple (W1), 84 Margaret Street, Sat–Thu 9.30am–5pm

London Library (SW1), 14 St. James's Square, Mon–Wed 9.30am–8pm, Thu–Sat 9.30am–5.30pm; daily, weekly, or annual membership necessary

London Scottish Regimental Museum (SW1), 95 Horseferry Road, Mon–Fri by appointment only www.londonscottishregt.org

London Silver Vaults (WC2), 53–64 Chancery Lane, Mon–Fri 9am–5.30pm, Sat 9am–1pm

London Transport Museum (WC2), Covent Garden Piazza, Mon–Thu, Sat & Sun 10am–6pm, Fri 11am–6pm

Lower Grosvenor Gardens (SW1), daily 10am–6pm (earlier in winter)

M. Manze (SE1), 87 Tower Bridge Road, Mon 11am–2pm, Tue–Thu 10.30am–2pm, Fri 10am–2.30pm, Sat 10am–2.45pm

Maggs Bros. Rare Books (W1), 50 Berkeley Square, Mon–Fri 9am–5pm

Magic Circle Museum (NW1), 12 Stephenson Way, Magic Circle Experience tour Mon 11.30am–1.30pm by appointment only www.themagiccircle.co.uk

Madame Tussauds (NW1), Marylebone Road, Mon–Fri 9.30am–5.30pm, Sat & Sun 9am–6pm; pre-booking advisable www.madametussauds.com

Marx Memorial Library (EC1), 37a Clerkenwell Green, daily 1–2pm

Monument (EC3), junction of Monument Street and Fish Street Hill, Apr–Sep 9.30am–6pm, Oct–Mar 9.30am.5.30pm

Marylebone Cricket Club Museum (NW8), Lord's, St. John's Wood Road, daily 10am–4.30pm except Major Match days

Michelin House (SW3), 81 Fulham Road, Bibendum Restaurant Mon–Fri 12am–2.30pm, 7–11pm, Sat 12.30am–3pm, 7–11pm, Sun 12.30am–3pm, 7–10.30pm, Oyster Bar Mon–Sat 12am–11pm, Sun 12am–10.30pm, Crustacea Stall Tue–Sat 9am–5pm, Café Mon–Fri 8.30am–5pm, Sat 9–12am; Conran Shop, Mon, Tue & Fri 10am–6pm, Wed & Thu 10am–7pm, Sat 10am–6.30pm, Sun 12am–6pm

Museum of London (EC2), 150 London Wall, daily 10am–6pm

Museum of the Order of St. John (EC1), St. John's Gate, St. John Lane, Mon–Sat 10am–5pm (for exceptional closures www.museumstjohn.org.uk)

National Gallery (WC2), Trafalgar Square, daily 10am–6pm (Fri 9pm)

National Portrait Gallery (WC2), St. Martin's Place, daily 10am–6pm (Thu & Fri 9pm)

National Theatre (SE1), Upper Ground, Mon–Sat 9.30am–11pm, Sun 12am–6pm; backstage tours Mon–Sat www.nationaltheatre.org.uk

Natural History Museum (SW7), Cromwell Road, daily 10am–5.50pm; Wildlife Garden Apr–Oct daily 10am–5pm; Spirit Collection and After Hours tours www.nhm.ac.uk

New London Architecture (WC1), Building Centre, 26 Store Street, Mon–Fri 9.30am–6pm, Sat 10am–5pm

Old Bailey, see Central Criminal Court

Old Operating Theatre and Herb Garret (SE1), 9a St. Thomas Street, daily 10.30am–5pm

Old Spitalfields Market (E1), Commercial Street, Mon–Wed 10am–5pm, Thu & Sun 9am–5pm, Fri 10am–4pm, Sat 11am–5pm

Old Truman Brewery (E1), 91 Brick Lane, opening times vary www.trumanbrewery.com

Olde Wine Shades (EC4), 6 Martin Lane, Mon 9.30am–9pm, Tue–Fri 9.30am–10pm

Palace of Westminster, see Houses of Parliament

Park Lane Hotel (W1), Piccadilly, Afternoon Tea in the Palm Court Mon–Fri 3–5.30pm, Sat & Sun 2–5.30pm by appointment only www.palmcourtlondon.co.uk

Paul Rothe & Sons (W1), 35 Marylebone Lane, Mon–Fri 8am–6pm, Sat 11am–5pm

Petticoat Lane Market (E1), consisting of Middlesex Street Market Sun 9am–2pm & Wentworth Street Market Mon–Fri 8am–4pm

Petrie Museum of Egyptian Archaeology (WC1), University College London, Malet Place, Tue–Sat 1–5pm

Phoenix Garden (WC2), St. Giles Passage off New Compton Street, 8.30am–dusk

Photographers' Gallery (W1), 16–18 Ramillies Street, Mon–Sat 10am–6pm (Thu 8pm), Sun 11.30am–6pm

Pollock's Toy Museum (W1), 1 Scala Street, Mon–Sat 10am–5pm

Princess Louise (WC1), 208 High Holborn (WC1), Mon–Fri 11am–11pm, Sat 12am–11pm, Sun 12am–6.45pm

Queen's Chapel of the Savoy (WC2), Savoy Street, Mon–Thu 9am–4pm, Sun 9am–1pm

Red Cross Garden (SE1), Redcross Way, daily 7.30am–sunset

Red Lion (SW1), 2 Duke of York Street, Mon–Sat 11.30am–11pm

Regency Café (SW1), 17–19 Regency Street, Mon–Fri 7am–2.30pm, Sat 7–12am

RIBA (W1), Royal Institute of British Architects, 66 Portland Place, Florence Hall (First Floor), Mon–Fri 10am–3.30pm

Roman Bath (WC2), Strand Lane, Mon–Fri by appointment only with Westminster City Council tel. 0044 (0)207 641 5264, dcreese@westminster.gov.uk

Royal Academy of Arts (W1), Burlington House, Piccadilly, Mon–Thu, Sat & Sun 10am–6pm, Fri 10am–10pm; Keeper's House Mon–Thu 10am–11.30pm, Fri & Sat 10am–12pm, Sun 10am–6pm

Royal Academy of Music Museum (NW1), Marylebone Road, Mon–Fri 11.30am–5.30pm, Sat 12am–4pm

Royal Festival Hall, see Southbank Centre

Royal Geographical Society (SW7), 1 Kensington Gore, Foyle Reading Room and Pavilion (during exhibitions www.rgs.org) Mon–Fri 10am–5pm

Royal Mail Archive (WC1), Freeling House, Phoenix Place, Mount Pleasant Sorting Office, Mon–Wed, Fri 10am–5pm, Thu 10am–7pm

Rules (WC2), 35 Maiden Lane, Mon–Sat 12am–11.45pm, Sun 12am–10.45pm

Russian Orthodox Cathedral of the Dormition of the Mother of God (SW7), 67 Ennismore Gardens, Divine Liturgy Tue–Sat 10am, Sun 11am

Salisbury (WC2), 90 St. Martin's Lane (WC2) Mon–Wed 11am–11pm, Thu 11am–11.30pm, Fri 11am–12pm, Sat 12am–12pm, Sun 12am–10.30pm

Sandys Row Synagogue (EC3), 4a Sandys Row, services Mon–Fri 1.30pm, Sat 9.30am

Sarastro (WC2), 126 Drury Lane, Mon–Fri 12.30am–10.30pm, Sat 12.30am–11.30pm, Sun 12.30am–4pm, 6–10pm

Science Museum (SW7), Exhibition Road, daily 10am–6pm

Selfridges (W1), 400 Oxford Street, Mon–Sat 9.30am–9pm, Sun 11.30am–6.15pm

Serpentine Gallery & Serpentine Sackler Gallery (W2), Kensington Gardens, West Carriage Drive, during exhibitions Tue–Sun 10am–6pm

Shakespeare's Globe (SE1), 21 New Globe Walk, exhibition daily 9.30am–5pm, guided tours Mon 9.30am–5pm, Tue–Sat 9.30am–12.30pm, Sun 9.30am–11.30am

Sherlock Holmes Museum (NW1), 221b Baker Street, daily 9.30am–6pm

Sherlock Holmes Pub (WC2), 10–11 Northumberland Street, Mon–Thu 11am–11pm, Fri–Sat 11am–12pm, Sun 11am–11pm

Sikorski Museum (SW7), 20 Prince's Gate, Tue–Fri 2–4pm, first Sat each month 10.30am–4pm

Simpson's Tavern (EC3), 38 Ball Court, Mon 11.30am–3.30pm, Tue–Fri 8.30am–3.30pm

Sir John Soane's Museum (WC2), 13 Lincoln's Inn Fields, Tue–Sat 10am–5pm; candlelit visits first Tue of each month 6–9pm

Smithfield Market (EC1), West Smithfield, Mon–Fri 3–12am

Somerset House (WC2), Strand, daily 10am–6pm

Sotheran's (W1), 2–5 Sackville Street, Mon–Fri 9.30am–6pm, Sat 10am–4pm

Southbank Centre (SE1), Belvedere Road, Hayward Gallery, Mon 12am–6pm, Tue & Wed, Sat & Sun 10am–6pm, Thu & Fri 10am–8pm; Queen Elizabeth Hall, daily 5–11.30pm; Royal Festival Hall, foyers daily 10am–11pm; Poetry Library, Level 5, Tue–Sun 11am–8pm

Southwark Cathedral (SE1), Cathedral Street, Mon–Fri 8am–6pm, Sat & Sun 8.30am–6pm

St. Christopher's Chapel (WC1), Great Ormond Street Hospital, Variety Club Building (Level 2), daily all hours

St. George's Cathedral (NW1), 1a Redhill Street, Mass Sun 11am

St. Pancras Renaissance Hotel (NW1), Euston Road, guided tours Sat & Sun 10.30am, 12am, 2pm & 3.30pm by appointment only tel. 0044 (0)20 8241 6921, info@luxuryvacationsuk.com

St. Paul's Cathedral (EC4), St. Paul's Churchyard, Mon–Sat 8.30am–4pm; Triforium tours by appointment only Mon & Tue 11.30am & 2pm, Fri 2pm www.stpauls.co.uk; café Mon–Sat 9am–5pm, Sun 10am–4pm

Pickering Place where duels were
once fought (see no. 78)

Stafford (SW1), 16–18 St. James's
Place, American Bar Mon–Fri
11.30am–1am, Sat 12am–1am, Sun
12am–12pm

Stanfords (WC2), 12–14 Long Acre,
Mon–Fri 9am–8pm, Sat 10am–8pm,
Sun 12am–6pm

Strand/Aldwych Station (WC2), corner
of Strand and Surrey Street,
occasional guided tours only with
London Transport Museum www.
ltmuseum.co.uk in conjunction with
Transport for London www.tfl.gov.uk

Subway Gallery (W2), Kiosk 1, Joe
Strummer Subway, Edgware Rd and
Harrow Road, Mon–Sat 11am–7pm

Sweetings (EC4), 39 Queen Victoria
Street, Mon–Fri 11.30am–3pm

T. J. Boulting (W1), 59 Riding House
Street, Tue–Sat 11am–6pm

Tate Modern (SE1), Bankside, Sun–Thu
10am–6pm, Fri & Sat 10am–10pm; the
Tate to Tate boat service operates
daily every 40 minutes during gallery
opening times

Tattershall Castle (SW1), Victoria
Embankment, Whitehall, daily 11am
onwards

Temple Church (EC4), Inner Temple
Lane, opening times vary www.
templechurch.com

Theatre Royal Drury Lane (WC2),
backstage tours Mon, Tue, Thu & Fri
2.15 & 4.15pm, Wed & Sat 10.30 &
11.45am

Topolski Bar and Café (SE1), 150–152
Hungerford Arches, Mon–Thu
9.30am–11pm (Thu 12pm), Fri & Sat
9.30am–1am

**Tower Bridge Exhibition and Victorian
Engine Rooms** (SE1), Tower Bridge,
Apr–Sep 10am–5.30pm, Oct–Mar
9.30am–5pm

**Tower of London including Fusiliers
Museum** (EC3), Tower Hill, Mar–Oct
Tue–Sat 9am–5.30pm, Sun & Mon
10am–5.30pm (last Yeoman Warder
tour at 3.30pm), Nov–Feb Tue–Sat
9am–4.30pm, Sun & Mon
10am–4.30pm (last Yeoman Warder
tour at 2.30pm); Chapel Royal of St.
Peter ad Vincula open during last hour
of normal opening times and as part of
a Yeoman Warder tour (Beating the
Bounds on Ascension Day every three
years); Ceremony of the Keys by
written application only to Ceremony
of the Keys Office, Tower of London
EC3N 4AB

Truefit & Hill (SW1), 71 St. James's
Street, Mon–Fri 8.30am–5.30pm, Sat
8.30am–5pm

Turnbull & Asser (SW1), 71–72 Jermyn
Street, Mon–Fri 9am–6pm, Sat
9.30am–6pm

Twining's Tea Shop (WC2), 216 Strand,
Mon–Fri 9am–5pm, Sat 10am–4pm

Two Temple Place (WC2), 2 Temple
Place, Jan–Apr during exhibitions or by
appointment www.twotempleplace.
org

Tyburn Convent (W1), 8 Hyde Park
Place, crypt tours daily 10.30am,
3.30pm & 5.30pm

Unseen Tour of Shoreditch (EC1), Old
Street Tube station, guided tours Fri
7pm and Sat & Sun 3pm by
appointment only www.unseentours.
co.uk

Veeraswamy (W1), 99 Regent Street,
Mon–Fri 12am–2.15pm, 5.30–10.30pm,
Sat & Sun 12.30am–2.30pm,
5.30–10.30pm (Sun 10pm)

Victoria and Albert Museum (SW7),
Cromwell Road, daily 10am–5.45pm;
Café Sat–Thu 10am–5.15pm, Fri
10am–9.30pm

View from the Shard (SE1), 32 London
Bridge Street, Sun–Wed 10am–7pm,
Thu–Sat 10am–10pm; advance booking
advisable www.theviewfromtheshard.
com

Village Underground (EC2), 54
Holywell Lane, for events www.
villageunderground.co.uk

Wallace Collection (W1), Hertford
House, Manchester Square, daily
10am–5pm

Welsh Church of Central London (W1),
30 Eastcastle Street, Sun 11am

West London Synagogue (W1), 34
Upper Berkeley Street, Shabbat
Service Fri 6am & Sat 11am

Westminster Abbey (SW1), Dean's
Yard, Mon–Sat www.westminster-
abbey.org; Cellarium Café Mon–Fri
8am–6pm, Sat 9am–5pm, Sun
10am–4pm

Westminster Cathedral (SW1),
Ambrosden Avenue, Mon–Fri
9.30am–5pm, Sat & Sun 9.30am–6pm

White Cube (SE1), 152–154
Bermondsey Street, Tue–Sat
10am–6pm, Sun 12am–6pm

White Cubicle (E2), George & Dragon
Pub, 2 Hackney Road, daily 6–11pm

Whitechapel Gallery (E1), 77–82
Whitechapel High Street, Tue, Wed,
Fri–Sun 11am–6pm, Thu 11am–9pm

Wolseley (W1), 160 Piccadilly, Mon–Fri
7am–12pm, Sat 8am–12pm, Sun
8am–11pm

Women's Library (WC2), 10 Portugal
Street, London School of Economics
and Political Science, Lionel Robbins
Building, Mon–Fri 10.30am–5pm

Yacht (WC2), Victoria Embankment,
Temple Pier, restaurant Tue–Sat
12am–4pm, 6–8pm (Tue–Thu), 6–10pm
(Fri & Sat), Sun 12am–8pm, bar Wed–
Fri 5pm onwards

Ye Olde Cheshire Cheese (EC4), 145
Fleet Street, Mon–Fri 11am–11pm, Sat
12am–11p, Sun 12am–4pm

Ye Olde Mitre (EC1), 1 Ely Court,
Mon–Fri 11am–11pm

Ye Olde Watling (EC4), 29 Watling
Street, Mon–Fri 10am–11pm, Sat
12am–10pm, Sun 12am–5pm

Bibliography

GUIDEBOOKS

Blue Guide London (Emily Barber), Blue Guides, 2014

The Traditional Shops and Restaurants of London (Eugenia F. Bell), Little Bookroom, 2011

The City of London: A Masonic Guide (Yasha Beresiner), Lewis Masonic, 2006

London Shops: The World's Emporium (Tara Draper-Stumm & Derek Kendall), English Heritage, 2003

Walking London (Andrew Duncan), New Holland, 2010

Nairn's London (Ian Nairn; revisited by Peter Gasson), Penguin, 1988

Literary Guide to London (Ed Glinert), Penguin, 2007

The Mini Rough Guide to London (Rob Humphreys), Penguin Books, 2008

Walking Dickens' London (Lee Jackson), Shire Publications, 2012

London Film Location Guide (Simon James), Batsford, 2007

Walking Haunted London: 25 Original Walks Exploring London's Ghostly Past (Richard Jones), New Holland, 2009

Tired of London, Tired of Life (Tom Jones), Virgin Books, 2012

The City of London: A Companion Guide (Nicholas Kenyon), 2012, Thames & Hudson

The London Market Guide (Andrew Richard Kershman), Metro Publications, 2008

London's Theatres: A Guide to London's Most Famous and Historic Theatres (Mike Kilburn), New Holland, 2011

Eyewitness Travel Guide London (M. Leapman), Dorling Kindersley, 2013

London Cemeteries: An Illustrated Guide & Gazetteer (Hugh Mellar), The History Press, 2011

London's Canals (Derek Pratt), Shire Publications, 2004

London's Royal Parks (Paul Rabbitts), Shire Publications, 2014

Book Lovers' London (Lesley Reader), Metro Publications, 2009

The London Blue Plaque Guide (Nick Rennison), The History Press, 2009

Walking Shakespeare's London (Nicholas Robins), New Holland, 2004

Time Out London (Various), Time Out, 2013

SECRET AND UNUSUAL LONDON

London Peculiars (Peter Ashley), English Heritage, 2004

More London Peculiars (Peter Ashley), English Heritage, 2007

London's Secrets: Museums & Galleries (Robbi Atilgan & David Hampshire), Survival Books, 2014

London's Hidden Secrets Volume 1 (Graeme Chesters), Survival Books, 2011

London's Hidden Secrets Volume 2 (Graeme Chesters), Survival Books, 2012

London's Secrets: Bizarre & Curious (Graeme Chesters), Survival Books, 2014

Secret London: Exploring the Hidden City (Andrew Duncan), New Holland, 2009

The London Nobody Knows (Geoffrey Fletcher), The History Press, 2011

The London Compendium: A Street-by-Street Exploration of the Hidden Metropolis (Ed Glinert), Penguin, 2004

London's Secrets: Parks & Gardens (David Hampshire & Robbi Atilgan), Survival Books, 2013

101 London Oddities (J. Edward Hart), J. R. Stallwood, 1994

A London Peculiar (Rafe Heydel-Mankoo), New Holland, 2015

Secret London – Unusual Bars and Restaurants (Rachel Howard), Jonglez, 2012

Secret London (Rachel Howard and Bill Nash), Jonglez, 2009

Discover Unexpected London (Andrew Lawson), Phaidon, 1979

Ben le Vay's Eccentric London (Benedict le Vay), Bradt, 2012

A Curious Guide to London (Simon Leyland), Bantam Press, 2014

Bizarre London (David Long), Constable, 2013

Tunnels, Towers and Temples: London's 100 Strangest Places (David Long), The History Press, 2007

Hidden City: The Secret Alleys, Courts and Yards of London's Square Mile (David Long), The History Press, 2011

London's Hidden Walks: Volume 1 (Stephen Millar), Metro Publications, 2011

London's Hidden Walks: Volume 2 (Stephen Millar), Metro Publications, 2012

Eccentric London (Tom Quinn & Ricky Leaver), New Holland, 2005

Quiet London (Siobhan Wall), Frances Lincoln, 2011

Discovering London's Curiosities (John Wittich), Shire Publications, 2012

SUBTERRANEAN LONDON

London Under (Peter Ackroyd), Vintage, 2012

Subterranean City (Antony Clayton), Historical Publications, 2010

London's Disused Underground Stations (J. E. Connor), Capital Transport Publishing, 2001

London's Sewers (Paul Dobraszczyk), Shire Publications, 2014

Discovering Subterranean London (Andrew Emmerson), Shire Publications, 2009

The London Underground (Andrew Emmerson), Shire Publications, 2013

Subterranean London: Cracking the Capital (Bradley Garrett), Prestel, 2014

Underground London: Travels Beneath the City Streets (Stephen Smith), Abacus, 2005

London's Lost Rivers (Paul Talling), Random House, 2011

London Under London (R. Trench & E. Hillman), John Murray, 1984

ART AND ARCHITECTURE

Banksy Locations & Tours Volume 1: A Collection of Graffiti Locations and Photographs in London, England (Martin Bull), PM Press, 2011

Wren's City of London Churches (John Christopher), Amberley Publishing, 2012

Discovering London Railway Stations (Oliver Green), Shire Publications, 2010

Lost London (Richard Guard), Michael O'Mara, 2012

London: A Guide to Recent Architecture (Samantha Hardingham), Ellipsis, 1995

London's 100 Best Churches: An Illustrated Guide (Leigh Hatts), Canterbury Press, 2010

London's Churches and Cathedrals (Stephen Humphrey), New Holland, 2011

Spectacular Vernacular: London's 100 Most Extraordinary Buildings (David Long), The History Press, 2006

London Bridges (Peter Matthews), Shire Publications, 2008

London's Statues and Monuments (Peter Matthews), Shire Publications, 2012

London's City Churches (Stephen Millar), Metro Publications, 2011

The Buildings of England – London (in 6 volumes) (Nikolaus Pevsner), Yale University Press, various

The Buildings of England – London: The City Churches (Nikolaus Pevsner), Yale University Press, 1998

London Above Eye Level: Glimpses of the Unexpected (John R. Murray), Frances Lincoln, 2009

London's Landmarks (Cara Frost-Sharratt), New Holland, 2011

Derelict London (Paul Talling), Random House, 2008

Parliament and its Buildings (Richard Tames), Shire Publications, 2012

London's Houses (Vicky Wilson), Metro Publications, 2011

HISTORY

London: The Biography (Peter Ackroyd), Vintage, 2001

Thames: Sacred River (Peter Ackroyd), Vintage, 2008

Old Customs and Ceremonies of London (Margaret Brentnall), Batsford, 1975

The Victorian City: Everyday Life in Dickens' London (Judith Flanders), Atlantic, 2013

Lost London: An A–Z of Forgotten Landmarks and Lost Traditions (Richard Guard), Michael O'Mara Books, 2012

Discovering London Guilds and Liveries (John Kennedy Melling), Shire Publications, 2008

London: A Social History (Roy Porter), Penguin, 2000

London's Strangest Tales: Extraordinary but True Stories (Tom Quinn), Anova, 2008

London Lore: The Legends and Traditions of the World's Most Vibrant City (Steve Roud), Arrow, 2010

London Stories (David Tucker), Virgin, 2009

The London Encyclopaedia (Christopher Hibbert, John Keay, Julia Keay, Ben Weinreb), Macmillan Reference, 2010

I Never Knew That About London (Christopher Winn), Ebury Press, 2007

Discovering London Street Names (John Wittich), Shire Publications, 2003

ILLUSTRATED BOOKS

London: Hidden Interiors (Philip Davies), English Heritage/Atlantic Publishing, 2012

Unseen London (Pater Dazeley & Mark Daly), Frances Lincoln, 2014

The Gentlemen's Clubs of London (Anthony Lejeune), Stacey International, 2012

London Dawn to Dusk (Jenny Oulton & David Paterson), New Holland, 2013

London: Portrait of a City (Paul Smith), Taschen, 2012

Great Houses of London (James Stourton & Fritz von Schulenburg), Frances Lincoln, 2012

TRAVEL MEMOIRS

London Journal 1762–1763 (James Boswell), Penguin Classics, 2010

Down and Out in Paris and London (George Orwell), Penguin Classics, 2001

The Illustrated Pepys (Samuel Pepys), Penguin, 2000

FICTION

A Christmas Tale, Bleak House, Little Dorrit, Oliver Twist (Charles Dickens), Various

A Study in Scarlet, The Sign of Four (Arthur Conan Doyle), Collector's Library, 2005

London (Edward Rutherford), Arrow, 2010

WEBSITES

www.visitlondon.com (Official visitor guide; formerly London Tourist Board)

www.cityoflondon.gov.uk (City of London visitor guide)

www.londonunveiled.com (Great places to visit off the beaten path)

www.londonopenhouse.org (Visiting buildings rarely open to the public)

www.opensquares.org (Visiting gardens rarely open to the public)

www.walks.com (Award-winning London walking tours)

www.insider-london.co.uk (Alternative London walking tours)

www.alternativeldn.co.uk (East End alternative walking tours)

www.londonist.com (A celebration of London old and new)

www.unseentours.co.uk (Unseen Tours led by the homeless)

www.hidden-london.com (Hidden places in London)

www.secret-london.co.uk (More hidden places in London)

www.leglondon.co.uk (London Explorers' Group monthly walks)

Acknowledgements

For kind permission to take photographs, as well as for arranging access and the provision of information, the following people are most gratefully acknowledged:

Chris Abbott (Luxury Vacations UK), Tom Almeroth-Williams (Goldsmiths' Company), Jack Ashby (Grant Museum of Zoology), Mike Baker (United Grand Lodge of England), Bank of England Press Office, Kevin Baumber, Ian Bishop (www.londonunveiled.com), Caroline Bowden, Michelle Brown and Katy Green (London Transport Museum), Kevin Brown (Alexander Fleming Museum), Rory Cook (Science Museum), Kay Coombs and Clementine Power (Garden Museum), Kate Crowther and Parveen Kaur Sodhi (Imperial War Museum), Adolfo Crawford-Garcia (St. Etheldreda), David Creese (Westminster Council), Richard Dabb (Museum of London), Ryan de Oliveira (Noir Espresso/The Attendant), Del'Aziz restaurant, Clive Dellow, Dirty Dick's, Angela Dunmore, Caroline Drayton and Madeleine Duxbury (St. Pancras Renaissance Hotel), Roger Dreyer (Houdini Museum of New York), Andrea von Ehrenstein (Sherlock Holmes Museum), Stephen Evans (St. Marylebone), Martin Fletcher, Ed Holmes and Simon Carter (St. Paul's Cathedral), Friends of City Churches, Colin Jenkins (Kirkaldy Testing Museum), Nicky Gardner and Susanne Kries (Hidden Europe), Adey Grummet and Kathy Taylor (All Hallows-by-the-Tower), Tim and Jane Hale, D. R. Harris & Co. Ltd., Nick Hern, Laurence Heyworth (Look and Learn History Picture Library), Stuart Hosker (London Library), Ruth Howlett (View from the Shard), Martin Humphries (Cinema Museum), David Iliff, Richard Ives (Map-Logic), Veronica Jacobs, Rachael Jones (Caro Communications/Sir John Soane's Museum), Nicola Kalimeris and Sophie Jackson (Museum of London Archaeology), Akoula Kadio (Notre Dame de France), Elizabeth Kaye (National Trust), Major Rupert Lendrum (Buck's Club), London Fo Guang Shan Temple, Londonist (www.londonist.com), Stewart Macfarlane, Herwig Maehler, Geoff Marshall, Caroline McDonald (Museum of London), Tim Meehan (St. Andrew Holborn), Kieran Meeke (www.secret-london.co.uk), Gareth Miles (Old Operating Theatre), Cordelia Morrison (Shakespeare's Globe), Museum of the Order of St. John, Elinor Newman (St. Martin-in-the-Fields), Mark Noad Design (www.london-tubemap.com), David Osborn (St. Clement Danes), Polly Parry (Natural History Museum), Judi McGinley (Museum of the Order of St. John), Mick Pedroli (Dennis Severs' House), Eric Perez (Fantasma Toys), Geoff Poole (M. Manze), Natalia Pourichko (Cathedral of the Dormition of the Mother of God), Louisa Price (Charles Dickens Museum), Marek Pryjomko, Max Putnam (Zetter Town House), Eugene Quinn, David Reed (Cinema Organ Society), Maria Rivas and Guy Stephenson (Transport for London), Ella Roberts (Handel House Museum), Judith Robinson (Bulldog Trust/Two Temple Place), Jasmine Rogers (Science and Society Picture Library), Maureen Rose (Taylors Buttons), Jayde Russell (London Central Mosque), Adrian Scarbrough Photography, Rudi Schmutz, Scotland Yard, Scotty and Kathy (Ye Olde Mitre), Phillip Shervington (James J. Fox), Clare Skinner (Marylebone Cricket Club), Dominic Stevenson and tour guide Henri (Unseen Tours), Pauline Stobbs (Historic Royal Palaces), Tamara Tadevosyan (Banqueting House/Historic Royal Palaces), Tai (Horse Hospital), Justine Taylor (Honourable Artillery Company), Kristin Teuchtmann and James Linkogle, Theatre Royal Drury Lane, Nick Thompson (Westminster City Council), Louise Tomsett (Natural History Museum), David Tucker (London Walks), Leigh Tuohy and Young's Brewery (The Lamb), Paul Turp (St. Leonard's Shoreditch), Matthew Turtle (Open House London), Andrew Wallis (Guards Museum), John Walters (London Pearly Kings and Queens Society), Chris and Joe Ware, Tricia Ware, Vicky Williams (Berry Bros. & Rudd), Amy Wilson (Lambeth Palace), Kathryn Wilson and Lewis Ashman (Foundling Museum), and Wang Yujie.

For very comfortable accommodation, Bob Barber and Marie-Christine Keith.

Particular thanks to Ekke Wolf for creating the layout and editing the photos, and Franz Hanns for creating the cover.

Thanks also to my mother Mary, brother Adrian, and great cousin James Dickinson for bringing many interesting items of London news to my attention, and Richard Tinkler for managing my websites, and Martina Bauer for design work. And not forgetting Andreas Eberhart, Zoltán and Sophie Farkas, and Simon Laffoley for their invaluable help with the photo selection.

Finally, very special thanks to my late father Trevor for encouraging me to track down things unique, hidden and unusual in the first place and to Roswitha Reisinger for her enduring love and inspiration and for making trips to London so much more enjoyable. This book could not have been written without her.

1st Edition published by The Urban Explorer, 2015
A division of Duncan J. D. Smith
contact@duncanjdsmith.com
www.onlyinguides.com
www.duncanjdsmith.com

Graphic design: Stefan Fuhrer
Typesetting and picture editing: Ekke Wolf
Cover design: Franz Hanns
Maps: Central London base map © www.maproom.net
Tubemap courtesy of www.london-tubemap.com
Printed and bound by GraphyCems, Spain

ISBN 978-3-9503662-5-9